BOOK JA

The book jacket was designed by the author and graphic designer Dora Cora. My father's crew wings were photographed by Jerry Wallace. The image of Stalag Luft IV was taken in the summer of 1944, while the photograph of Allied airmen on the back cover, intentionally set above snow drifts in the foreground, symbolic of the early days of the evacuation, was taken in late March, or early April 1945. The epic itself is characterized, in part, by the last two paragraphs of the Congressional Record for 8 May 1995. The photograph of my father was taken while training as an air cadet in late 1943.

C-LAGER

Stalag Luft IV & the 86-Day Hunger March

A triumph of the American spirit

David Dorfmeier

ISBN: 0692211136
ISBN: 13:9780692211137
Library of Congress Control Number: 2016913294
David Dorfmeier, Paso Robles, CALIFORNIA

PREFACE

In March 1945, an estimated 73,535 soldiers and airmen of the US Army and Army Air Force were interned as German prisoners of war in the European Theater of Operations (ETO). From 1942 until late 1944, the majority of these POWs were airmen, shot down over the Third Reich and other German-occupied countries of Europe. Over 10,000 of these airmen, including those who flew for the British Royal Air Force, were eventually sent to Stalag Luft IV, the largest and most notorious of the camps administered by the German Luftwaffe. In early February, 1945, the Soviet Winter Offensive into Eastern Europe forced the evacuation of their camp, resulting in an epic 86-day forced "Hunger March" across northern Germany.

The story of *C-lager* is about one of these young men, Sergeant Donald Dorfmeier, and the other airmen in his compound who participated in the 86-day trek across northern Germany. Fittingly, the story chronicles the heroism and spirit of the airmen who served in the Army Air Corps and exhibited the courage and inspiration to persevere in spite of great hardships and suffering that would haunt them "for many years to come."

DEDICATION

For our fathers . . .

This book is dedicated to the servicemen of the US Army Air Force "who participated in the world's first combined, and most sustained strategic bombing campaign. These servicemen are widely acknowledged to have endured more hardships and made greater sacrifices than almost any group of combatants in modern warfare." The largest organizational entity to participate in this endeavor was the US Army Eighth Air Force, which lost 46,456 aircrew while conducting air operations over England and occupied Europe from 17 Aug 1942 through 25 Apr 1945.

EPIGRAPH

"Prisoners of War [endure] . . . a melancholy state. You owe your life to [another's] humanity, and our daily bread to his compassion. You must obey orders, go where he tells you, stay where you are bid . . . [and] possess your soul in patience."

Winston Churchill,
Former POW,
Second Boar War
1899–1902

Cadet Don Dorfmeier, 1943   Author's collection

INTRODUCTION

Two photographs occupied prominent positions on my grand-mother's fireplace mantel. Yet, it was the confident smile and gaze of the young air cadet that always caught my attention. This compelling, captivating image of a handsome adolescent, dressed in the olive-brown hues of an Army Air Corps uniform, always fascinated me. The other photograph on the mantel was a more formal and somber image of my paternal grandfather, taken in his late thirties. In contrast to the portrait of his son, the depiction of the family patriarch was dark and dated, and seemed to accentuate his absence following an untimely death years earlier.

A narrative for my father's photograph could be found in the family scrapbook, among the other pictures and newspaper clippings announcing the births, weddings, and deaths of friends and relatives. There, amid the usual announcements, was the striking image of the young cadet featured in an article declaring, "Fresno Gunner is Missing." The notice never failed to elicit a sense of shock and apprehension just as subsequent articles, published months later, acknowledging his escape and safe return home, evoked feelings of excitement and relief.

Incredulously, my father had escaped captivity with another Fresno airman, Paul McNally. The two men had taken flight with three other POWs during the closing days of the war in Europe. Moving only at night, the group evaded capture for a week before making contact with British forces advancing toward the Elbe River. Only later would I discover that the June 1945 article announcing the escape of these two airmen was inaccurate and that segments of the story were presented out of context. Yet, there was no denying that the account of their ordeal, printed with accompanying images of the two winsome youths, captured the essence of a dramatic achievement. Perhaps the airmen, still traumatized by their past experiences or emotionally overwhelmed by their recent return home, could not have provided a more coherent account of their experiences. Or possibly the newspaper reporter was too excited by the stories of the two former prisoners of war to have asked more exacting or clarifying questions.

Regardless, the inaccurate and disjointed article, along with the promise of the two youths, remained fixed in time in the Fresno family scrapbook. However, I frequently found myself wondering about the character of these young men, and in particular, about the man who was my father. I was curious about the developmental influences in his life–what events during the closing days of the Second World War in Europe compelled him to risk his life by escaping captivity? The answers to these questions, as well as others, are embedded in the fabric of my father's family history and the times in which he lived.

TABLE OF CONTENTS

C-LAGER:
Stalag Luft IV & the 86-Day Hunger March

1

FRESNO

Many adolescents and young men who joined the US Army Air Corps during WWII came from small towns and farming communities across America. My father, Donald D. Dorfmeier, was born in such a place–in Fresno, California. It was in this town, located in the state's vast Central Valley, that his childhood and character were shaped by the values of an agricultural economy. A generation earlier, his family, to include my paternal grandfather, Albert, moved from Missouri to southern California. A few years later, Albert and his family moved again, from Los Angeles to Fresno. Early immigrants to the Central Valley were drawn initially by the gold rush of 1859; yet the area around the present day city was considered uninhabitable. The later introduction of irrigation and the cultivation of grapes eventually brought some prosperity to the county. However, the actual development of the city was attributable to the Central Pacific Railroad, which established a station stop at Fresno in 1872.[1] Leland Stanford, a co-owner of the Central Pacific, had envisioned the new town evolving into the major city in the Central Valley and the main shipping points for the county's agricultural products.

Eight years after arriving in California, 21-year-old Albert A. Dorfmeier married Mary F. Turpen. Mary, known more affectionately to her family and friends as Marie, was four years younger than Albert and the youngest of 12 siblings. After marrying in Stanislaus County, the young couple moved to Fresno, a small, ethnically diverse and developing community of some 30,000 inhabitants. Author William Saroyan, later characterized this small parish of his youth stating, "When I sold papers in Fresno, it was a town you could walk across in less than half an hour."[2] In this emerging setting, the couple established their first residency on Platt Avenue. Once settled, Albert learned a trade as an electrician and later promoted himself as an independent contractor. A first son, Alton, was born in 1916. A second son, Glenn,

---

[1] Waiczis & Secrest, *A Portrait of Fresno*, 3
[2] Ibid., 173

was born four years later. Shortly thereafter, the couple purchased residential property in what was then considered the north side of town.

The new residence, at 1411 Poplar Avenue, was a 1,650 square foot, single story, wood-framed house designed by Albert. Although modest in style, the home, with three large bedrooms and two tiled baths, was more than adequate for a small family. The functional center of the house was a large formal dining room situated between an open, front living room and a modest sized kitchen in back. Attached to the kitchen was a small, screened porch that served as a utility room. A detached garage in the backyard, some 40 feet from the house, served as storage for the family car and Albert's shop.

The development of new neighborhoods in the northern part of Fresno was a reflection of an "economic postwar boom" at the end of WWI.[3] A productive agricultural base, augmented by an industry limited to the manufacture of locally produced material, was supporting the city's expansion. Raisins, one of the primary agricultural crops of the region, were in demand, and vineyards in full production were selling for "as [much] as $1,500 an acre."[4] With increased revenues, the city built a second high school, paved new streets, and lay tracks for streetcars to expand public transportation as the city developed into a major urban center of 45,000. The Sun-Maid Raisin Corporation completed the construction of a large plant in 1920, a city newspaper was founded two years later, followed by the opening of the elegant Hotel California.

Two years after moving into their new home, Marie gave birth to another child, Donald, on 12 April 1924. The couple now had three sons, separated by four and eight years in age. This difference in maturity would limit their interaction as children, yet Don benefited from having older brothers who modeled responsible behavior. The age differences between the brothers also minimized the effects generalized to birth order. Don's need for achievement, a characteristic usually associated with a firstborn, was balanced by a more relaxed and fun-loving disposition typical of later or last-born children. His temperament was also markedly different from that of his two older brothers who were more reserved. Marie would later describe her

[3] Rehart, *The Heartland Heritage*, 117
[4] Walker, *Fresno County Blue Book*, 56

youngest son's distinctive temperament, noticeable at an early age, as "good-natured, outgoing, and charming."

A year after Don's birth, the price of raisins in Fresno fell sharply signaling the forthcoming crash of the New York stock exchange, shattering the economic prosperity of the United States. Further hardship occurred the following year with the Southern Drought of 1930, which forced thousands of families to immigrate from Oklahoma and Arkansas to California in hope of finding employment in the fertile fields of the Central Valley. By 1932, "half of Fresno County's farms faced foreclosure,"[5] and "nearly 3,500 banks nationwide had closed," including several Fresno institutions that held billions of dollars in uninsured deposits.[6] "Soup kitchens and breadlines opened in downtown Fresno"[7] and elsewhere; 12,000,000 persons, representing 25 percent of the nation's workforce, lost their jobs. The "pain and suffering [from the Depression was] as tragic as any in modern history."[8]

In Europe, the world depression was an "economic catastrophe of unprecedented proportions,"[9] resulting in the collapse of the German banking system in 1931. The following year, unemployment in the country approached 40 percent of the workforce.[10] These conditions created nationwide instability as various ideological parties fought for control of the country's political leadership. One of these factions was Adolph Hitler's National Socialist (Nazi) party, which attracted significant membership and public support. In 1932 Hitler's party received 37.4 percent of the popular vote for representation in the national Reichstag election. Although the election would not control the legislative assembly of the country, Adolph Hitler had emerged as the most powerful politician in Germany and was appointed chancellor on 30 January 1933.* The following year, the new chancellor

---

* The threat of the German Communist Party in the 1920's increased Hitler's popularity among those voters "who were terrified by the specter of Bolshevism."[11]

[5] Rehart, *The Heartland's Heritage*, 118
[6] Jennings & Brewster, *The Century*, 149
[7] Rehart, *The Heartland's Heritage*, 120
[8] Jennings & Brewster, *The Century*, 149
[9] Garraty, *The Great Depression*, 2
[10] Ibid., 44
[11] Keegan, *The Second World War*, 35

consolidated his political power and assumed ultimate authority of the national government after the death of Germany's president, Paul von Hindenburg. Several months later, all members of the newly designated armed forces, the Wehrmacht, swore an oath of personal allegiance to Adolph Hitler in elaborate ceremonies held throughout the country.[12] Hitler then initiated various rearmament programs, re-instituted military conscription, and embarked on extensive public works projects to eliminate massive unemployment. This singular achievement, skillfully portrayed to the world as the "German Miracle," magnified Hitler's popularity at home and his prestige abroad.

Zeppelin Field, Nüremberg, Germany 1936   German Federal Archives

Five weeks after Hitler assumed power in Germany, Franklin Delano Roosevelt was inaugurated as 32nd president of the United States. Desperate for a change in national leadership, Roosevelt won 60 percent of the popular vote in the previous year's presidential election, defeating incumbent Herbert Hoover. A *New York Times* article, printed after the balloting, reported that "the country was ready and anxious to accept any leadership [and] inclined to accept [Roosevelt] as the heaven-sent man of the hour."[13] Amid an unprecedented level of public expectation, Roosevelt received "no fewer than half a million letters" from persons expressing concerns and support.[14]

---

[12] Cooper, *The German Army*, 30
[13] Brendon, *The Dark Valley*, 270
[14] Jennings & Brewster, *The Century*, 155

The new President was "buoyant, charismatic, and extremely confident," as he sought to reassure the country with masterful oration and a "strong belief in using government to actively aid the lives of ordinary people."[15] During the next several years, "Roosevelt became the most important president of the century, changing the office so completely that historians would measure all those who succeeded him against his extraordinary accomplishments."[16] Many of these feats, which included 15 major pieces of legislation drafted with the collaboration of Congress, were initiated and passed within the first three months of Roosevelt's first administration.

Both Roosevelt and Hitler were propelled to national prominence by their persuasive rhetoric and established themselves as powerful world leaders shortly after assuming public office. However, each man articulated a vastly different explanation for the world's economic collapse. Hitler appealed to a national consciousness seeking to avenge Germany's defeat in the First World War and to restore the German nation to its perceived rightful position of world dominance. Conversely, Roosevelt was sensitive to the plight and concerns of the individual and focused primarily on "reinvigorating public service and the resources of democracy" to master the national crisis.[17] He also used numerous public works programs to relieve unemployment in the United States by building roads, parks, and dams. In Fresno, the Public Works Administration (PWA) built the Hall of Records and the Fresno Memorial Auditorium, in addition to other smaller structures.[18] The Works Project Administration (WPA) cleared "obstructions to irrigation on the Kings River", while the Civilian Conservation Corps (CCC) built and "maintained camps in the mountains to take care of unemployed youth."[19]

In spite of Roosevelt's optimism and initial accomplishments after he assumed public office, the United States remained acutely affected by a national depression. The lingering economic distress and hardship in California's Central Valley and Fresno were also perceived by Albert's family to have been causal factors in his sudden and fatal

[15] Jennings & Brewster, *The Century*, 157
[16] Ibid., 157
[17] Brendon, *The Dark Valley*, 271
[18] Walker, *Fresno County Blue Book*, 58
[19] Ibid., 58–59

heart attack in April 1934. Albert's unexpected death at age 42 was a traumatic incident for his entire family. His death also left his family destitute. A local church refused to pay for Albert's services, and an alleged inheritance dispute with a younger brother left his estate without financial assets. However, 10-year-old Donald may have suffered the most from this loss, which occurred during his transition from childhood to early adolescence–a critical developmental period characterized by the establishment of a stable identity and consistent relationships with others.

Albert's death changed the dynamics in Don's family, which struggled to meet pressing financial needs. Some of these demands were alleviated later when Marie found employment outside of the home and Alton was offered an apprenticeship in an advertising department upon graduating from high school. Glenn also found part-time work in a butcher shop after school and, during the summer months, he cleared brush for the CCC in the Sierra Mountains. Don's contribution to the family's financial struggle was initially limited to an occasional odd job and delivering evening newspapers. Later, he would recall this period in his life as a time of "social isolation," noting that his "mother and brothers worked late every night." Yet, he also perceived that his family relationships were strengthened by this encounter with adversity. Both experiences would leave lasting impressions of the importance of personal responsibility and working collaboratively with others.

Marie also rented the front bedroom of their home to male students attending Fresno State College. The former Normal School and later Teachers College, at Poplar and McKinley Avenue, was just three city blocks from the family residence. Initially, Marie only rented to male students. However, in the summer of 1936, she abruptly changed her "males only" policy and, for the first time, rented her front bedroom to two female students attending FSC. One of these women was June Martin, a 22-year-old day student who worked part-time for the college. June, who earned a salary of $7.50 a week, would later recall that her "rental agreement, which included kitchen privileges for ten dollars a month, was very satisfactory." While June lived in the family home, Don shared a bedroom with his brother Glenn. He also attended Hamilton Junior High where he excelled in drama, literature, and social science.

Fresno State College 1936   Claude Laval

That same year, Adolph Hitler reestablished the German Air Force, which had been banned in perpetuity by article 198 of the Versailles Treaty.[20]* This newly recognized branch of service, the Luftwaffe, was to become the instrument of power that enabled Hitler to intimidate Europe for the next three years. Although the efficacy of airpower was primarily a theoretical construct in the early 1930s, early advocates, such as Billy Mitchell and Italian Air Marshall Giulio Douhet, foresaw the effective employment and the destructive capabilities of such a force.

The threat of the new German Luftwaffe served as leverage for Hitler to pursue his aggressive political policies in Europe. The first of these provocations was the reoccupation of the Rhineland in spring 1936. The following year, Germany repudiated the financial obligations imposed by the Versailles Treaty and suspended payment for war reparations. Later, the German Condor Legion was sent to the Iberian Peninsula to provide air support for General Franco's nationalists during the

*The Treaty of Versailles, signed on 28 June 1919, forced Germany to accept responsibility for causing WWI, disarm, and make large territorial concessions, in addition to paying heavy reparations.

[20] Cooper, *The German Air Force*, 1

Spanish Civil War. Then, in mid-March 1938, German troops occupied Austria without opposition, exploiting "the enthusiasm among German nationals for union (*Anschluss*) with the Third Reich."[21]

Hitler's next provocation was to annex the Sudetenland of Czechoslovakia in September 1938. This incitement created a three-week international crisis, which was ultimately resolved at Munich when England's Prime Minister, Neville Chamberlain, conceded to the demands of Adolph Hitler. At the height of this crisis, when war seemed imminent, Joseph Kennedy, the US Ambassador in London, informed Washington that Germany possessed the largest and most destructive air force in Europe.[22] Kennedy's assessment was endorsed by Colonel Charles Lindbergh, the famous and influential American aviator. However, both men had been successfully manipulated by German propaganda portraying the Luftwaffe as a totally overwhelming and irresistible force. In reality, the new service "possessed only two-thirds of the authorized aircrew strength."[23] Moreover, neither the Wehrmacht nor the Luftwaffe was ready to fight a prolonged conflict.

President Roosevelt was appalled by the Sudetenland incident, and had seen the inevitability of American involvement in a European conflict. Recognizing the role of the German Luftwaffe in forcing an agreement at Munich, Roosevelt called for the expansion of an almost nonexistent US Army Air Corp in 1938.[24] He also sought to draft the required legislation to purchase additional aircraft and expand the army pilot training program, along with initiating other plans necessary to prepare the country for war. Other Western democracies also realized that they too must rearm to challenge Hitler's outright aggression in Europe. However, the German leader had become emboldened by Britain and France's lack of resolve and "abandoned caution in his campaign of aggressive diplomacy."[25] Thus, when Hitler started to turn his attention toward the Polish Corridor,* he dismissed the guarantees

---

* A strip of former German territory, consisting of Posen, West Prussia, and part of Pomerania, ceded to the newly reconstituted Polish Republic at the end of WWI.

[21] Keegan, *The Second World War,* 38
[22] Cooper, *The German Air Force,* 84
[23] Hoyt, *Angels of Death,* 129
[24] Jablonski, *Flying Fortress,* 22
[25] Keegan, *The Second World War,* 40

issued by other countries to defend the beleaguered east European nation.

Confident that England and France would not act militarily, Germany attacked Poland on 1 September 1939. Days earlier, German and Soviet Foreign Ministers had signed a nonaggression pact after months of secret negotiations that enabled Hitler to move against Poland without provoking a Soviet military response. The Soviet Union, in exchange for their cooperation, would be allowed to "annex eastern Poland and the Baltic states of Latvia, Lithuania, and Estonia."[26]

Two weeks later, the Soviets joined in the attack on Poland, which sealed the country's fate. However, contrary to Hitler's earlier expectations, England and France honored their agreements to Poland by declaring war on Germany just days after the country was invaded.* The day German mechanized units crossed the Polish border Don was beginning his second semester of high school. School transcripts and yearbook entries from his freshman year at Fresno High noted an initial involvement in student government and an active participation in school sports. The following spring, while competing as a weight man in the shot put and discus events for the varsity track team, he met Jean Lamoure. At the time, Jean was a senior in the same division and the two athletes spent the season competing against each other and other schools in their athletic conference. Although the two competitors were separated in age by as many years, their acquaintanceship developed into a warm and affectionate lifelong friendship.

That same spring, the war in Europe erupted into a larger conflict. On 10 May 1940, the German Wehrmacht launched an explosive 36-day campaign that overran Western Europe and defeated France, reputed to have the most powerful army in the world.[27] The British Expeditionary Force in France was also routed and forced to evacuate the continent at Dunkirk several weeks later. The defeat was a terrible shock for Londoners. The sight of injured, disheveled, and shaken soldiers "brought home the nearness of the [conflict], and the fear of

---

* Germany and the Soviet Union were eager to recover territory relinquished at the end of WWI that re-established the Polish state, as the Second Republic, in 1918.

[26] Keegan, *The Second World War*, 43
[27] Cardozier, *The Mobilization of the US in WWII*, 10

imminent invasion."[28] Yet, amid the chaos, the newly appointed Prime Minister, Winston Churchill, refused to negotiate a peace with Hitler. Rather, Churchill inspired the nation when, days later, he addressed the British Parliament, declaring, "We shall go on to the end. Whatever the cost may be, we shall fight on . . . we will never surrender."[29]

Following Churchill's refusal to negotiate peace, Hitler ordered preparations for the invasion of England. The initial phase of this operation required the German Luftwaffe to gain mastery of the skies over the English Channel and adjacent provinces. To accomplish this, the German Air Force assembled an array of 2,500 bombers and other supporting aircraft. The size of this force alone seemed to validate the Luftwaffe's reputation as the most powerful and dominant air force in the world. However, this position of prominence was achieved against smaller nations that possessed technically inferior aircraft. Against Britain the Luftwaffe would face a competent air force, whose pilots were highly skilled.

Roosevelt responded to the initiation of hostilities in Europe by declaring a limited national emergency and, in September 1940, signed the Selective Service Act requiring men between the ages of 21 and 36 to register for conscription. The following year, the "United States initiated a first [peace] time use of a military draft to expand the strength of its regular Army, which was ranked 18th in the world."[30] However, more than 40 percent of those men called for induction failed to pass the physical examination.[31] This failure rate was attributed to the high illiteracy rate in the country and the lingering effects of the Depression, where an estimated 45,000,000 Americans still suffered from a pervasive mild malnutrition. Eventually almost 1,000,000 men were called to military service for an initial period of one year, then extended to 30 months by a House vote of 203 to 202 in August 1941.

Most Americans followed the developing events in Europe through weekly print periodicals and live radio broadcasts. By 1940, *Life* magazine, available for 10 cents an issue, or $4.50 for a year, was one of the nation's most popular publications. The magazine's success

[28] Mark & Humphries, *London at War*, 23
[29] Churchill, *The War Speeches of Winston Churchill*, 195
[30] Ross, *America 1941*, 27
[31] Ibid., 74

was largely attributed to pictorial coverage of the war, although the journalistic reporting was also comprehensive and accurate. The most exciting news source, however, was live radio broadcasts from the four national networks, featuring Charles Collingwood, Edward R. Murrow, William L. Shirer, and Howard K. Smith. The most dramatic coverage of the war was provided by Murrow's nightly reports from London during the Battle of Britain and the London Blitz.[32]

Prior to the political crisis in Europe escalating toward armed conflict and war, Don's two older brothers were leaving home. Alton was the first to depart when he married June Martin in February 1939, and the couple established a separate residence in another part of town. The following year, Glenn married Elizabeth Fiske, then transferred from Fresno State College to the University of Washington in Seattle. Jean Lamoure also graduated from Fresno High in the spring of 1940, yet elected to enroll at Fresno State College in the fall, where he played football as an offensive lineman. Fortunately for Don, the college's close proximity to Fresno High, and Jean's part-time employment as a local elementary school grounds supervisor, allowed the two young men to maintain their friendship. Years later, Jean recalled, "Don would frequently stop by after school to just talk," then concluded . . . "he was very serious and focused in those days." However, Jean's assessment may have just been a reflection of the tension and general anxiety that engulfed the entire country.

[32] Ross, *America 1941*, 3

BALTIC SEA

DANZIG · EAST PRUSSIA

HAMBURG ·

Polish Corridor

BERLIN ·

WARSAW ·

RUHR

POLAND

Rhine-land ·

Sudetenland

FRANKFURT ·

CZECHOSOLAKIA

NÜREMBERG ·

MUNICH ·

VIENNA ·

GERMANY 1937

Regions of interest and early conflict   Author's collection

Germany lost significant territory to other countries at the end of WWI. Recovery of these former territories, to include provinces ceded to the newly reconstituted Second Polish Republic in 1918, was the driving force behind Adolph Hitler's aggressive foreign diplomacy after coming to power in 1933. The first of these provocations was the reoccupation of the Rhineland in 1936. Two years later, Germany annexed Austria and the Sudetenland in Czechoslovakia prior to invading Poland 1 September 1939.

German *Reichsadler* 1933–1945

2

COLLEGE TRAINING DETACHMENT

The public mood of the United States at the beginning of 1941 was, according to author Gregory Ross, "a time of high drama, insecurity, and indecision."[33] Adolph Hitler stood as the undisputed master of all Europe, and by spring, tensions were escalating between the United States and Germany. German submarines were routinely harassing American merchant ships and later sank several US Navy destroyers. The United States government retaliated to these provocations by seizing all German and Italian merchant ships in American ports and freezing all their financial assets, as well as the resources of countries occupied by these belligerent powers.[34] A national draft was also implemented in March 1941, along with congressional authorization to provide material aid to Great Britain.

In Europe, German air and ground units were re-deploying from France to occupied Poland in preparation for a summer invasion of the Soviet Union. The massing of these formations and the recalling of recently demobilized soldiers represented the prelude to Operation Barbarossa. Hitler's decision to attack Russia, while necessary to secure victory in Europe, was also driven by a long, deep-seated political hatred of the Communist Party, and loathing of the Slavs as an inferior and degenerate ethnic group. This latter perception influenced the planning of the forthcoming invasion as a racial war of annihilation that would be "conducted without compassion or decency,"[35] and characterized by a sustained and pervasive use of terror.

The meticulously planned German invasion of Russia was unprecedented in its scope and complexity. The Wehrmacht mobilized almost 3.2 million men for the operation that was launched 22 June 1941. The German Field Army alone deployed some 152 divisions for

---

[33] Ross, America 1941, ix
[34] Cardozier, *The Mobilization of the United States in WWII*, 27
[35] Seaton, *The Russo-German War*, 55

the campaign, in addition to other forces from Finland and Romania.[36] However, while impressive in size, this force structure possessed three fundamental weaknesses. First, the allocation of men and material was insufficient in number and type of divisions. Equally deficient, the Luftwaffe could not provide the necessary air assets to adequately support the strategic objectives of the campaign.

The fundamental problem with the German Air Force was that the operational strength of the service had remained primarily static during the past two years of war and possessed no more than 3,340 combat aircraft at the time of the Soviet invasion.[37] More significantly, only 2,770 front line units were available for the Eastern Front as another 1,500 aircraft were required for service in other theaters. The limitations of the Luftwaffe were also not readily apparent at the onset of the campaign after initially destroying a more numerically superior Russian Air Force.* Only the ensuing pace of operations, characterized by extensive battles of encirclement, in addition to an early and severe winter, would expose these deficiencies.

The German offensive in Russia faltered in late November. Shortly thereafter, the Japanese Navy attacked the US Pacific fleet at Pearl Harbor. The preemptive, 7 December 1941 strike, initiated as part of Japan's expansion into the South Pacific, caught the United States by surprise. The following morning, thousands of eager and resolute young men waited in long lines at recruiting stations throughout the country.[38] On that same morning, Don and the rest of the Fresno High student body gathered in the school's assembly hall to hear President Roosevelt address the nation. Don, a seventeen-year-old high school senior, recalled "there was a hush over the [assembly] as we sat, anxiously awaiting the President's message. [An excitement] overcame me as his booming voice rang through the auditorium, declaring the previous day's attack, as 'a date that will live in infamy,' and concluded his speech 'requesting that Congress declare war on Japan.' Later that

---

* A German in-service audit verified over 2,000 Soviet aircraft were destroyed on the first day of Operation Barbarossa, a finding that was more astonishing than the earlier claims of the German pilots.[39]

[36] Ziemke, *Stalingrad to Berlin*, 7–9
[37] Cooper, *The German Air Force*, 219
[38] Jennings & Brewster, *The Century*, 238
[39] Bekker, *The Luftwaffe War Diaries, 221*

afternoon", Don continued, "I practically ran all the way home and breathlessly pleaded with my mother to let me go. I was graduating in January and wanted to go join [the army] right away." However, Don was underage and could not enlist for military service without parental consent. His mother acknowledged her son's enthusiasm, yet wisely insisted he "first finish high school and one semester of college" prior to joining the service.

Roosevelt's request for a declaration of war against Japan passed by the unanimous vote of the United States Senate, and by one vote short of a similar endorsement in the House of Representatives. Three days later, Germany and Italy declared war on the United States. These subsequent events unleashed another world war and a torrent of patriotic idealism, which compelled men and women of all ages to enlist in the armed forces. However, these enlistments were also motivated by other psychological considerations. For some, military service offered escape from drudgery or other responsibilities, in addition to providing a tremendous sense of immediate excitement.

Philosopher and author, J. Glenn Gray, attributes man's enduring excitement and attraction to war as derived from the universal appeal of participation, comradeship, and destruction. Gray further argues that danger enhances our awareness of living "by calling attention to our physical selves . . . [and provides an opportunity] to establish a sense of mastery over [our] environment."[40] Author John Laffin characterized the country's enthusiasm for war following the events of December 1941 noting, "the American soldier was imbued with the sense of sharing 'a great adventure,' when only the young officers of other armies retained such a notion."[41]

Don would have willingly enlisted in the nation's armed forces following the attack on Pearl Harbor had his mother not insisted otherwise. Instead, her obedient son finished his senior year of high school and graduated 30 January 1942. The following week he applied for enrollment at Fresno State College. In the school's one-page application for admission, Don identified his intent to specialize in scientific study and teach high school after graduation. Presumably, this focus was based on his earlier studies in geometry, physics, and

---

[40] Gray, *The Warriors*, 43
[41] Laffin, *Americans in Battle*, 5

chemistry. Still, pursuit of a formal education in the early 1940s was unusual, regardless of one's academic accomplishments in high school. Fewer than eight percent of the nation's population attended any form of college and the percentage of those completing a degree program was even smaller. Prewar college enrollment throughout the United States in the fall of 1941 was only 1.5 million men and women, of which 1,867 students were attending classes at Fresno State College.[42]

Once admitted to Fresno State, Don registered for 13 units that included spring training with the football team and competing as a weight man in track. He also worked part-time for a pharmacy and a men's clothing store while the United States initiated a full-scale mobilization that would ultimately induct over 15,000,000 men and woman into the country's armed forces.[43] The magnitude of this effort was reflected in every facet of national life, including education. Enrollment at Fresno State dropped by 320 students in spring of 1942, and another 110 students left the following semester.[44]

Part of this national mobilization included an anticipated expansion of the new US Army Air Force to an end-strength of one million men. A January 1942 *Life* magazine article reported the intent of the service's new chief, Major General "Hap" Arnold, to create the greatest air force the world has ever seen. To accomplish this goal, the former Army Air Corps was reorganized as an independent service; "an elite organization, with distinctive uniforms, badges, and insignia."[45] Pilot training programs were cut from nine to seven months as recruiting advertisements promoted "simplified requirements [and] new opportunities," with enticements of $75 a month to train as an air cadet. The article was a direct appeal to a generation yearning to be aviators and for those who had a fascination with the danger of flying.

Prior to the expansion of the Air Corps, the senior leadership of the service sought to establish a separate identity and a service song that "expressed some of the idealism and aspirations of aerial flight." Hundreds of scores were submitted for review before a committee of wives unanimously selected a composition titled, "The Army Air

[42] CSU-Fresno, Special Collections Library
[43] Cardozier, *The Mobilization of the United States in WWII*, 92
[44] CSU-Fresno, Special Collections Library
[45] Wells, *Courage & the Air War*, 92

Corps Song," by Robert Crawford. Crawford's entry was sung for the first time by its composer on 2 September 1939, and opened with the rousing lyrics, "Off we go into the wild blue yonder . . . ," which received a standing ovation. The senior officer of the Corps' Training Command, Brigadier General Barton Yount, was equally impressed with Crawford's work, and ordered command performances at every training facility in an effort to imbue the fledging service with its new song. Aviation cadets also found the lyrics of the song inserted inside their newly issued service caps, and marched everywhere in step with the compelling meter and cadence of their service anthem, aspiring to "live in fame."

The youth of the country was captivated by the glamour of this new service, and perceived opportunity for individual accomplishment and recognition. The appeal was so compelling for Don, that, after completing his first semester of college, he reported to the recruiting station at Hammer Air Field, seven miles northeast of Fresno, and enlisted in the Army Air Force pilot training program. A required physical examination noted that the now eighteen-year-old Fresno youth was 72 inches in height, had a medium build, and weighed 172 pounds. Other identifying information recorded a history of few childhood illnesses, a "ruddy complexion, blue eyes, and dark brown hair." However, the most salient annotation on Don's medical form was an examiner's comment, "desirable material," indicating the college freshman represented the prototypical all-American youth that Hap Arnold wanted for the expanding Air Force. The following week, Don was inducted into the Air Corps Enlisted Reserves (ACER).*

The ACER program had been established only 10 weeks earlier, on 1 April 1942, to "enlist qualified candidates in a reserve aviation cadet grade and place them on inactive status until such time as they would be called to active duty to fill training school quotas."[46] The program was "widely publicized in newspapers and college publications" and special recruiting teams were sent to colleges throughout the country. Three flexible enlistment options were available to attract and "insure

---

* The new US Army Air Corps remained a functional entity of the new Air Force, and strong sentimental attachment to the former branch persisted throughout the war, especially among combat aircrew.

[46] Carter & Mueller, *The Army Air Forces in WWII*, 494

a constant pool of 54,000 qualified applicants."[47] Don's enlistment allowed him to remain in school full-time, "with the understanding that the deferment could be terminated at any time by the Secretary of War."[48]

In late June 1942, just two weeks after Don enlisted in the ACER, the German Wehrmacht launched a new, although limited, offensive operation into the southern Ukraine of Russia. The war on the Eastern Front of Europe had remained inactive for months following the intensity of the previous year's campaign, and the harsh winter of 1941–42 left the German and Red armies' exhausted. The resumption of a new campaign in Russia, even on a limited scale, was only possible with further conscription and culling of personnel occupying administrative or support positions, in addition to a significant augmentation of Romanian, Hungarian, and Italian forces.

German infantry advancing on Stalingrad 1942   German Federal Archives

The strategic objective of the 1942 German offensive in Russia was to capture the mineral rich Donetz Basin and the oil production facilities in the Caucasus region, between the Black and Caspian Seas. Similar to operations conducted the previous year, German panzer and mechanized units moved across the southern steppes of Russia, well in advance of their infantry, at a distance of thirty to forty kilometers a day. Yet the Red Army refused to allow encirclement, and withdrew

---

[47] Ibid., 495
[48] Ibid., 496

further into the vast interior, resulting in the Wehrmacht overextending itself on its approach to Stalingrad and the ensuing battle for the city.

The protracted six-month struggle for the possession of Stalingrad was fought during Don's second semester of college as German forces attempted to subdue a stubborn Soviet resistance. Finally, on 19 and 20 November 1942, the Russians launched a winter offensive that encircled 285,000 men of the German Sixth Army amid the ruins of a destroyed city. Adolph Hitler responded to this crisis by ordering his army to "stand fast," as relief efforts were initiated to sustain, then relieve, the beleaguered garrison. Yet, both endeavors were beyond the logistical capabilities of the Wehrmacht, and effective resistance within the city collapsed after 10 weeks of encirclement.* The remnants of the exhausted army, an estimated 90,000 men, surrendered on 2 February 1943.[49] The epic battle for Stalingrad was the most savage engagement fought in Europe during WWII, resulting in an estimated 2,000,000 causalities. The Wehrmacht alone lost over 300,000 soldiers, in addition to four Romanian, Hungarian, and Italian armies.[50]

Don was called to active duty service on 19 February 1943–just two weeks after the German surrender at Stalingrad. Months earlier, the United States Secretary of War announced that all students in the Air Corps Enlisted Reserve would be mobilized at the end of the fall semester. Regional commands, however, were allowed to determine when each reservist would report.[51] The flexibility of this order enabled Don to finish his second semester of school, completing a total of 28 units for his freshman year of college. Following induction, the "[reservists]

---

* The decision to resupply Stalingrad by air was based on an earlier success of maintaining the Demyank pocket where two army corps were surrounded for three months in early 1942. Yet in November 1942 the Luftwaffe was under exceptional stress with the opening of a second front in Africa following the American landings in Morocco and Algeria. Not only had 400 combat aircraft been redeployed to Africa, but the Luftwaffe was conducting a massive airlift of men and material to Tunisia. On 25 November 1942, the German Air Force only "had 298 JU-52 transports to supply Stalingrad, [yet] needed 500."[52]

[49] Cooper, *The German Army*, 335
[50] Ibid., 336
[51] Cardozier, *Colleges & Universities in WWII*, 13
[52] Ziemke, *Stalingrad to Berlin*, 61

were supposed to complete basic training and be sent to a classification center to determine whether they qualified for [assignment] as a pilot, bombardier, or navigator."[53] However, the activation of such a large number of personnel overwhelmed the service and Don, along with thousands of other ACER reservists were assigned to the Army Air Force Air Crew College Training Program (AAFTP). The program's curriculum, implemented at 153 colleges and universities throughout the United States, was designed to give future aviation cadets solid preparation for the ground instruction they would receive following their classification and selection for further training.

Don Dorfmeier, along with hundreds of other AAFTP cadets was assigned to the 318th College Training Detachment (Aircrew) at Utah State Agricultural College in Logan, Utah. The state college was notified in early January 1943 that they had been selected to participate in the service program. The school contracted with the War Department to teach four-hundred and twenty hours of freshman level courses in mathematics, physics, history, geography, and English to two groups of five-hundred students. This number, later revised to include a total of seven-hundred fifty cadets, was scheduled to arrive on 1 March and 15 April. Don arrived in Utah with the first group of airmen and, according to medical records, was hospitalized for sinusitis on 27 March 1943 at Bushnell General Hospital in Brigham City, Utah. He returned to duty 12 days later and attended classes that summer, excelling in physics and martial arts.

The daily activities for Don and the other cadets at Utah State were very structured. Demanding classes and study schedules, in addition to a system of disciplinary control, regulated personal privileges and limited the social life of the airmen. Yet, town's people would "invite trainees to their homes, particularly for Sunday dinner" and women at the university hosted frequent USO dances.[54]* These social encounters resulted in a number of servicemen developing romantic attachments to young women residing within the local community. Author Glenn Gray has acknowledged, "these war-wartime romances had an urgency . . . that peacetime seldom [knew]," and further cites the sociological

---

* The United Service Organizations Inc. (USO) is a nonprofit agency established in 1941 to support the war effort during WWII.

[53] Ibid., 88

[54] Cardozier, *Colleges & Universities in WWII*, 105

explanation for this phenomenon as "the uprooting character of war experiences."[55]

Don recalled that he and "the other cadets were well received and cared for by the residents of Logan, Utah. The Mormons were wonderful people who took us into their homes and into their hearts. Logan was also a place where I spent six months of the happiest days of my life. I had met a Mormon girl at a dance, and fell in love. We were terribly happy during those days. We would have picnics in a [secluded] canyon and ski in the snow country. We had many happy times together, and time [passed] quite rapidly." Soon, however, it was time for the detachment to depart, and the residents of Logan, "literally lined the streets of this small town, bidding us farewell, as we marched through."

Completing their training in Utah, Don and the other members of his detachment were sent to Santa Ana Army Air Base in California. Riding across the country, he and a close friend "laughed and joked about [their recent assignment]." Recalling their collective experiences, they reflected on the "one day where we were struggling through mud, weighted down with all of the equipment carried by soldiers in the infantry, thinking, this isn't what we signed up for." At that moment, "a Major stopped the disheveled and forlorn group of cadets to berate the noncommissioned officer (NCO) in charge and said, 'Sergeant, make these men straighten up and fly right. They're going to be officers in the United States Air Force and they'd better look like it!'" The acknowledgement caused the cadets' morale to soar.

The Army Air Base at Santa Ana in southern California was one of three "training centers for classification and preflight instruction of candidates for pilot, bombardier and navigator training," replacing the former two-year college prerequisite. Earlier assignments to a particular specialty were "based on aptitude, individual preference, and quota availability."[56] However, after 2 July 1942, all cadets were administered a series of written and physical tests that included an exacting two-day physical examination and psychiatric interview "to determine each applicant's adaptability for military aeronautics."[57]

---

[55] Gray, *The Warriors*, 62
[56] Carter & Mueller, *The Army Air Forces in WWII*, 553
[57] Ibid., 551

An additional two days were devoted to aptitude tests designed to "measure speed and accuracy of perception; use of tables, graphs and charts, and resourcefulness in practical problems."[58] The last phase of the classification process, consisting of psychomotor tests "to measure motor coordination, steadiness under pressure and reactions to candidate's aptitude for successful completion of training.

The new classification program at Santa Ana was very exacting, "normally last[ing] eighteen days" and "those men qualified for aircrew training were a carefully selected group."[59] All cadets completed a series of 20 written and physical tests, known as the "'classification battery' or 'stanine tests' [where] individual scores were weighted and cited as composites that measured potential for future assignment."[60] Don's clearance for further training in aeronautics was noted on his 23 August 1943 flight physical, which cited a passing "adaptability score, and composite aptitude scores for B-5 (bombardier), N-6 (navigator), and P-4 (pilot)." The examination also documented the Fresno youth's continual physical development, noting his height at 73 inches, his stocky build, and 190 pound weight.*

Aviation cadets, once assigned to a specific classification for training, were usually "motivated and enthusiastic student[s]."[61] In spite of this dedication, some parts of the training program, such as radio code instruction, were very unpopular. All students were required to attend one hour of daily instruction and by 1944, the required proficiency for an aviation cadet was to send and receive six words of Morse code per minute.[62] The task was considered dull and repetitious, and required great attention. Don, along with others students who struggled with mastering this standard, recalled "I couldn't pass Morse code because I kept focusing on the word instead of the letters [of the alphabet]." Yet, prior to sitting for his final examination, a compassionate instructor

---

* "Ten to 15 percent [of all cadets were rejected] on the original psychiatric interview," while qualifying scores for flying specialties were frequently adjusted to reflect the needs of the service.[63]

[58] Ibid., 551
[59] Ibid., 549
[60] Wells, *Courage and the Air War,* 7
[61] Carter & Mueller, *The Army Air Forces in WWII,* 560
[62] Ibid., 560
[63] Ibid., 8

told the anxious youth, "go drink a beer then come back and take this test." Don complied with the directive, and said, "the [the alcohol] relaxed me just enough to pass." Other instruction taught at Santa Ana covered thirteen subject areas, with significant concentration in physics, squadron tactics, and physical training. Service records indicate that Don completed 332 hours of instruction in this phase of his training and received a "weighted grade of 85.7," in spite of obtaining a minimum passing grade in code, and failing 18 hours of instruction in "Maps and Charts," truly an inauspicious beginning for a future navigator.

While training at Santa Ana, Don and the other cadets learned of the losses suffered by the US Army Air Force (USAAF) striking deep into Germany to bomb Schweinfurt and Regensburg on 17 August 1943. These missions, intending to destroy German ball bearing and aircraft production facilities, resulted in the loss or damage of 118 heavy bombers, which represented approximately one-third of the 376 aircraft launched to attack these targets. The losses were so severe that the air offensive over Europe was halted for a week so senior staff officers could reevaluate the viability of a strategic bombing campaign. However, just three weeks later, the Fortresses returned to Germany. This time they struck Stuttgart, 6 September 1943, and lost another 45 bombers. The following month, 14 October 1943, the US Army Eighth Air Force launched a second mission to bomb Schweinfurt, and again the losses were catastrophic. Moreover, the second Schweinfurt raid, known as Black Thursday, became legendary for the greatest loss of bombers dispatched to attack any single target during the war. Sixty of 291 B-17s were lost en route or over the city. Another 17 aircraft crashed on landing, or were salvaged due to extensive battle damage after returning to home station. However, neither Don nor the other cadets in his class considered the losses of the Army Air Force (AAF) in that summer and fall of 1943 as a harbinger or fatalistic indication of things to come. Rather, the eager young men derived some sense of reassurance from these events, perceiving them as almost a "guarantee" that they would all now have to graduate to replace the recent loss of so many personnel. Yet, few of these cadets realized that many of them would be interned within a year as POWs in the same camps as the airmen shot down during these ill-fated missions.

From Santa Ana, Don was sent to Las Vegas Army Air Field, Nevada, for six weeks of flexible gunnery training with the .50 caliber machine gun.[64] The purpose of this instruction was to teach sighting procedures, turret orientation, and other skills necessary for crew members in a heavy bomber. Current AAF doctrine stipulated that bombers would proceed to enemy targets without fighter protection, and training was essential for self-defense when attacked by enemy aircraft. Beginning in 1942, navigator trainees were given gunnery instruction in addition to their specialty training. Two years later, gunnery familiarization was provided for all students before their entry into navigation schools.

Don Dorfmeier   Author's collection

After graduating from gunnery school, Don was allowed to take nine days of personal leave, yet he had no way to get home. In desperation, the young cadet had "gone all the way to the base commander, but there just weren't any ships available." In the commander's office, looking sad and despondent, the young cadet was approached by a staff sergeant in the training group known as "Blackie the Greek," who asked, "What's the matter, son?" Don explained his situation, and the NCO, known for a "getting more things done on that base than the commanding general," had the forlorn cadet on a plane heading back to Fresno within 24 hours. Don was elated by this opportunity. It allowed him to spend five days at home with his family before reporting to his

---

[64] Carter & Mueller, *The Army Air Forces In WWII*, 591

next duty assignment. "It was," he recalled, "the only days my mother, family, and I spent together for [the next] two years."

Departing Fresno, Don reported to the AAF Navigational School at Hando, Texas, in early March 1944. The navigator training program had expanded rapidly the previous year, and this new facility was built to meet the escalating needs of the service. The objective of the training was to qualify students as precision, dead reckoning navigators with basic pilot skills, along with radio and navigation techniques. The attrition rate for this training "was approximately 20 percent" of any given class "for failure to meet basic proficiency requirements during . . . training."[65]

At his new duty station in Texas, Don completed eight training flights before he received a letter from his Mormon girlfriend informing him she was dating another man whom she planned to marry. Recalling the incident years later, Don said, "It seemed she had met some clown and they were getting pretty serious. So I went to town, proceeded to get drunk and reported AWOL for [the next] three days." After returning to base, the despondent 19-year-old cadet was called before the Training Review Board and informed by the presiding officer that he was being "washed back six weeks." The officer, according to Don, was a "nice guy who was willing to dispense leniency." Yet, the offended cadet, still smarting over his recent rejection, responded to the board's recommendation with several disrespectful and sarcastic comments. "I have waited 15 months to get into this man's war," Don said, "and I'm not there yet! Now, if you think I can make it after being [recycled] then do it. [However], I want to get there and I want to get there [now]!" Stunned by the insolent remarks, the board reversed its decision, dismissed Don from the navigational school, and terminated his status as an aviation cadet. Days later the reprimanded youth, now reduced in grade to the rank of private, reported as an aerial gunner to 18th Replacement Depot in Salt Lake City where he would start the third and final phase of crew training, prior to overseas deployment. After arriving at Salt Lake, all new personnel were assembled in a large theater and assigned to form training replacement crews to fly the B-17 Flying Fortress. Don, along with eight other individuals, three officers, and five enlisted men was assigned to crew B-10, under the command of Lieutenant Wallace Blackwell.

---

[65] Carter & Mueller, *The Army Air Forces in WWII*, 589

Boeing's legendary B-17 Fortress, which now served as the premier heavy bomber of the US Army Eighth Air Force in Europe, had experienced numerous modifications since the first prototype was built in 1935. Extensive revisions and alterations of the original design had extended the length of the fuselage to 74 feet, and increased the size of the vertical fin and rudder of the tail section to produce a magnificent and glamorous aircraft with a wingspan of 103 feet. The frame of the larger and new G-model Fortress was now propelled by four modified 1,200-hp Wright R-1820-97 Cyclone turbocharger radial piston engines capable of flying a distance of 2,000 miles with a 5,000 lb. bomb load. Flying such a distance to conduct a combat mission required a 10-man crew to perform a variety of complex tasks. Four officers served as pilot, copilot, navigator, and bombardier, while two of the six enlisted crewmen performed primary duties–radio operator and flight engineer– in addition to functioning as aerial gunners.

The intended purpose of this third and final phase of training was to integrate individual and collective training to form a crew that would function as a cohesive unit. This transformation was as much a psychological process as an exercise in advanced technical training. The emergence of a crew identity also required that the airmen accept the different backgrounds and temperaments of other crew members. This process was essential in order to develop a sense of trust in the judgment and performance of other crew members under trying circumstances. The technical aspects of this phase of training focused on extensive exercises in high-altitude formation flying, long-range navigation, target identification, and simulated combat missions.

During this last phase of stateside training, Don developed a strong friendship with another enlisted gunner, John E. Bell. Their friendship was enhanced significantly by their similar backgrounds in college and the ACER. Although slightly older, John was also a student, playing football at Mississippi State College when the Japanese attacked Pearl Harbor. Two months later, the 20-year-old college student enlisted in the Air Corps Enlisted Reserve and finished his second semester of college before called into the active Army Air Force. Once mobilized, the cadet was sent to Maxwell Airfield, Alabama, to wait preflight training in Santa Ana, California.

Awaiting his orders, Bell attended a local dance and met freshman student, Gincie Dollaheit, who was enrolled at Huntington College, an all-women's school in Montgomery, Alabama. The couple dated and maintained contact with each other as John progressed through his phase training and his later termination from the pilot program. This was a similar, if not greater,disappointment than Don's dismissal from his navigational training. Both programs were challenging, yet the pilot program was, according to John, more demanding as "[an instructor's] judgment [regarding] flying proficiency was [more] subjective." Regardless of reasons, a total of " . . . 124,000 students failed to complete the primary, basic or advanced stages of pilot instruction. This figure, which includes fatalities, amounted to almost 40 percent" of the cadets who entered the training program.[66] However, "students eliminated from pilot training were not lost to the AAF, since most of them were reassigned to other types of instruction or service."[67]

John fondly recalled Don as " . . . a person everyone liked. He had a physically dominating presence, enjoyed perfect health, and possessed a wonderful spirit that was kind and lovable." Bell also recollected how Don's physical stamina served to benefit the crew while participating in a simulated escape and evasion exercise. "With most of the group succumbing to fatigue and exhaustion," John continued, "Don's prodding and exhortations kept the crew moving."

Early that spring, Gincie Dollaheit was granted a leave of absence from her position at the Pentagon in Washington, DC, and traveled to Rapid City, South Dakota to marry John Bell prior to his overseas deployment. The service was conducted at the First Methodist Church on 9 April 1944 and all of John's crew attended the wedding, with several individuals actively participating in the ceremony. Crew member Adrian Bacon served as John's best man and Don gave the bride away. "They all looked so good in their dress uniforms," John recalled, "and Don seemed as proud as he escorted Gincie down the aisle."

Weeks later, Blackwell's crew completed their final phase training and prepared for overseas deployment. "We had some good times . . . we were a good crew," recalled Wallace Blackwell, reflecting on the quality of their training and their development as a cohesive group.

---

[66] Carter & Mueller, *The Army Air Forces in WWII*, 578
[67] Ibid., 578

From Grand Rapids, the airmen moved by rail to Kearney, Nebraska, to draw new equipment before proceeding by troop train to Brooklyn Navel Shipyard. There, Don and the others members of his crew boarded a converted luxury liner for a 30 June departure for England. Aboard ship, Don wrote to his mother describing his cross-country journey. "This is beautiful, lovely country with lovely weather. Maybe some day we'll all [vacation] together when the lights of the world are lit again."

The airmen in Wallace Blackwell's crew were one of twenty replacement crews traveling with other Army Air Force ground and administrative personnel. These 400–600 airmen were a small component among the thousands of soldiers assigned to the Army Ground Forces. John Bell recalled that his contingent of airmen quickly incurred the resentment of other soldiers, "for failure to adhere and abide by the Army regulations" used to enforce a daily routine aboard ship during the 10-day voyage. "The airmen," according to John, "stayed up late at night playing cards after 'lights out,' failed to make morning formations and slept late into the day." Although irritating to the regular Army, this behavior was in keeping with all "elite forces . . . [who consider themselves] relatively free from ordinary administration and discipline."[68]

In contrast to John's assessment, Don recalled that, "aboard ship there were about 600 of us flying guys," and the rest were in the regular Army. To provide some structure and entertainment, boxing matches were conducted every day on the top deck. As an athlete, Don appreciated the competition of these matches and enjoyed watching them until, "everybody wanted to know if there was somebody from the 'chicken shit' Air Force who could box, and my crew came looking for me. Well, I watched these guys and they were good. They had the moves . . . they were quick, [and] I wasn't going to climb in there with any of them. I had three bouts in college [as part of my physical education] and I could hit, but not like these guys. So for six days I hid [until we reached England]."

[68] Beaumont, *Military Elites*, 2

Prop and Wings insignia

This insignia was used by the US Army Air Corps, which was a separate branch of the US Army, from 1926 to 1947. During WWII, all commissioned aviators, in addition to most enlisted aircrew, identified with the elite status of this smaller corps rather than with the larger Army Air force.

US Army Air Corps shoulder sleeve patch

3

ENGLAND: 1942–43

In late February 1942, shortly after Don started attending classes at Fresno State College, Brigadier General Ira Eaker departed for England to consult with military representatives of the British government. Eaker and his advance party arrived with instructions to identify and coordinate the logistical requirements necessary to base the newly activated US Army Eighth Air Force.[69] It was during this official visit that the flat open countryside of East Anglia, north of London, was selected for the numerous airfields required to deploy the largest of all US air forces stationed overseas in WWII. The first contingents of administrative and ground crew personnel arrived later, on 12 May 1942; however, construction of the new airfields would not proceed until mid-summer.

The strategy for directing the American air campaign in Europe was only completed six months earlier, following the reorganization of the former Army Air Corps. The plan, written as an annex to a broader global strategy, was based on an anticipated conflict with Germany and Japan, and a mutual agreement with England to "attack Germany first" in the event America became embroiled in a European conflict. The annex, designated AWPD-1, was drafted in just days by the recently activated Air War Plans Division, yet reflected a generation of analysis and study by the Corps Tactical School at Maxwell Field, Alabama. The primary objectives of the plan were to conduct a daylight bombing campaign against Germany in order to disrupt and destroy the nation's electric power grid and transportation system, as well as their synthetic and petroleum refining industries. The confidence exhibited by the staff planners to achieve these objectives was based on the Air Corps' earlier acquisition of two technological advances during the past ten years. The first service procurement was the Norden bomb sight, a sophisticated instrument that could automatically calculate a bomb release point by factoring altitude, air and ground speed, in addition to wind drift. The other service acquisition was the 1937 purchase of the Boeing B-17

[69] Jablonski, *The Flying Fortress*, 85

Flying Fortress, the world's only heavy, four-engine bomber.

B-17 production line   Boeing

Following Germany's declaration of war against the United States, President Roosevelt and England's Prime Minister, Winston Churchill, conferred in Washington to "[reaffirm] their joint decision to concentrate on the defeat of Germany."[70] The British public, however, was generally ambivalent regarding America's late entry into the war and the deployment of US forces to their country. Others resented the fact they had been at war for two and a half years while the United States had remained neutral. The war in Europe had caused great anxiety throughout England, especially among the people of London who feared they would be subjected to massive aerial bombardment.[71] The apprehension felt in the nation's capital and elsewhere was based on the country's lack of resolve and limited military capability to wage war.[72] After suffering several million casualties during the First World War, and the financial devastation of the 1929 Depression, British politicians were reluctant "to jeopardize the frail economic recovery by spending more money on [rearmament]."[73] However, the British Royal Air Force (RAF) received enough funding to begin a limited production program in 1934. Still, at the onset of hostilities, deliveries of the new British aircraft were "six months behind schedule."[74]

---

[70] Forster, *The World at War,* 201
[71] Mark & Humphries, *London at War*, 10
[72] The Dark Valley, 409
[73] Ibid., 414
[74] Ibid., 64

In early September 1939, the British government initiated forced evacuations of 750,000 Londoners in anticipation of mass aerial bombings.[75] Another 2,225,000 persons "left their homes during the first month of the war"[76] as the "fear of air attack closed cinemas, theatres, and football grounds."[77] Ultimately, the perceived threat of an attack by air, in addition to actual damage sustained from aerial bombardment, caused marked shifts in the country's population, when millions of Britains either voluntarily relocated or were displaced to new residences.

The war also forced England into a general mobilization. National conscription, first introduced in spring 1939, and expanded to require that all men, aged eighteen to fifty, be inducted into the military or other services designated as essential by the state. Unmarried women aged twenty to thirty were also required to perform similar duty, and the number of women in military service increased dramatically over the next eighteen months. By spring 1941, over 100,000 women were serving in the Royal Air Force alone, manning communication sites, plotting tables and, in some instances, performing aircraft maintenance.[78] The country's mobilization for war also caused a marked decline in the nation's standard of living. German U-boat operations in the Atlantic Ocean, which sank one quarter of the British Merchant Fleet, dramatically affected a nation that imported "half her food, and two-thirds of her raw materials from abroad."[79] Food rationing, first introduced in January 1940, varied each month according to shipping losses and seasonal supplies.

A sense of resolve and confidence only started to emerge in England following Winston Churchill's appointment as prime minister in May 1940. Soon after, British industry converted to 24-hour operations, and productivity increased significantly in the weeks following Dunkirk. Then, on 10 July 1940, the long anticipated German air assault against England commenced. Initially, the Luftwaffe attacked shipping, airfields, and communication sites located south of London prior to concentrating on bombing the nation's capital. This shift in focus, while

---

[75] Mark & Humphries, *London at War*, 14

[76] Ibid., 11

[77] Marwick, *Britain in Our Century*, 106

[78] Deighton, *The Battle of Britain*, 183

[79] Mark & Humphries, *London at War*, 110

dramatic, surrendered the tactical initiative to the RAF as German fighters were forced to fly protective escort for their smaller, lightly armed bombers. These fighters were further restricted by fuel limitations that curtailed their range and their ability to remain over London for more than a few minutes. Eventually, mounting losses of aircraft and aircrew forced the Luftwaffe to suspend daylight operations. A final 10-week phase of nightly bombings, known as the "London Blitz," began on 6 October 1940.

The following spring, German air and ground units in northern France redeployed to Eastern Europe in preparation for Operation Barbarossa, the forthcoming assault on the Soviet Union. This shift in operational focus forced the Luftwaffe to acknowledge that they had failed to achieve air supremacy over England. The defeat was attributable to multiple causes. First and foremost, British command and control procedures, in addition to the performance of their fighter aircraft, were superior to the poorly conceived and executed German strategy and the use of their air assets. The air campaign also exposed serious deficiencies in the operational doctrine and the tactical execution of the Luftwaffe; most notable being that the German air service was not organized to perform the role of a strategic air force and did not possess a heavy bomber with sufficient load-carrying capacity or operational range. Equally problematic, German production schedules for existing aircraft were not increased to offset combat losses, which allowed the British RAF to replace lost aircraft at a faster rate than their adversary.

While London survived the Blitz of 1940, the British Army continued to suffer further defeats in Greece, Crete, and the African desert prior to the arrival of the first deployed elements of the US Army Eighth Air Force in June 1942. The British public greeted the American's arrival with uncertainty while the nation's military strategists were openly skeptical of the American proposal to conduct a daylight bombing campaign. Both England and Germany had tried unsuccessfully to conduct similar operations earlier in the war, yet neither country achieved satisfactory results. Significant daytime losses of aircraft forced the British Royal Air Force to revert to a nighttime campaign, while the German Luftwaffe eventually suspended their sustained air assault against England altogether. British sensibilities were further offended by the assuredness of the inexperienced Americans and their "reckless spending of money and the wild parties for which they became notorious."[80] Moreover, arrogant and condescending comments such as, "We've come over to win the damn war for you,"[81] were infuriating; and British resentment, in some segments of society, persisted throughout the war. Still, the prime minister welcomed the American entry into the European conflict, knowing that this act alone ensured England's survival and Germany's ultimate defeat. Churchill knew the history of the United States, and he appreciated the fierce nature of the American spirit. He also recognized the determination of the American soldier, whose tenacity, courage, and valor were notable in other conflicts. The Yanks, Churchill noted in mid-1942, were "wonderful material and will learn very quickly."[82]

The initial deployment of the US Army Air Force to England and the start of subsequent air operations over German-occupied northern Europe were limited and slow developing. Preparation alone for movement of an air unit overseas was complex and required months of coordination.[83] Once deployed, the task of conducting a strategic daylight bombing campaign to destroy the industrial production capacity of the Third Reich was daunting. The German Luftwaffe had benefited significantly from almost three years of operational experience that enhanced their command and control procedures, as well as their tactical skills.

By mid-August 1942, the recently deployed Eighth Air Force had assembled sufficient number of aircraft in England to conduct a limited first mission, and bombed the Sotteville marshaling yards near Rouen in Northern France. While all aircraft returned from the mission, subsequent operations would prove that heavy bombers were vulnerable to a determined air attack, despite their defensive armament. However, the greatest difficulties encountered by US Army Eighth Air Force initiating air operations in Northern Europe were bad weather and the diversion of air assets to support the forthcoming American landings in North Africa.

Following the liberation of French Morocco and Algeria, Roosevelt and Churchill conferred again at Casablanca in January 1943 to plan an

---

[80] Laffin, *Americans in Battle*, 152
[81] Kaplan & Smith, *One Last Look*, 78
[82] Laffin, *Americans in Battle*, 148
[83] Carter & Mueller, *The Army Air Forces in WWII*, 625

overarching strategy for conducting war against Germany. Achieving air supremacy over the Third Reich was identified as an absolute necessity for a " . . . successful invasion of continental Europe."[84] To achieve this most primary of goals, both nations agreed to initiate a Combined Bomber Offensive. The British RAF would continue their two-year campaign of night bombing, while the US Army Air Force would make the necessary tactical adjustments to implement daylight operations. The objectives of this campaign were to dislocate and destroy the German military, industrial, and economic structure by attacking submarine construction and aircraft production facilities, in addition to transportation and other industrial targets.[85]

In January 1943, American aircrews of the US Army Eighth Air Force started flying bombing missions inside Germany. However, the bomb groups lacked fighter escort for a significant part of their mission, and losses of aircraft and crews mounted dramatically. Most targets were well-defended by effective German antiaircraft batteries directed by electrical transmission tracking data, generated from an analog computer. These batteries, under the operational control of the Luftwaffe, were the primary defensive weapon of the German Air Force and initially thought to prove sufficient for the defense of German air space. By 1940, 10,000 light, medium, and heavy *flieger abwehr kanones* (referred to as "flak" in Allied operation reports) were deployed around major cities and "vulnerable targets in the Ruhr, or in the Western Defense Zone."[86] This defensive belt, established behind the Rhine River, was hundreds of kilometers in length, varied between 18 to 100 kilometers in depth, and was designed to "provide a three-fold overlapping field of fires against aircraft flying at an altitude in excess of 23,000 feet."*

The standard and most versatile antiaircraft gun in the German Luftwaffe was the famed 8.8cm model 36, otherwise known as the "88" that fired an 18-pound shell to a maximum effective altitude of 20,000

---

* By 1944, the German flak service "numbered more than 900,000 [personnel] who manned 14,250 heavy . . . and almost 35,000 lighter weapons." [87]

[84] Overy, *The Air War*, 73
[85] Jablonski, *Flying Fortress*, 114
[86] Cooper, *The German Air Force*, 56
[87] Wells, *Courage and the Air War*, 43

feet. Clock fuses in each round were used to determine the altitude at which the shell would explode, splitting the casings into hundreds of pieces of jagged shrapnel to inflict lethal damage to aircraft within the bursting radius of 20 meters. A well-drilled crew could track and engage a target in 20 to 25 seconds, and maintain a sustained rate of fire of one round every five seconds for a period of two minutes.

German 8.8 cm Flak 36   German Federal Archives

Although the German flak service was initially designated as the primary air defense system of the Third Reich, newly formed fighter groups were soon deployed through Western Europe and Germany to intercept and attack the incoming British and American bomb formations.[88] These defensive interceptors groups consisted of heavily-armed, high-powered, single engine Messerschmitt and Focke-Wulf fighters that would attack the Allied bomb groups en route to their targets.* The German fighters would then circle in waiting for the bomb groups to finish their attack, thus avoid being hit by their own antiaircraft fire, and strike the departing formations again as they turned toward England. During this phase of the operations, the interceptors concentrated their attack on damaged aircraft unable to keep pace with the main group. German fighters initially preferred to attack the American bombers from the rear. However, this approach left the attacker exposed for an extended period before closing within the optimum range of 400 meters necessary to deliver the required 18–20

* The ME-109 was the primary interceptor of the German Luftwaffe during WWII. A total of 33,984 models of this aircraft were produced between 1933 and 1945.

[88] Westermann, *Flak*, 181

rounds of 20 mm cannon fire that would bring down a B-17.* However, an alternate tactic, soon adopted by the German fighter command, was to attack American bombers head on. In this instance, the actual time of attack was limited to a few seconds. The increased rate of speed at which the combatants approached each other, limited the time available for the gunners to spot and accurately fire on the attacking aircraft.[89] Accurate gunnery was further affected by "the challenges of deflection shooting, extremely cold temperatures and cumbersome equipment, which limited [an individual's], reaction time" to an attack.[90]

German Focke-Wulf 190   German Federal Archives

Throughout the spring of 1943, USAAF bomb groups flew deeper into occupied Europe, testing the quality of the German opposition and adjusting their tactics to provide a greater concentration of firepower against harassing enemy fighters. The current B-17 model Fortress, armed with eleven flexible .50 caliber machine guns, only carried enough ammunition for each gun to sustain a continuous rate of fire for 60 seconds.

Yet, when these bombers were arranged in multiple group formations of 18 and 36 aircraft, the volume of defensive fire was formidable. By 1943, this so called "combat box" had evolved as the ideal defensive formation, comprised of "three staggered squadron formations, [flying] at different altitudes so as to provide maximum

---

* German gun-camera film clearly show "that Luftwaffe fighters often came well within 100 yards before delivering their deadliest blows."[91]

[89] Wells, *Courage & Air Warfare*, 40
[90] Ibid., 41
[91] Wells, *Courage and the Air War*, 99

defensive fire to all aircraft of the bomb group." Although the combat box provided significant protection, only fighter escorts would keep the German Air Force from inflicting unacceptable losses.

Combat missions, in addition to routine air operations over Europe, were inherently stressful. An aircrew's "fundamental reliance on a number of mechanical systems for their safety meant airmen faced long hours of life-threatening hazards related to human error, malfunctions, and other problems related to weather."[92] Moreover, operations were conducted at 20,000 to 25,000 feet, which limited the effectiveness of German antiaircraft batteries, yet exposed individuals to temperatures that ranged between 25 to 50 degrees below zero. The heavyweight flying suits available in 1942 were not adequate to protect the aircrews at this altitude. The Air Force eventually conducted an investigation of the unsatisfactory performance of the flying clothing used by the AAF operating from England, citing, frostbite constituted 70 percent of all combat casualties. Furthermore, the report noted, the "number of bombers [sent] out on a combat mission was determined more by the amount of adequate clothing available than by any other factors."[93] Beginning in 1944, improvements in flight suits and improved training programs in the proper use of this clothing reduced frostbite casualties to acceptable levels.

In spite of these difficulties, most airmen considered the hardest part of any mission as the time spent aboard aircraft prior to launch. The wait required mastery of both boredom and dread after preparing oneself to "face the hazards of combat."[94] However, the one stress that affected every crew member was the inevitable "stand downs" required because of weather or other operational considerations. "Few [aspects of the air war] caused more anxiety, stress, or anger." Yet, once airborne and engaged, the unique characteristics of air combat also placed extraordinary strains on the airmen.[95] The operational environment was overwhelmingly demanding, life threatening, and "the unremitting carnage of combat [with the attending] frequency . . . and the randomness of death was shocking, and tested [everyone's] confidence."[96] The most

---

[92] Ibid., 28
[93] Sweeting, *Combat Flying Clothing,* 5–6
[94] Kaplan & Smith, *One Last Look,* 97
[95] Wells, *Courage & Air Warfare,* 60
[96] Ibid., 60

stressful moments in aerial combat occurred after sustaining battle damage, for crew members had only brief moments to make life or death decisions. Thousands of bombers were shot down under these circumstances, usually killing several, if not most of the aircrew. Between August 1942 and August 1944, an even greater number of bombers "sustained battle damage during the air campaign over Europe and returned to bases carrying [thousands of killed and wounded crew members]."[97] One study, conducted between January and June 1944, noted returning Eighth Air Force "aircraft brought back 1,175 dead and 4,689 wounded airmen."[98]

The most reliable aircraft to bring the majority of these airmen back to their respective home stations in England was the Boeing B-17F model Fortress, first flown in May 1942. The latest model bomber, with more than four hundred modifications to the original prototype, possessed greater utility and survivability than the newer B-24, which could not absorb the same degree of battle damage. In comparison, the Fortress would become legendary for its ability to reach its target and bring its crew home in spite of horrific damage. This record would later prompt Lieutenant General Ira Eaker to state, "The B-17 . . . was the best combat airplane ever built. It combined, in perfect balance, the right engine . . . wing and . . . control surfaces. The [Fortress] was . . . rugged . . . and it could sustain . . . [significant] battle damage. You wouldn't believe they could stay in the air."[99]

Eaker's sentiments were captured in the lyrics of a popular song of that era, "Coming in on a Wing and a Prayer." The idea for the song came from a letter written by a B-17 pilot to Jimmy McHugh, recounting a return from a particularly difficult mission being made on "one engine and a prayer." The recording, released in 1943, eventually registered as one of the nation's most popular songs, and reflected the country's awareness and fascination with the prominent role of the US Army Air Force in the first eighteen months of war in Europe.

Although USAAF combat operations in the European Theater were initially limited in 1942–43, it was not long before psychiatric casualties, which confused and confounded medical authorities,

---

[97] Wells, *Courage & Air Warfare*, 47
[98] Ibid., 101
[99] Jablonski, *The Flying Fortress*, xiv

began to occur. All the US Armed Forces, and in particular the Army Air Force, had gone to great lengths to use psychological testing and psychiatric interviews to identify those individuals thought to be vulnerable to psychological stress and potential psychiatric causalities. This initial screening, conducted prior to induction, rejected over one million men for military service based on "emotional disorders, and/or mental deficiency."[100]

Once enlisted and in training as a member of the USAAF, an individual's sense of invulnerability and omnipotence was sustained by narcissism and elitism. Later, as exposure to the operational intensity of flying increased during combat, "peer pressure, self-esteem, [and unit] cohesiveness served as the under-pinning of crew moral."[101] In recognition of these group dynamics, crew integrity was maintained whenever possible. Unfortunately, loss of a crew member from illness, injury, or death frequently demanded that these positions be filled by replacements. Sadly, such occurrences increased the stress level of both the newly assigned individual and the gaining crew, until the replacement proved to be reliable.

Ultimately, all aircrew members were affected by stress associated with combat operations, and attempted to manage the anxiety associated with disfigurement and death. However, the most common coping behavior of many airmen involved the excessive use of alcohol to numb their emotional reactions, intrusive thoughts, or nightmares.[102] Such behavior was readily understandable given that the Army Air Force officially sanctioned the use of alcohol during crew debriefings following combat operations. In these settings, airmen were routinely provided whiskey or other spirits for its sedating effects, which enabled them to focus. Outside formal debriefings, alcohol "was freely available at cheap prices to officers and enlisted men, and the drinking of American fliers in England during the Second World War was legendary."[103] Only years later would countless numbers of airmen learn of the problems associated with alcohol use as a primary means of calming their anxieties.

---

[100] Ginzberg, *The Lost Divisions*, 36
[101] Wells, *Courage and the Air War*, 93
[102] Ibid., 97
[103] Laffin, *Americans in Battle*, 131–132

Not everyone, however, could cope with the anxiety and fear inherent in air operations, even with alcohol. The dilemma then faced by the medical authorities of the AAF was attempting to distinguish and differentiate between those men experiencing emotional distress and potential psychiatric collapse from those individuals who were malingering. This confusion was reflected in the use of a wide variety of terms to characterize the phenomena of psychological breakdowns: "operational fatigue or exhaustion," in addition to the pejorative, "lack of moral fiber," noted as LMF in reports and individual medical records. Regrettably, the variations of terminology used to describe the condition contributed to further confusion of identification and treatment.[104]

By 1943, American authorities were starting to recognize that emotional collapse could happen to anyone, especially if the affected person had already flown several combat missions. This change in attitude caused a shift in emphasis from a predisposition orientation to a stress-related model of mental health based on three supporting considerations. First was the intensity and duration of the stress. Second was the realization that everyone was vulnerable to the effects of combat. And last, emotional distress was recognized as noninfectious. Service physicians were then tasked with taking a more active role in talking with aircrews to acknowledge their anxieties, bolster individual coping skills and, when appropriate, recommend a temporary "stand down" to prevent a pending psychological break.

Flight surgeons assigned to the Eighth Air Force were assisted in their efforts to practice preventive medicine soon after US forces deployed to England. Beginning in 1942, various "English manors and hotels were used as rest homes," providing an atmosphere of "ease and freedom" for operationally fatigued airmen. Despite joking references to these rest sites as "flak farms," 15 facilities were eventually established, "providing an average stay of six to eight days."[105] One veteran characterized his rest and recreational leave as having " . . . a whole group of activities . . . with dances every night. A joyous experience . . . . You got no sleep at all, but it was worth it!"[106]

---

[104] Wells, *Courage and the Air War*, 165
[105] Wells, *Courage and the Air War*, 80
[106] Kaplan & Smith, *One Last Look*, 143

In spite of these efforts, aircrew morale had flagged precipitously in early 1943 in response to the dramatic losses of aircraft and personnel. Enemy fighters and effective antiaircraft defenses were destroying as much as 12 percent of all formations attacking targets in Europe. Finally, in March 1943, the AAF was forced to establish a tour of duty policy, limiting the number of required combat missions to twenty-five before an airman could rotate back to the United States. Yet, many crew members thought the policy unfair and unattainable, believing the odds were against them. A later study conducted by the Eighth Air Force validated this perception. The study tracked the status of 2,085 airmen who represented six bomb groups, and concluded that an individual was statistically most at risk of becoming a casualty during his first ten missions. However, "only 25 percent of the [participants] survived their operational tours unscathed."[107]

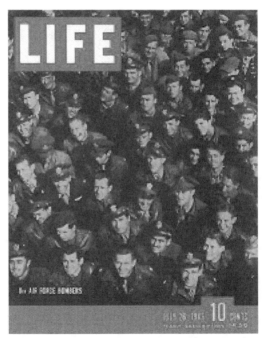

US airmen 1943   Life Magazine

By midsummer 1943, the Germans recognized that they had initially underestimated the threat posed by the daylight raids of the Eighth Air Force. Mistakenly, they believed that the 260 interceptor

---

[107] Wells, *Courage and Air Warfare*, 46

fighters deployed in France and Germany would make these incursions too costly. However, the success of the early Eighth Air Force missions, conducted in spring and early summer of 1943, illustrated the necessity to respond more aggressively to this new threat.[108] Additional German fighters and antiaircraft batteries were subsequently transferred to the West to counter the growing threat of the punishing raids and the increasing frequency of deeper penetrations into northwestern Germany.

The US Army Air Force responded to the increasing presence of German air units by attacking the aircraft production plants and other installations with the intended purpose of eliminating the Luftwaffe as an effective fighting force. Despite this determined effort, deliveries of new German fighter aircraft increased to an overall production of almost 1,000 units a month by June 1943.[109] This increased productivity occurred primarily because of the recuperative powers of the German aircraft industry and the effectiveness of a decentralization program implemented by Albert Speer, the new Minister of Armament. However, German aircrew could not be replaced as readily as lost aircraft, nor could the Luftwaffe curtail the growing momentum of the Combined Bombing Campaign. Enraged by this turn of events, Hitler went so far as to "accuse the German fliers of cowardice and threatened them with court-martials, executions, and other reprisals."[110]

As the American air campaign intensified over Germany, the Eighth Air Force attacked the ball bearing plants in Schweinfurt and the Messerschmitt production factory in Regensburg. These attacks, conducted 17 August 1943, represented the deepest penetration into Germany and employed the largest number of heavy bombers for any single day operation to date. The raids were also a disaster, costing the USAAF the loss of 60 of the 376 Fortresses dispatched for the day's mission, along with 565 aircrew. Another 130 bombers returned to their bases damaged. Moreover, the Americans had hoped the British RAFs would conduct a follow-on strike to Schweinfurt that evening to eliminate the ball bearing production capability of all five plants located in the city. However, the RAF's evening mission had already been determined by other priorities. Weeks earlier, Winston Churchill and his advisors had selected an even more important target than

---

[108] Freeman, *The Mighty Eighth*, 74
[109] Bekker, *The Luftwaffe War Diaries*, 304
[110] Jablonski, *Flying Fortress*, 143

Schweinfurt, an obscure experimental facility located near Peenemünde on the Baltic coast of northern Germany.

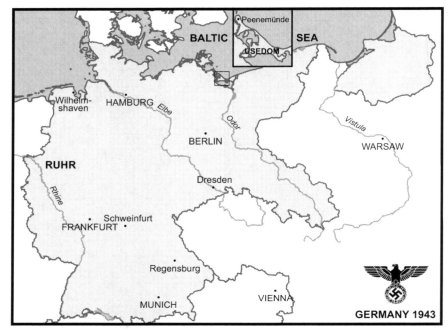

Strategic Targets 1943   Author's collection

The first bomb groups of the newly organized US Army Eighth Air Force arrived in England late summer of 1942. Months later, these same units attacked the submarine yards in Wilhelmshaven. Subsequent missions targeted industrial cities in the Ruhr prior to initiating the ill-fated strikes on Schweinfurt and Regensburg.

4

PEENEMÜNDE

Early in 1940, British Intelligence received information that Germany was pursuing a rocket propulsion program. The report was initially dismissed as implausible or a ruse initiated by the German *Abwehr* to mislead and divert British intelligence efforts.* However, similar reports of scientific achievement and production efforts to build new weapons continued to surface through 1942. Several months later, British aerial reconnaissance finally confirmed the existence of a secret development site, and what appeared to be multiple firing stands, near

RAF reconnaissance photo   NCPA

the Baltic coast fishing village of Peenemünde. Shortly thereafter, on 29 June 1943, Winston Churchill and his advisors reviewed the latest intelligence reports on this secret facility during a critical cabinet meeting, concluding that immediate action must be taken. The prime minister then directed the full weight of the British Royal Air Force (RAF) to attack the recently discovered location during a nighttime raid when weather conditions would allow for the most favorable results.[111]

The secret activity at Peenemünde was an extension of a rocket

---

* The Abwehr was a German Army intelligence organization that gathered raw intelligence reports from field agents and other sources. The organization was abolished by Hitler on 18 February 1944.

[111] Shirer, *Rise & Fall of the Third Reich*, 1009

program and experimental center established in 1930 by the German Army near Kummersdorf, Germany. The program was initiated to circumvent the restrictions of the Treaty of Versailles that ended WWI and sought to limit Germany's development and production of heavy artillery. The primary purpose of the original facility was to conduct research and experimental test firings of solid-fuel artillery rockets, in addition to investigating the possibilities of using liquid-fuel rockets for long-range bombardment of military targets.

Following Adolph Hitler's rise to power and the country's accelerated rearmament initiative of 1935–36, the German Army and the newly formed Luftwaffe agreed to cooperate on the research and development of a liquid-fuel rocket propulsion program. The German Army was interested in long-range ballistic missiles, while the Air Force wanted to develop and produce jet aircraft. To maintain secrecy, the joint service program was relocated to the northeast peninsula of Usedom Island near the Baltic fishing village of Peenemünde, some 250 kilometers north of Berlin. The selection of this remote and forested site would provide the necessary isolation to conduct unobserved test firings of experimental rockets into the Baltic Sea.

The development of the new research facility was financed by both the Wehrmacht and the German Air Force, although the actual construction of the site was funded and built by the Luftwaffe in 1937.[112] Eighteen months later, the new location had been transformed into a self-contained community with living quarters for the families of scientists and technicians, along with social and medical services near the town of 20,000 inhabitants. The development was also supported by a power station, oxygen plant, and a labor camp for manual workers, in addition to an airfield and wind tunnels in support of specific projects for the German Air Force. The new site, known as the Peenemünde Experimental Works, became operational the following year.

In spring 1939, Adolph Hitler visited the older, yet still functional, Kummersdorf Experimental Station to view a demonstration of the latest rocket design and learn of the progress made at Peenemünde. The briefings were conducted by project commander, Oberst Walter Dornberger, and Director of the technical department, Wernher von Braun. Dornberger and other members of the tour would later recount

---

[112] Middlebrook, *The Peenemünde Raid*, 15

that Hitler seemed initially disinterested in the new technology. Still, the Experimental Works received increased priority for all essential raw materials several months later, following the onset of war in Europe. Yet, the priority for developing the army's latest design model rocket, the A-4, was again curtailed after Germany's stunning defeat of France in summer 1940.[113] Most military and political leaders in Germany regarded the war in Europe as all but won, and all research and development programs were subsequently reappraised. Those projects that could not be put into production during the forthcoming year were canceled.

German industry lacked sufficient quantities of raw materials to meet the demands of the Wehrmacht and a prolonged conflict. These problems were further aggravated by a poorly organized economy that was easily affected by political intrigue and military strategy, in addition to an ineffectual military command structure. Hitler further complicated Germany's production requirements for specific items such as new aircraft, after rescinding the Luftwaffe's priority for materials. His focus, and that of the nation's industry, was now dedicated to the production of tanks and other motorized vehicles required for the pending invasion of Russia.

Hitler's intention to invade the Soviet Union, while a defiant England required the deployment of military forces in Western Europe and North Africa, made senior German military officers apprehensive. However, the initial success of the German Armed Forces in earlier campaigns suggested that Russia would be defeated quickly during a brisk summer operation. This miscalculation, based on faulty analysis by the Wehrmacht, was the greatest intelligence failure of the war. Moreover, Germany's attack on the Soviet Union in June 1941 completely changed the strategic balance of power in Europe.[114] Instead of a brief campaign, the Russo-German war lasted four years, and became one of the cruelest conflicts in modern history.

Following the Wehrmacht's initial setback in Russia, the German economy was reorganized in spring 1942, and industrial output improved dramatically under direction of the newly appointed Minister for Production, Albert Speer. The funding priority for Peenemünde

---

[113] Middlebrook, *The Peenemünde Raid*, 19
[114] Cooper, *The German Air Force*, 62

was also reinstated. However, the primary effort at the secret facility was now directed toward the research and development of the army's A-4 rocket. Other programs, such as the development of the A-9/A-10, intercontinental missiles designed to target New York and Washington, were postponed. The curtailment of funding for the air force's jet propulsion program, in addition to earlier cancellations, and conflicting ideas pertaining to utilization, would later have far-reaching consequences for the hard-pressed German Luftwaffe.[115]

The expansion of German industry to replace the material losses in Russia required an increase in the hours of operations at all industrial and administrative agencies. It also required all males, ages 16–65, and females, ages 17–50, to register for work. However, the following year's increase in production was still insufficient. Belatedly, Hitler was forced to order the country's commitment to a total war effort in January 1943. This same month, the fifteen-year-old age group of the Hitler Youth was called up to augment the women auxiliaries and Russian POWs who were already manning the antiaircraft batteries that defended the country.

As the nation's industrial production struggled to sustain an expanding war effort, the German Field Army was "never able to recover from their overall losses of 900,000 casualties during the severe Russian campaign of 1941."[116] Moreover, the loss of Stalingrad the following year was a catastrophe for the Third Reich that unnerved the leadership of the government and citizens alike. In the aftermath of this disaster, hundreds of thousands of skilled workers were drafted to fill the depleted ranks of the Wehrmacht.[117] Yet, in spite of various initiatives to replace the increasing losses of the army, German manpower difficulties were becoming more acute. Permanent losses on all fronts, including dead, missing, and disabled, was close to 2,000,000 men by summer 1943.[118]* The earlier 800,000-man draft order for skilled

* In September 1942, the German strength on the Eastern Front totaled 2,490,000 men, some 560,000 fewer men than at the start of the Russian invasion the previous summer.[119]

[115] Cooper, *The German Air Force*, 219
[116] Cooper, *The German Army,* 407
[117] Ziemke, *Stalingrad to Berlin*, 213
[118] Ziemke, *Stalingrad to Berlin*, 213
[119] Ibid., 19 & 34

workers failed to deliver the required replacements–a result of intense resistance from industry and civilian bureaucracy. The nation's industrial mobilization for total war was competing with the needs of the Wehrmacht, and the German Field Army, in particular, was having difficultly finding a source of new recruits. This pressing requirement of the German Army led to large-scale recruiting and drafting of foreigners after propaganda skillfully presented the war against the Soviet Union as a battle of European states united against communism.[120] These measures attracted over one and a half million volunteers who served throughout the war with the German Armed Forces. Hitler also authorized an expansion of the Waffen-SS following the terrible winter of 1941–1942, when these units had demonstrated cohesiveness and an ability to retain their fighting spirit even in defeat.[121]*

Following the loss of Stalingrad, Germany suffered a second strategic defeat when 250,000 German and Italian soldiers were forced to surrender in Tunisia in mid-May 1943. Elements of Erwin Rommel's once-vaunted Africa Korps had retreated to Tunisia after being defeated by the British Eighth Army at El Alamein. Although later reinforced, the German and Italian forces defending the Atlas Mountains south of Tunis were eventually overwhelmed by converging American and British armies advancing from Algeria and Egypt. The Axis surrender and defeat in North Africa resulted in a loss for Germany in yet another theater of operations. Equally significant, the Luftwaffe was also losing its capacity to prevent Soviet bombers from attacking Germany from the east and the American and British air forces from penetrating the nation's airspace from the West.

On 26 May 1943, just weeks after the surrender of Axis forces in Tunisia, the research team at Peenemünde successful launched a test trial of the A-4 rocket. The demonstration was acknowledged by military and civilian leaders in attendance as having immense military potential. The exhibition also persuaded Adolph Hitler to reconsider the rocket's capability, yet it wasn't until mid-summer, after another

---

* The Waffen-SS was the combat arm of the Nazi Party's paramilitary organization known as the *Schutzstaffe*. It became a de facto branch of the Wehrmacht as it expanded from an initial force of three regiments to 38 divisions by 1945.

[120] Buss, *Hitler's Germanic Legions*, 21
[121] Ziemke, *Stalingrad to Berlin*, 312

briefing by von Braun on the theory of rocket propulsion, that he became excited by the possibilities of the A-4 program. The war of attrition in Russia had already cost Germany significant casualties, and the possibilities of the A-4 seemed to offer the promise that Germany could reclaim the strategic initiative in the European conflict. Hitler then ordered the rocket be given top priority in the armament program with a projected production of 2,000 units a month. The A-4, Hitler asserted, would be the "decisive weapon of the war."[122]

A-4 rocket at Peenemünde   German Federal Archives

Later that summer, as Allied air raids into Germany were increasing in size and scope, the residential sections of the city of Hamburg were targeted for destruction by the RAF. In the last week of July 1943, British Bomber Command conducted four nights of intense bombing of the city. These attacks were initiated after a long period of hot and dry weather, with the specific intent of creating a firestorm. The ensuing conflagration ultimately burned "62,000 acres and destroyed 80 percent of the buildings in the German port city. Thirty thousand inhabitants were also killed and another 800,000 persons were left homeless."[123]

The destruction of Hamburg and the horrific loss of life caused by these attacks, enraged Hitler, creating an irrational desire to retaliate at any cost. Frantic and delusional, Hitler and other leaders within the country's political hierarchy perceived the A-4 as the ideal weapon with which to achieve retaliatory satisfaction, and regain the strategic

---

[122] Overy, *Why the Allies Won*, 239
[123] Jennings & Brewster, *The Century*, 259

initiative.[124] Reich minister Joseph Goebbels was so optimistic about the weapon's potential he renamed the A-4, the *Vergeltungswaffe 2*, or V-2, for propaganda purposes, hoping the army's rocket would become another of Germany's vengeance weapons. A smaller, pulse-jet powered rocket, designated the V-1, had been developed earlier at Peenemünde by the Luftwaffe, and was already moving toward mass production.

Churchill and his advisors only recognized the threat of the German rocket program just a month prior to the razing of Hamburg, and directed the full weight of the British Bomber Command to attack the Experimental Works at the earliest opportunity. However, six weeks would pass before weather conditions were favorable for a nighttime strike. Utilizing the advantage of a full moon, every available Lancaster, Halifax, and Stirling bomber in the RAF (a total of 596 aircraft) were launched in the first nighttime raid requiring precision bombing.[125] The specific targets for the mid-August raid were the Experimental Works, the Production Plant, and the main Housing Estate, a residential community of 4,000 persons. The objectives of the mission were to destroy the German facilities and kill the scientists and technicians who were assigned to the experimental program.[126] The selection of the Housing Estate as a specific target was not an isolated incident. Rather, it was the stated policy of British Bomber Command throughout the war to intentionally target residential areas of German cities.[127]

To ensure the element of surprise over Peenemünde, the British RAF launched a diversionary effort earlier that same evening against Berlin. This secondary mission reached the German capital at 2300 hours on 17 August 1943, eliciting the anticipated response from the city's flak batteries and the dispatch of all German night fighters in the city's defense.[128] The diversion had been so well planned and executed that the primary attack on Peenemünde, initiated two hours later at 0115 the following morning, was met with limited resistance. Only three or four batteries of heavy flak, along with several batteries of smaller caliber antiaircraft guns on land and nearby ships, offered any opposition.

---

[124] Gander & Chamberlain, *Weapons of the Third Reich*, 32

[125] Middlebrook, *The Peenemünde Raid*, 13

[126] Ibid., 66–68

[127] Keegan, *The Second World War*, 420–421

[128] Middlebrook, *The Peenemünde Raid*, 109

RAF Target Map   Author's collection

The attention of the German Luftwaffe was focused on defending Berlin as the lead squadrons of 560 British bombers approached Peenemünde. Descending to an altitude of 7,500 feet, pilots in these lead elements were looking for targets identified by the marking ordnance of Pathfinder aircraft prior to initiating an hour long raid. Once located, three separate formations released a total of "1,795 tons of incendiary and high-explosive [ordnance] into the residential housing area" alone before the last group was chased off by the late arrival of German aircraft. Some 30 Focke-Wulf night fighters, acting on their own initiative, had flown from Berlin to join in the defense of Peenemünde and shot down an equal number of the attacking bombers as the last RAF squadrons departed for England.

The British raid on the Peenemünde Experimental Works cost the RAF 40 heavy bombers and 290 aircrew, while another 32 aircraft were damaged.[129] Yet for all the preparation and sacrifice, the mission failed to achieve its primary objectives. The bombing inflicted very little damage to the secret facility and only a limited number of scientists or technicians were killed. British bombers, utilizing new marking techniques in the initial attempt to conduct precision strikes on a specific objective, had missed their targets by as much as three kilometers. Material damage was "[greatest in] the domestic quarters and the wind-tunnel workshops," while German personnel casualties

---

[129] Bekker, *Luftwaffe War Diaries*, 314

from the raid were also limited.[130] Only one hundred and seventy-eight persons of the 4,000 individuals of the in the housing area were killed, although hundreds of others, interned in the labor camp located south of the main target also perished.

Another indirect casualty of the early morning operation over Peenemünde was General Hans Jeschonnek, Chief of Staff of the German Luftwaffe. Commissioned as a young lieutenant in 1915, Jeschonnek had served as a fighter pilot during WWI, where he earned two German Iron Cross decorations. Ten years later, the young officer again distinguished himself as class valedictorian, graduating from General Staff training in 1928. He then served in several staff positions in the new German Air Force before returning to the air ministry, where he was promoted to Chief of the General Staff of the Luftwaffe on 1 February 1939. In this critical role, Jeschonnek orchestrated the early successes of the new German Air Force. However, he endured increasingly harsh and scathing criticism from Hitler for the Luftwaffe's later failures to defeat the British RAF during the Battle of Britain, and to prevent the raids that recently leveled Hamburg. With each new debacle, Jeschonnek became evermore disillusioned and dismissive of Reichsmarschall Hermann Goering's failed role as Chief of the Luftwaffe.* The morning of 18 August 1943, the 44-year-old Chief of Staff, already shaken by the previous day's raids against against Schweinfurt and Regensburg, was stunned to learn of the RAF's bombing of Peenemünde. After receiving the 0800 call informing him of this latest attack, the senior Luftwaffe officer went to his room and shot himself.[131] Aside from the anticipated criticism he would receive from Hitler, Jeschonnek's suicide was undoubtedly influenced by his recognition of the increasing strength of the Allied air forces, and realization that Germany had already lost the war.[132]

---

* Goering was promoted to the senior rank of Reichsmarschall following the Luftwaffe's early success in Poland and Western Europe.

[130] Middlebrook, *The Peenemünde Raid*, 222
[131] Bekker, *Luftwaffe War Diaries*, 314
[132] Ibid., 315

5

FIRST MISSIONS

Almost a year after the RAF raid on Peenemünde, Corporal Don Dorfmeier and other members of the 20 replacement crews arrived in England. They had been at sea for 10 days without incident. Disembarking on 13 July 1944, the airmen were processed through a reception station near the old market town of Stone in Staffordshire before being sent to various bomb groups located throughout East Anglia. Lieutenant Wallace Blackwell's crew, along with several others, was assigned to 398th Bomb Group at Nuthampstead, 50 kilometers north of London. The group, commanded by Colonel Frank P. Hunter Jr., was activated 1 March 1943, and trained replacement crews for six months before their own deployment a year later.

Months prior to the arrival of the 398th Bomb Group, the air war over Europe still hung in the balance. German fighter production had increased in 1943 because of the recuperative powers of the nation's aircraft industry and the effectiveness of decentralization. The availability of additional aircraft enabled the Luftwaffe to mount a more aggressive defense of Western Europe, culminating in an unprecedented concentration of 300 day fighters against US bombers making a first strike on Schweinfurt. On 14 October 1943, Lieutenant General Eaker launched a second bombing mission against the city's ball bearing plants, "convinced of the strategic and economic necessity of completely eliminating production at these key facilities."[133] However, the mission was as difficult as the one conducted eight weeks earlier, and a total of 60 B-17s were shot down during the operation, and another 138 aircraft were damaged.

Later that year, the US Army Air Force in the European Theater was reorganized. On 1 November 1943, the Fifteenth Air Force was activated from elements of the Ninth and Twelfth air forces operating in North Africa. The newly organized air force, with six subordinate bomb groups, was located near the recently occupied city of Foggia,

---

[133] Jablonski, *Flying Fortress,* 141

Italy.* This location provided the USAAF with a southern approach into Germany to bomb targets located in the eastern part of the country, in addition to reaching sites in France, Poland, and the Balkans. The rest of the Ninth was redeployed to England and designated a tactical air force to support the US Army Ground Forces gathering for the invasion of France. During this reorganization, the Eighth Air Force continued to expand in size and complexity. By September 1944, some 200,000 airmen were assigned to one of the 40 bomb groups subordinate to the largest US Air Force deployed overseas during WWII.**

In January 1944, the numbers of US combat aircraft in England increased significantly to 4,242 units.[134] Months earlier, in August

Boeing B-17G Flying Fortress   USAAF

and September 1943, the new B-17G Fortresses began to arrive at various air bases in East Anglia. The new, iconic models were modified to include a front turret with two .50 caliber machine guns mounted below the bombardier window that provided additional protection against German fighters mounting head-on attacks. However, the most significant development that fall was the arrival of the P-51

* Foggia was liberated by the British Eighth Army in late September 1943 after Allied forces invaded southern Italy weeks earlier.
** Only 31,000 airmen in these groups were assigned to aircrew positions flying combat missions over Europe.[135]

[134] Russell, *Leaping the Atlantic Wall,* 7
[135] Wells, *Courage and the Air War,* 161

fighter, designed for long-range escort. With these additional assets, the reorganized US Army Eighth Air Force was directed to destroy the German Luftwaffe as part of the strategic campaign to invade Western Europe later that spring. The campaign designed to achieve this objective was initiated in February 1944. A force of 1,000 AAF bombers conducted five days of intensive operations against the German production factories at Regensburg, Augsburg, Furth, and Stuttgart. Several days later, a force of 2,000 heavy bombers from The Eighth and Fifteenth air forces struck the same factories again. The raids cost the Army Air Force 244 bombers with the loss of 2,200 aircrew, yet destroyed 600 German fighter aircraft during the same period. Equally significant, German aircraft production fell to an 18-month low and the Luftwaffe was severely crippled from these losses. No longer could the German Air Force challenge the penetration of airspace over Western Europe, except in the rare occasion where they had local superiority or when high-priority targets were under attack.[136]

The 398th Bomb Group arrived in England on 22 April 1944 and was assigned to the reorganized Eighth Air Force. The Group headquarters and all four subordinate bomb squadrons were co-located at Nuthampstead, also known as station 131. The airfield was ringed with separate parking hard stands and revetments for the individual aircraft of each squadron, while clusters of buildings and small huts were located at the base of and between the two longest runways. The base, like most installations in East Anglia, was hurriedly built, with mostly single story structures that were functional, yet austere, dispersed somewhat arbitrarily to complement the settlement of the countryside. This collection of approximately 400 buildings included the primary structures: a group headquarters, operation center, and briefing rooms for approximately 2,800 men of the bomb group. Billeting for personnel assigned to the four squadrons was established at separate sites, along with the infirmary, the laundry, and the combat mess–a separate dining facility provided for combat aircrew that required a restricted diet. These facilities, in addition to the American Red Cross, Aero Club, and the recreation room were supported by the 325th Station Complement Squadron, the 244th Medical, and the 1226th Quartermaster Detachments.

To distinguish separate bomb groups from similar organizations, a

---

[136] Jablonski, *The Flying Fortress,* 148

marking system was implemented in spring 1944 that used a division symbol, a group letter and a squadron code. All aircraft assigned to the 398th were identified with distinctive white "W" placed inside a black triangle located on a red vertical tail band. Additional identification codes for the squadron and individual aircraft letters were painted on the aircraft's fuselage behind the waist gunner's window. The markings were, according to Wallace Blackwell, "a [pleasing] color arrangement." Individual aircraft within various squadrons of the bomb groups were also assigned colorful names as an expression of personal attachment. Most often the names assigned to these aircraft established individual or crew identities, reflecting an alter ego or the acknowledgement of a wife or girlfriend, in an effort to project a sense of strength or maternal protection. These names, usually painted with artful motifs and combat histories, imbued the aircraft with a personality, and were frequently referred to in diaries and memoirs of the men who flew them. The most common motif was the female figure in some seductive pose. Although many of these themes were provocative, group commanders tolerated this practice as an expression of unit morale.

This sense of identification with a specific aircraft was most pronounced in 1942–43, when crews were assigned, whenever possible, to the same aircraft through the duration of their tour. However, by 1944, more aircrews than aircraft were available in theater, and most crews would fly a half dozen different Fortresses or Liberators during their overseas assignment.[137] Still, many airmen developed emotional attachments to particular aircraft and attributed to them unique distinctions responsible for their safe return from a mission. Highly superstitious, these same men were frequently emotional and, at times, tearful when their aircraft was taken out of service for maintenance or repair of major battle damage.*

One man who witnessed multiple incidents of this emotional grieving was Master Sergeant George Hillard. As the Senior NCO and Line Chief for the 603rd Bomb Squadron's maintenance section, Hillard coordinated and directed the mechanics, armorers, and other specialists who were responsible for maintenance and logistical tasks

---

* Between January and June 1944, 2,128 Eighth Air Force aircraft were shot down and another 15,346 returned with battle damage.[138]

[137] Forman, *B-17 Nose Art Name Directory*, 286
[138] Wells, *Courage and Air Warfare*, 108

for the aircraft assigned to the squadron. The competence and dedication of these men was critical in keeping the squadron's aircraft serviced, repaired, and operational. Hillard characterized the technicians who performed these functions as "hard workers, who, at times, would work through the night to ready an aircraft for the following day's mission." The Line Chief was equally appreciative and complimentary of the men in the 478th Sub Depot at Nuthampstead, who performed third echelon maintenance for the 398th when the group's aircraft were severely damaged.

Now, arriving at Nuthampstead, Don and his crew were assigned to the 601st Bomb Squadron, where the officers and enlisted members were billeted in separate facilities. The crew was then allowed almost two weeks of orientation training prior to conducting their first combat operation. During this familiarization, the airmen attended classroom briefings and flew cross-country training flights to orient themselves with the regional topography, to identify landmarks unique to their airfield and, most important, to practice close-formation flying. All training fights and combat missions were conducted following a standard briefing, after which crew members would move out to their assigned aircraft and conduct various preflight procedures while "sweating out" the weather. Once ready, the airmen waited for the firing of a green flare across the airfield, signaling the launch of the mission. For many airmen, waiting for clearance to start their engines was "the hardest part of a mission." Having prepared psychologically to face the hazards of flying and combat, the "wait" allowed too much time for boredom . . . and anxiety to create a sense of fear.

Routine missions, as well as combat operations, were frequently hazardous. The first task in either circumstance required the pilot and his crew to negotiate a successful launch. This was usually complicated by the excessive weight of the aircraft, which were frequently overloaded with thousands of gallons of fuel, in addition to the ordnance for their missions, and having to launch from confined airfields with short runways. Such conditions created what some crew members referred to as "nervous moments."

Although weight was an important consideration for any launch, weather was the greatest uncertainty affecting takeoff and assembling of a group, once in flight. Wallace Blackwell would later recall that his first "indoctrination flight" was to dump an entire bomb load in the North Sea following an earlier mission that was "scrubbed because of weather or such."[139] Thick fog, low ceilings and rain were common considerations, which required aircraft to increase their intervals between departures from the normal thirty-second span, when clear, to one-minute intervals when not. Once airborne, all aircraft would have to circle over their designated assembly area, utilizing radio beacons to facilitate assembly and the correct assignment within the group's formation. The procedure was tedious and, at times, costly. Adverse weather across northern Europe caused numerous incidents of aircraft colliding with each other on the ground or in the air. During the last 18 months of the war, a total of 1,660 aircraft were involved in such incidents. In another study, sixty-five percent of all noncombat deaths reported between June 1942 and June 1945 were attributed to weather-related accidents.[140]

Once airborne, the next critical task for an aircrew was the assembly and preservation of a tight formation as it maneuvered to and from a designated target. Holding one's assigned position within the group was critical to provide maximum defensive fire to protect all aircraft. The maintenance of these formations required that each bomber of a particular box fly within 100 yards of each other, and the "[slipping] of 50 or 60 yards [out of formation]" would invite the attack of enemy fighters.[141] The ability to fly and maintain one's position within a formation was an absolute necessity for survival in the air war over Europe.[142] American bombers straggling over German-held territory rarely survived. A 1943 USAAF survey indicated that "over half of all heavy bombers lost during [missions] on targets in Europe were shot down after they had left the formation for one reason or another."[143]

Training to achieve proficiency in these tasks during the day, most airmen, whenever possible, went out drinking at night. Corporal Don Dorfmeier and the other members of his crew were no exception and, shortly after arriving at Nuthampstead, went out on pass to London. "The group," according to John Bell, "eventually found themselves

---

[139] Wallace Blackwell, "Timeless Voices," www.398th.org
[140] Wells, *Courage and Air Warfare,* 31
[141] Ibid., 99
[142] Ibid., 102
[143] Price, *The Bomber in WWII,* 124

in an English pub, crowded with predominately British servicemen." After a few drinks, the crew started to goad Don, the more extroverted one of the group and known for his entertaining impressions, to "do Churchill." After much prodding, Don hopped up on the bar in a manner that demanded attention. Furrowing his brow and affecting a low baritone delivery suggestive of the English prime minister, he started to passionately incite the crowd with exhortations from one of Winston Churchill's more famous speeches, asserting, "' . . . we shall not flag or fail. We shall go on to the end, we shall fight in France, we shall fight on the seas and oceans, we shall fight with growing confidence and growing strength in the air, we shall defend our island . . . we shall never surrender!'"[144] "The audacity of this delivery," Bell said, "stopped all conversation," and for a brief moment, complete silence hung over the patrons "as the lone group of Americans began to think they might have to fight their way out of the bar." Then, to the Yank's relief, "The tension was broken with a loud and thunderous applause."

Several days later, Don and another crew member were reassigned to other crews in the bomb group. This was upsetting for everyone. Established relationships developed during their previous four months of training were severed at a critical time. Yet, the reassignment of individuals to serve as replacements or to fill vacant positions with other crews was a reality of modern combat. Wallace Blackwell acknowledged this many years later, recalling, "Not many crews stayed together for entire tours of duty. I flew my 35 missions with 34 different crew members." Still, administrative transfers, regardless of the reason, were awkward for all concerned. The individual being reassigned felt inadequate; while the gaining crew would be guarded and apprehensive about any replacement whose quality and character might be suspect.

Don was reassigned to the crew of Lieutenant Nigel B. Carter, one of Blackwell's former classmates. "Carter", according to Don, "wasn't happy when I reported as the replacement for the ball turret gunner," a position requiring a man of much smaller stature. The renowned Sperry ball turret, used in both B-17 and B-24 bombers, was intentionally small by design to reduce drag during flight, and the position was usually assigned to the smallest member of the crew. Don, noted at that time for his six foot and 198 pound stature, was much too large to fit into the small, cramped turret. After some angst, Carter reassigned one

---

[144] Churchill, *The War Speeches of Winston Churchill*, 195

of his smaller crew members, Corporal William R. Carr, to the vacant position.

Twenty-five-year-old Bob Carr, a native of Centralia, Illinois, joined the US Army in September 1942. An early fascination with flying motivated him to enlist for training as a glider pilot, yet the program was disbanded just after his completion of school. However, Bob elected to remain in the Army and transferred to the Air Force for further instruction as a radio operator and an aerial gunner, prior to reporting for crew assignment in Rapid City, South Dakota. Following another six weeks of training, the new radio operator and crew deployed overseas and arrived in Liverpool, England on 14 July 1944. However, the crew's ball turret gunner was not deployed after he developed a problem with his eyesight.

Bob Carr clearly remembered the circumstances of Don's reassignment to his crew. In a letter written to the author years later, he noted, "There was no way [Don] could get into that ball turret. I only weighed about 150 lbs., so I took that job and your father [was assigned] the waist gunner [position]." What Bob did not mention, however, was that he and Don recognized that the ball turret, protruding from under the fuselage of the aircraft, was isolated and exposed. The ball was also so small and cramped that some men could not enter the position with their parachute. Visibility in the turret was restricted as well, which required cooperation from other crew members to provide the location of approaching enemy fighters. Recognition of the ball turret's vulnerability caused the two men to make a "blood oath" one night while out drinking. "The agreement," according to Don, "required me, as the closest available crew member, to get Bob out of the ball and back into the fuselage of their aircraft in the event of a [pending crash landing or necessity to abandon ship]." Yet the ball turret position, although precarious, was not the most dangerous assignment on a B-17. Rather, the waist gunners, standing behind their gun at an open window, "incurred the largest number of casualties of all the Fortress crew positions" during the war.[145]

Lieutenant Carter's displeasure and irate comments pertaining to Don's late transfer was most likely a reflection of the young pilot's anxiety regarding his crew's pending certification. Don's assignment

---

[145] Editor, "Crew Positions," *Flak News* 22.1 (Jan 2007) : 10

and Carr's subsequent detail to the ball turret meant that two crew positions were being manned by individuals whose capabilities were yet unknown, suggesting a heightened sense of vulnerability in future combat operations. Carter's annoyance, however expressed, should have been directed toward the group's personnel or operations section responsible for the assignment of new crew members. Instead, Carter's attitude and comments caused Don to react defensively, creating an underlying tension that would later provoke a confrontation.

This tension within Carter's crew, exacerbated in part by Don's recent transfer, was attributable to "the normal result of stress."[146] For some airmen, their anxiety was significant enough to cause "changes in appearance, speech, or behavior." The more discernible changes in behavior included "weight loss, irritability, and aggressiveness."[147] Don, who readily acknowledged his fear of flying, attempted to manage his anxiety by waking up early before a mission and riding out to the revetment area to conduct his own inspection of the aircraft. Another strategy Don employed to calm himself at the start of every mission was to conduct a through visual inspection of his parachute, which he wore throughout the duration of each flight, stating, "I never did take my chute off, where the other boys had theirs in the corner. But I heard . . . too many stories where our planes got shot to pieces and fellows went flying by with nothing on. I figured that's not going to happen to this guy."

While Don and his new crew were conducting their orientation and certification training, the Eighth AAF was continuing to fly support missions for the Army Ground Forces in Normandy. "The Allied air campaign for the invasion of France consisted of three phases."[148] The first phase, requiring the destruction of the German Luftwaffe, had been conducted during the first five months of the New Year. The second phase of "isolating the battlefield by interdicting road and rail networks" was accomplished after the Allies achieved air superiority as well as supremacy over France.* The third and final phase required

---

* "The [air] campaign against the French railway system cost [the USAAF] 2,000 aircraft and 12,000 airmen in a little over two months."[149]

[146] Wells, *Courage and Air Warfare*, 68
[147] Ibid., 68
[148] Hallion, *D-Day 1944; Air Power . . .* , 2
[149] Keegan, *The Second World War*, 415

Allied air forces to "concentrate on battlefield interdiction and close air support."[150] Implementing the third phase of the air campaign required that Allied air forces target the German panzer divisions moving to the battlefront. The earlier placement of these armored formations, prior to the invasion, followed a contentious philosophical argument within the senior ranks of the Wehrmacht. However, Hitler ultimately backed the strategy that called for holding the panzer divisions in reserve and concentrating the German armor en mass for a later counterattack.

D-Day: US 1st Infantry Division   US Coast Guard

Two of the German formations held in strategic reserve that suffered grievously from this failed policy were the 12th SS Panzer "Hitlerjugend" and the Panzer Lehr divisions. On the evening of the Allied invasion, both formations were positioned some 60 to 100 kilometers behind the Normandy sector in northern France. While en route to the beachhead, each unit was continually interdicted and severely mauled by Allied aircraft, inflicting severe losses, and delaying the arrival of both divisions on the field of battle. The Panzer Lehr division alone lost "more than 200 vehicles" on just one of its two-day road marches to the battlefront.[151]*

---

* The hard-pressed German Seventh Army defending Normandy was further degraded by the lack of personnel and material replacements, receiving only 10,000 personnel to offset the 116,000 causalities suffered from 6 June to 20 July 1944.

[150] Ibid., 2
[151] Hallion, *D-Day 1944; Air Power* . . . 7

Eight weeks after the initial Allied landings, the massive buildup of men and material remained confined to a very limited bridgehead in Normandy, despite the success of the earlier AAF missions supporting the Army Ground Forces. The planned breakout across France had bogged down in the infamous bocage, where thickly banked hedgerows afforded the German defenders excellent antitank positions. Advancing against these placements cost the Allies over "40,500 casualties during the first two weeks of the invasion."[152] Later Allied efforts to capture Caen during the last two weeks in June, and the Falaise Plain in mid-July, also ended in failure despite heavy bombardment from the Allied air forces. To break the ensuing stalemate, the US Army Ground Forces requested a massive concentration of heavy bombers, the largest to date, to saturate a rectangular box, four miles long and one and three quarter miles deep, running parallel to the Allied line. Previous supporting missions, flown by the USAAF during the past two months, had failed to sufficiently subdue enemy resistance. Yet, staff members planning this operation "were enthusiastic . . . [to have] an unrivaled opportunity to test the feasibility of saturation bombing."[153]

On 24 July, the Eighth Air Force launched a force of 1,500 heavy bombers to support the planned operation, yet were later recalled when a low ceiling of clouds over the target area failed to lift. Unfortunately, 352 bombers had already bombed the target area prior to receiving the recall notification. This formation, flying perpendicular to the target area, released their bomb loads early, killing and wounding 156 soldiers of the US Army's 30th Infantry Division. The following day, another formation of a similar number of bombers from the Eighth and the Ninth Air Force, supported by all four squadrons of the 398th Bomb Group, executed "the most effective carpet bombing of the campaign."[154]

While the mission was successful, and allowed for the Allied breakout of the Normandy bridgehead, the operation had unintended consequences when the American positions were mistakenly bombed for a second time. This day 600 US soldiers from the 9th and 30th Infantry Divisions were killed or wounded. One of these casualties was Lieutenant General Lesley J. McNair, the highest ranking American officer killed during the war. Another 164 men were evacuated as

[152] Laffin, *Americans in Battle,* 154
[153] Rust, *The Eighth Air Force Story,* 31
[154] Levine, *The Strategic Bombing of Germany, 1940–1945,* 140

psychological casualties.* Don acknowledged this episode years later stating, "This was an unfortunate, tragic [incident]. But these are the tragedies of war. Whenever there is a human element involved, there is a chance for error." While generous in his assessment of the command and control procedures used in the execution of this mission, others in England at the time were not so forgiving. The incident generated much animosity between the soldiers and airmen of the Army and Army Air Force, resulting in frequent fights whenever these two groups would meet in public. In truth, the errant bombing simply exacerbated a common rancor that already existed between the servicemen assigned to the Army Ground Forces and the Air Force. Soldiers of the US Army envied and resented the airmen, who they considered to be undeserving of their "excessive rank," doing much of nothing during the day and having the run of London at night. Conversely, the airmen thought of themselves as the true veterans of the war who had endured "endless hours of boredom, excessive cold, and fear while flying, then an hour of pure terror when over their targets, confronting German flak and fighter attacks."

During the first weeks of Don's orientation in England, he exchanged correspondence with his mother in Fresno and his two brothers. At that time, his brother Alton was training with the Army Air Force at Carlsbad, New Mexico and Glenn was serving with the US Navy in Australia. In these letters, Don expressed his admiration for the spirit of the British people and speculated that "the people in America could never fully understand the deprivation or the hardships experienced by the British." The most noticeable manifestation of these hardships was the degree of damage sustained during the earlier London Blitz, which occurred during Don's junior year in high school.

Now, four years later, it was the British Bomber Command who was attacking, with impunity, German cities at night. Furthermore, the Allies were starting to perceive an end to the war with Germany by late 1944. This was certainly the dominate theme expressed in the letters Don received from his mother and others. Everyone, it seemed,

* One of every five medical evacuations of US servicemen in WWII was a psychiatric casualty. "The alarming scale of these numbers was apparent even at the earliest stages of American involvement in the European war."[155]

[155] Wells, *Courage and the Air War*, 70

was focused on the recent comments of Walter Winchell, a prominent journalist, who proclaimed that the war in Europe "would be over soon, no later than Christmas." Winchell's proclamation was notable because of his celebrity status and his access to information. An estimated two-thirds of the adult population of America listened to his weekly radio broadcast or read his daily column syndicated in more than two thousand newspapers. Winchell's assessment of Germany's willingness to continue the war was most likely influenced by a recent attempt to assassinate Adolph Hitler and seize control of the national government. The German leader had been opposed throughout his twelve-year dictatorship by an active, albeit, small and covert resistance movement. Yet, serious resistance to Hitler only galvanized after the military disasters at Stalingrad, the loss of North Africa, and the successful Allied landing at Normandy. On 20 July 1944, a group of active and retired military officers in the Germany Army, supported by a number of mid-level government officials, attempted a military coup. Hitler was injured, but not killed by the bomb placed under a conference table at his headquarters in Rastenburg. Moreover, members of the Wehrmacht and the government, still loyal to Adolph Hitler, rallied quickly to restore order after the attempted assassination.

Referring to Winchell's prophecy 20 years later, Don recalled with some amusement, " . . . the war would [supposedly] be over by Christmas. That everyone in Germany wanted to revolt, if only they had a gun, they would turn on Hitler and the war would be over in a matter of weeks." Yet, the ordinary German soldier regarded "the unsuccessful revolt as treason of the most infamous kind,"[156] and Don would spend Christmas behind barbed wire. "It so happened," he said, "that when I landed in [Germany], there were about 20 guys standing around me, all of them had guns, and they weren't about to turn on Hitler."

Days after the attempted assassination, Carter's crew was certified to fly combat operations and participated in their first mission, 29 July 1944. The assignment required the squadron support 568 bombers targeting the synthetic oil production and storage facilities at Merseburg, Germany. It was a long flight, lasting more than 8 hours. "It was rough," recalled the crew ball turret gunner, Bob Carr, "but we made it all right. We did not have any [fighters attack] us, just flak from

[156] Hastings, *Armageddon, Battle for Germany, 1944–45*, 165

the antiaircraft guns. There were a few planes that went down in our group, but we didn't take any hits at all." Technical Sergeant Ben Core, a radio operation in the same squadron, was a little more reflective and noted in his diary the loss of "seventeen heavy bombers and six fighters" for the day's operation.

For the next two days, bad weather grounded the 398th Bomb Group at Nuthampstead. Then, on 3 August 1944, Don and his crew flew a second, more dramatic mission to bomb the marshaling yards in Saarbrucken, Germany, where they were hit by flak and experienced their first battle casualty. "We flew a long ways," Don recalled, "and we really got shot up badly. The navigator, [Lieutenant Harry Cowen] had his hand blown off. I had to crawl down through the [bomb bay] catwalk to put a tourniquet around his hand, [as] . . . he was in pretty bad shape." Technical Sergeant Derald R. Lyman, flying the same mission, corroborated part of Don's account, noting they encountered "lots of flak . . ." and that he "saw one B-17 explode like a firecracker."[157]

Corporal Bob Carr also recalled the mission, the intensity of the flak, and the wounding of their navigator, yet could not recollect Don's alleged medical intervention. Still, both men clearly remembered that their aircraft "broke" formation upon returning to Nuthampstead. "The practice was to fire a double red flare, to alert other aircraft of our priority to land first, and the ambulances would race to meet the identified aircraft at the end of the run-way."[158] "[With] wounded aboard," Don continued, "they let you down right now! The pilot did a magnificent job. He slipped that [aircraft] in, and you could look out that waist window at the wing and it was pointing straight down. Then he cranked her over and slid her in and we were on the ground in a matter of seconds. The ambulances were there and took the navigator off the plane. The war was over for him. He was going home, so it really wasn't that bad. It was at that point I stopped being bitter, because I should have been riding in that seat [instead], I still have both my hands."

After Cowen was transferred to a waiting ambulance, Carter taxied the Fortress "down to the end of the strip [where] we all got out. We were [all] pretty shaken up," Don recalled, when another crew member

---

[157] Derald R. Lyman, "Combat Diaries," www.398th.org
[158] Kaplan & Smith, *One Last Look*, 117

asked, 'Well, Dorfmeier, what do you think?'" The question apparently activated some unexpressed resentment, or simply allowed Don to vent his own personal feelings regarding the existing formality within the group. Yet, whatever the motivation, Don responded to the question by unloading on Carter, stating, "Listen, if you four SOBs," referring to the officers of the crew, "figure you can fly this ship, then fly it [by yourselves]! But there are 10 guys [on] this crate, and it takes all of [us] to make it go. Now, either we work as a team and we stop this nonsense of 'yes sir' and 'no sir' business or you can take this airplane and jam it!"

"Carter may not have liked what he heard," Don said, "yet, he took it. He could have had me thrown in jail or anything else, but he took it!" More significantly, the confrontation seemed to have changed, at least from Don's perspective, the dynamics within the group: "from that day on, [the officers agreed]" or professed an intent to share their "whiskey ration [or] anything [else] they had with us." This understanding still required adherence to all military courtesy "on the ground, because it had to be that way. But . . . in the air, we were . . . all one [team]. This was the esprit de corps that developed in the Air Force. This was what made us different from other branches [of the service]."

So for a brief moment, a heightened sense of camaraderie and group identity coalesced among the eight crew members, buoyed by their good fortune of having survived their first "baptism of fire." This transcendent experience and perception of being a "veteran crew," participating in an archetypical life and death drama, must have felt intoxicating. Yet, regrettably, "their moment was short-lived," according to Don, "as we got shot down the next raid out."

US Army Eighth Air Force shoulder sleeve patch

The US Army Eighth Air Force was activated in Savannah, Georgia on 2 January 1942. Five months later, the first forward deployed 97th Bomb Group arrived in England. By September 1944, some 200,000 airmen were assigned to one of 40 bomb groups subordinate to the largest US Air Force formed during WWII.

6

4 AUGUST 1944

The first three days in August 1944, the US Army Eighth Air Force conducted tactical operations in support of the Allied Ground Forces fighting in France. These missions included dropping supplies to the French resistance movement, and bombing German airfields, marshalling yards and supply depots in the vicinity of Paris and Northern France.[159] On 4 August 1944, favorable weather forecasts allowed a "dispatch in the late morning of a large-scale effort, utilizing forces from all three bomb divisions to [attack] targets in northern central Germany."[160] The objective of this mission, designated as Operations Number 514, was to attack 10 separate targets inside the country, employing 1,246 heavy bombers, supported by 15 Fighter Groups. Two smaller elements would serve as diversions by attacking coastal batteries and V-1 launch sites in Pas de Calais and northwestern France.

The scope of the Eighth Air Force's primary mission and the diverse locations of the designated targets in Germany, required that the supporting combat wings be grouped into four separate force structures. The 398th Bomb Group was allocated to Force II, which consisted of eleven combat wings of 36 aircraft each.[161] Six combat wings of this subordinate command, including the 398th, were designated to attack the German Experimental Establishment at Peenemünde, the secret test and launch site for the German rocket propulsion program. The other five wings would strike the Aircraft Component Plant, supply depot and airfield at Anklam, located 35 kilometers southwest of the experimental facility.

"On the morning of our third mission we went through the usual procedures," Corporal Don Dorfmeier recalled. "We were briefed, told where we were going . . . it was a long ride–Peenemünde. This was a

[159] Carter & Mueller, *The AAF in WWII: Combat Chronology, 1941–1945*, 412
[160] HQ Eighth AF, Tactical Mission Report-514, 4 Aug 1944, 1
[161] Ibid., 2

maximum effort [as] we were going to knock out their V-2 rocket site and . . . research facility." The "maximum effort" designation required the group commander, Colonel Frank P. Hunter, Jr. and his executive officer to fly as copilots in two of the group's 36 aircraft. Moreover, the 398th was selected as the "lead group of the 1st 'B' Combat Wing." Lieutenant Carter's crew, which included Don, was assigned to an aircraft known only by its tail number, 7098-Y, and would assemble with the "high group" of the formation. Lieutenant Wallace Blackwell and other members of Don's original crew would also participate in the Peenemünde mission and fly with the middle group.

Following the main briefing, Don and the other enlisted men and gunners in the group went to the flight line locker rooms to dress for frigid weather and gather their parachutes and flak vests. Once dressed, the gunners moved to the armament shop to secure the machine guns that had been removed from the aircraft and then proceeded to the squadron's revetment area. On arrival, the airman mounted the heavy 82-pound guns in their respective positions and conducted dry-fire function checks, then initiated the first phase of their preflight inspections. The four officers of Don's crew, including a new navigator, Lieutenant William W. Hembrough, arrived around 0915 hours after receiving more specific briefings. After all initial preparations were concluded, the crews waited for the firing of the green flare from the airfield's Operation's Center. This signal was the official acknowledgement that the mission would proceed and for the pilots to start their engines. Slowly, the roar of one hundred and forty-four, 1,200 horsepower, radial motors blanketed the airfield and engulfed the surrounding community. Minutes later, the collective roar of the group's engines increased in intensity as the long lines of fully loaded aircraft moved toward their launch point. Under ideal conditions, these bomb-laden aircraft would take off on 30-second intervals, but overcast weather this particular morning would cause some delay.

Once airborne, the group's lead aircraft flew east toward their assembly area some seven miles away. The aircraft then circled back to Nuthampstead to fly a continual racetrack pattern, some five miles in diameter, while climbing 300–400 feet per minute. Other aircraft followed in the same pattern until all 36 Fortresses had reached assembly altitude. "This procedure," according to Lieutenant Bob Kraft, lead navigator for the 602nd Bomb Squadron, "took the better part of 30 minutes."[162] Once assembled in the correct formation, the 398th proceeded to link up with the other two bomb groups of the 1st Combat Wing.* This collective force of 108 bombers climbed to an altitude of 12,000 to 14,000 feet en route to their designated assembly area before joining with other wings participating in the day's mission. The assembly of such a large formation, consisting of 1,246 heavy bombers and their fighter escorts, would have "extended 100 miles in length and 75 miles in width," according to operations officer Lieutenant Willis Frazier.[163] A force of this magnitude would also take almost an hour to pass over the English coast.[164] The sound of such a massive force departing Britain was deafening. Yet on the other side of the English Channel, the roar of the oncoming formation, announcing itself some 30 minutes before actually being sighted, was terrifying.

At 1120 hours, the 398th Bomb Group passed over the coastal town of Louth, flying on a converging course across the North Sea to join with Force III and IV. These elements joined to form a single formation of 927 heavy bombers at " . . . a point, approximately 100 miles west of Jutland." The three groups then continued to fly directly eastward to the North Frisian Islands, soaring on two parallel routes, Force I preceding the other formation by 45 minutes. Individual groups then broke formation, as required, to make the desired approaches to their respective targets.

The selection of this particular penetration into Europe was revised to limit the number of German aircraft that could be brought into the radius of action, as well as avoid extensive flak defenses while approaching specific targets.** Further, staff planners had hoped to confuse the Germans as to the actual purpose and intended targets selected for attack. German fighters from two separate groups, representing 100 single-engine aircraft, were put in the air to "make a determined effort"[165] to oppose the two separate AAF formations. Still,

* See Appendix D, Order of Battle
** By late 1943, the German Luftwaffe had deployed over "55,000 anti-aircraft guns to combat the [Allied] air offensive."[166]

[162] Kraft, Bob, "The Art of Bunching Up," *Flak News* 20.3 (Jul 2005) : 5
[163] Frazier, Willis, "Operations Officer," *Flak News* 21.3 (Jul 2006) : 4
[164] Ibid., 4
[165] HQ Eighth AF Tac Mission Report-514, Wireless Intel Service, 4 Aug 1944
[166] Overy, *Why the Allies Won*, 129

enemy controllers appeared confused, according to later reports, as to which element should be attacked first.[167]

Ultimately, the Luftwaffe fighters were directed to intercept Force I as it entered Northwest Germany around 1400 hours. "In the main, the German fighters were attacked by American escorts, and no more than 40 enemy fighters succeeded in attacking the bomb groups, where they shot down one B-17."[168] Later in the afternoon, another force of 10 German single engine fighters also engaged five bomb groups that were directed toward Anklam. A larger group of German twin engine fighters based at the airfield, and thought to be available for local defense, had been recently transferred to the Russian front. Last, 40 German fighters from the initial group assembled earlier attempted to intercept the withdrawal of the 1st Bombardment Division in the Schleswig-Holstein area.

After Force I turned to attack oil refineries at Bremen and Hamburg, the second larger formation continued to fly eastward. Fifteen minutes later, Forces III and IV turned south into northern Germany while Force II proceeded for another 140 kilometers as the only element flying into the Baltic Sea. The formation then made two course corrections to reach their designated IP (Initial Point), some 80 kilometers northeast of Usedom Island at 1441 hours (briefed). At that time, the eleven combat wings designated to attack the two farthest targets executed a 90-degree turn to the southeast. The six wings assigned to strike the Experimental Establishment turned to a 257-degree heading toward Peenemünde. The other five wings made a less severe turn and proceeded on toward Anklam.

Completing their adjustment, the 221 Fortresses of the six combat wings heading toward Peenemünde aligned their formation for their final approach. At this point, the airmen had been in the air for five hours and were fatigued by the physical stresses of the flight and subfreezing temperatures. They had also been in enemy territory for almost 90 minutes, which required a heightened sense of personal alertness. All crew members in the formation now felt a sinking feeling in their stomachs. Their bomb run had begun–along with their individual encounter with fate.

---

[167] HQ Eighth AF Tac Mission Report-514, 4 Aug 1944, 12–13
[168] HQ Eighth AF Tac Mission Report-514, Enemy Reaction, 4 Aug 1944, 1–2

The bomb run represented the time required for the aircraft of each group or wing to traverse the distance from the designated IP to their target. The run for Don's squadron started at 1458 hours and lasted a full seven minutes. During this time, the pilots and bombardiers were not allowed to maneuver their aircraft to avoid enemy flak or attacking aircraft. Any deviation in flight, however slight, would cause the bomb strikes to miss their intended targets by tens, if not hundreds, of meters. For most veterans, this phase of any mission, running the gauntlet of defensive fire, caused them their greatest fear in combat. "You couldn't do a darn thing about it," according to one airman, "[except] plow through it."[169]

Bomb run   398th Bomb Group

German flak batteries began to open fire as the six combat wings of Don's group started to close on their targets within the Peenemünde Experimental Establishment. The first of these batteries to engage the forward elements of the combat wings were the antiaircraft guns mounted on flak ships positioned near the Baltic coast to defend Usedom Island from a northern approach. Eventually all of the Luftwaffe batteries defending the Experimental Works would engage the slow-moving formation, while excited German gun crews calculated the correct course, distance, and altitude of the oncoming Fortresses.

The flak batteries, according to former battery crew member, Otto Suchsland, were initially alerted by "a sophisticated nationwide tracking

[169] Kaplan & Smith, *One Last Look*, 21

system . . . [that] allowed early identification of probable targets." Once a battery was alerted, an individual crew member would "optically zero the range finder . . . on the selected target," identifying elevation, traverses, and distance. This data was entered into a computer that transmitted information to the guns, which then fired barrage salvos calculated to intersect with the bomb formation's direction of flight. However, the one variable that could not be determined on the ground, and which could deflect the course of a projectile, was wind direction and velocity at altitude.[170]

The minutes slowly passed for Lieutenant Charles J. Mellis, Jr., a copilot flying his 20th mission with the 603rd Bomb Squadron. He later recalled, "I had to do most of the flying during the bomb run, especially when things got hot." At the point the group started getting hit, Mellis continued, "We really caught all the flak, too–our element was hardest hit of the whole wing. We only got 5 [hits] but the element leader got plastered. I shudder when I think of it. It happened 30 seconds after bombs away–had it happened before that, I'd not be here." [171]

Mellis's aircraft was buffeted by exploding flak as the high squadron of the 398th Bomb Group started dropping their ordinance. One of the bombs in Don's aircraft hung on a shackle preventing its release. "Events of this nature," according to Lieutenant Leonard Streitfeld, a bombardier assigned to the 602nd Bomb Squadron, "would happen periodically." Corrective action required that the bomb be freed manually. Describing this incident years later, Don said, " . . . the bombs got hung up. So I had to enter the bomb bay on the catwalk, [with] doors open at 22,000 feet and [force a release] . . . with a screwdriver. It wasn't a hard thing to do; just somebody had to do it."

Shortly after the bombs in Don's aircraft were released and he returned to his assigned duty position, the wing's "element leader" took a direct "hit in the main [fuel] tank and exploded. I got a glimpse," Mellis noted, "of the burning hulk, before it fell–it was horrible. The explosion rocked [our] ship and burning parts of the [other aircraft] hit near our right wing. I thought we were hit and had a wing fire. Even as I glanced out, I was wondering what to do next, [when] I saw their burning framework. It was awful. Only two other crew members saw

---

[170] Otto Suchsland, *Course Twelve*, unpublished article
[171] Charles J. Mellis, Jr., "Combat Diaries," www.398th.org

it and I am glad for their sake–especially the bombardier whose best buddy went down with the [aircraft]."

Former crew members John Bell and Adrian Bacon, flying in the middle formation of the 398th Bomb Group, also saw the explosion of the aircraft identified by Mellis. Moments earlier, the two airmen had mistakenly identified the same aircraft as the one flown by Carter and the crew to which Don had recently been assigned. In the next instant, the plane exploded and ceased to exist; displaced by a bright flash, followed by a spray of fluid and falling debris. Incredulous, John strained to spot any deploying parachutes that would indicate some men survived the explosion. Seeing none, his vision started to blur with tears. In shock, John turned to Adrian, to seek some sort of confirmation or to acknowledge what they had just witnessed, only to find him slumped over his gun, equally distraught.

The explosion that caught the attention of the two airmen, and thought to be Don's aircraft, was actually that of another plane flying in close proximity and almost directly in front of Carter's Fortress. This aircraft, number 7186-L, flown by Lieutenant John S. MacArthur, 603rd Bomb Squadron, had received a direct hit from a flak round and exploded mid-air, instantly killing the entire crew. The two airmen, thinking that Don had just been killed, struggled with their sense of shock and disbelief as they tried to contain their emotions and comprehend their loss of a beloved friend. Moreover, the incident forced both men to recognize, if only fleetingly, their own vulnerability.

In all probability, MacArthur and Carter's aircraft were hit from the same flak salvo as the two Fortresses were flying within 100 yards of each other. Although Carter's aircraft avoided a direct hit, it had been struck by multiple shards of shrapnel. Ball turret gunner, Bob Carr, recalled that the crew's radio operator, Sergeant Robert Doll, described the fragments striking the aircraft as sounding like "a bunch of rocks being thrown on a tin roof." Miraculously, no one in the crew was killed or wounded, although the plane's left wing had caught fire. Lieutenant Carter recognized the danger almost immediately and executed the standard procedure for such emergencies by breaking formation and sharply banking his aircraft to "dive out" the fire. Descending as rapidly as possible, Carter dropped several thousand feet in altitude within a matter of minutes. Later witness statements, from men flying in the group's formation, provided further insight regarding the fate of the two aircraft.

Lieutenant Richard T. Ostern, Jr. reported, "The high group had just made their rendezvous after the bomb run with the wing, when aircraft 7098 left the high [group] . . . dived for about 3,000 feet and . . . crossed under our formation. Navigator Lt. Marcus J. Woods recalled that his tail gunner announced the explosion of MacArthur's aircraft, then said, "there goes another ship into a dive . . . after losing about 2,000 feet, [Carter] leveled off, and started for Sweden, then started a wide circling descent." Lieutenant Van B. Campbell saw Carter's ship [take] "a sharp dive, then leave the formation and level off" near 10,000 feet AGL (above ground level). At the time he was on a heading for Sweden, but ran into some flak (a second encounter). He used evasive action and when the flak ceased he still appeared in control of his plane and headed for England."[172]

Carter's maneuver to extinguish the fire in their left wing was initially successful, yet there was still concern among officers of the crew regarding the mechanical worthiness of their aircraft. Bob Carr recalled Lieutenants Carter and Hembrough engaging in conversation for approximately two minutes as they considered the merits of attempting to fly across the Baltic Sea to Sweden, some 120 kilometers north of their present location. Sweden's declared neutrality at the onset of hostilities in Europe and her close proximity to Germany represented a safe haven for damaged German and British aircraft during the first years of the war.[173] In spring 1944, American Fortresses and Liberators started [arriving] in large numbers as the Combined Bomber Offensive began targeting the aircraft industry and fuel deposits in Northern Germany and the "USAAF started issuing maps of southern Sweden to guide damaged aircraft to safety."*

Carter momentarily considered the merits of flying to Sweden, yet

---

* "A total of 327 aircraft from belligerent countries found their way to Sweden during the war,"[174] of which 140 belong to the USAAF. Another 166 damaged US aircraft found safety in Switzerland.[175]

[172] WD, HQ AAF, Missing Air Crew Report - 7707, 8 Aug 1944
[173] Henningsson, Par, "Americans . . . in Sweden," *Flak News* 14.3 (Jul 1999) : 5
[174] Henningsson, Par, "Americans . . . in Sweden," *Flak News* 14.3 (Jul 1999) : 5
[175] Wells, *Courage and the Air War*, 108.

acquiesced to the more experienced assessment and recommendation of his navigator, William Hembrough. The veteran navigator, flying his 27th combat mission, had advised against making such an attempt, and Carter's decision to accept the recommendation was prudent. Only 38 percent of all B-17 aircrew that ditched or bailed out over the North Sea while returning to England were rescued, and a crew going into the more northern and colder Baltic waters would have certainly perished.[176] Carter then adjusted his heading for England in hope of returning to home station when his ship was hit a second time by flak, reigniting the fire in the previously affected wing. Carter called on other crew members for a damage assessment, although the waist gunner's position provided the clearest view of both wings and all four engines. Don responded to the inquiry, asserting, "The wing is starting to buckle!" Without hesitation, Carter replied, "All right–abandon ship!"

The order confirmed every crew member's worst fear–they would not make it back to England. Concern regarding this possibility first surfaced when Carter broke formation and plunged their aircraft into a sharp dive to extinguish the fire in the left wing. At that moment, every crew member's body was flooded with a surge of adrenaline, triggered by an involuntarily "fight or flight" response to perceived threats of danger. Once alerted, the crew's heightened anxiety remained elevated throughout the running conversation between Carter and the navigator, as the two officers deliberated the option of flying to Sweden. However, earlier distress and worry over what might happen were surpassed by Carter's last command, and a collective apprehension started to mount. Faced with the necessity of abandoning their aircraft, each man sought to recall the procedures for just such an eventuality and to control their fear of executing a parachute jump from a disabled aircraft. For such contingencies, the Air Force had established a written Standard Operating Procedure (SOP), yet not provided any practical training.

The procedure for exiting a B-17 while in flight was based on the position and location of each crew member in the aircraft. The bombardier and navigator were designated to exit from the front entrance door; the ball turret and waist gunners would exit from the main entrance door; the tail gunner would exit through a small emergency door located in the far tail section of the fuselage. The other four crew members–the

---

[176] Kaplan & Smith, *One Last Look*, 116

radio operator, engineer, pilot and copilot–would exit through the bomb bay. The pilot was designated as last man to exit in order to maintain control of the plane, if necessary, so that crew members would not be pinned inside by centrifugal force if an unstable aircraft fell or spun out of control.

After Carter activated the alarm bell, each crew member started attending to personal and crew-related tasks in preparation for making their exits. Don's first reaction resulted in a tense moment, which he later characterized as "humorous," when he tried to jettison his flak vest. The vest had been redesigned in response to a 1942 analysis of wounds sustained by airmen while in combat, indicating that "70 percent were caused by missiles of relative low velocity."[177] The resulting canvas flak vest consisted of overlapping, two inch squares of thinly, laminated manganese steel plates that prevented most 20mm aircraft and antiaircraft shell fragments from piercing the body. The armored vests, produced later in the war, weighed approximately twenty pounds, featured a single strap that, when pulled, detached the vest if bailout was necessary. Elaborating further, Don said, "I always wore a flak vest, which I could release by pulling a little cord, and the vest would fall from my shoulders. Well, [as I tugged on] the damn cord release, it wouldn't fall off. So I had to pull the vest off over the top of my head and I almost took my ears off doing it. But, I got out of it."

Don's next concern should have been to assist in extracting Bob Carr from his precarious position in the ball turret. He had sworn to do so one night drinking beer with Bob, vowing that he would "never leave the aircraft with him in the 'ball'." However, preoccupied with his own survival, Don completely forgot about his fellow crew member. Fortunately, he had given Bob his parachute shortly after he entered the ball turret at the start of their mission. This provided Carr with an alternate escape option. His first preference would have been to climb back into the fuselage of the aircraft, then exit from the designated door. But, under the circumstances, Bob was forced to exit the ball directly from a small escape door in the turret assembly.

Carr was fortunate to have had his parachute. Don's primary focus after jettisoning his flak vest was to move toward the main exit door.

[177] Freeman, *The Mighty Eighth*, 28

"Once in position," he recalled, "I reached down for the emergency handle on the door and that damn thing didn't work either. So I kicked the door out and sat down, my feet dangling in the slipstream [before] I realized if I'm going to evade [capture] I'd better get my shoes." The special boots worn by the airmen while flying were designed primarily for keeping their feet warm at high altitudes and were not adequate for moving over open terrain. "So I crawled back up into the radio cabin where I had my shoes. At this time I guess the plane was on automatic pilot, and I imagine she's [flying] about 160 [mph] indicated. I get my shoes, and that crazy radio operator, [Sergeant] Robert Doll, who was kind of a character–in fact I think we were all characters aboard that plane–came in and pushed the little red button that made the radio go 'poof,' then turned around and smiled at me." Doll's smile was an acknowledgement of his responsibility to destroy the radio by activating a thermite compound that burned metal components at extremely high temperatures. "Meanwhile," Don continued, "the plane was burning . . . as I moved back to the exit. I then sat in the door with my shoes in my hand, said a prayer, and tumbled out."

Don wasn't the only crew member who experienced difficulty and delay in exiting the burning aircraft. Tail gunner Corporal Sanford Lewis experienced problems opening the emergency door located in the tail of the fuselage. Bob Carr also experienced similar problems when he opted to exit the small escape door that was part of the ball turret assembly. A side pocket of his flight suit caught on a piece of metal, which prevented any further forward movement and may have saved him from a fatal jump. Carr's parachute was only attached to the left D-ring of the harness and most likely would have not fully deployed when activated. Once back inside the turret, Carr noticed this oversight and took the time to attach his parachute to the other side of his harness prior to making a successful exit.

The hindrances cited by Don and Bob Carr, attempting to exit their stricken aircraft, delayed their escapes by several critical seconds. This lag caused them to be separated from other crew members by a significant distance once on the ground. Other factors that affected the crew's dispersion pattern were the amount of time each airman remained under an open canopy, in addition to the force and direction of the prevailing winds.

Don and his crew wore one of three types of parachutes: a back, chest, or conventional seat type model. Most aircrew gunners wore the 1944 A-4 Chest Type parachute, a 24-foot, flat, circular, silk-nylon canopy that was attached to two D-rings located on the front side of the parachute harness. The harness itself was uncomfortable, and deployment caused frequent injury to the face or head of the jumper when slapped by the two-inch nylon risers of the parachute. More problematic was the fact that the parachute canopy could not be maneuvered during descent.[178]

Airmen who jumped with the attached chest parachute would free fall for an additional 168 to 240 feet after deploying their canopy. During this period, the jumper would reach the speed of terminal velocity, falling 32 feet per second. Once the airman's canopy, suspension lines, and raisers were fully extended, the canopy would start to fill with air slowing the jumper's rate of descent. After the parachute was fully deployed, the airman would experience a truly jarring, and at times, violent "opening shock."[179] This jolt was more severe at higher altitudes where the air was less dense, which increased descent velocity.

Don successfully exited his burning Fortress and fell to earth. While falling, he vividly, "remembered the training manuals advising an individual to conduct a long count from 'one to ten' before pulling the ripcord handle to activate the parachute. Well, instead of making a long count," Don continued, "I [quickly] counted 'one' . . . 'ten' . . . then pulled the ripcord, and bang! I damn near tore myself in half when my parachute deployed. [The opening shock was so forceful] my shoes snapped out of my hands and went tumbling below. If they'd hit somebody on the head they would have been knocked cold."

Don's parachute probably deployed around 9,500 feet above ground level, although he would have descended to a lower altitude before he regained his composure and orientation. At the time he discovered he had "unrestricted visibility" for approximately thirty miles,[180] which was, no doubt, exhilarating. However, it was also frightening, given his close proximity to the Baltic coast, and concern that his descent might take him out into the water. He also noticed that his aircraft continued

[178] Poynter, *The Parachute Manual, Vol I,* 165

[179] Poynter, *The Parachute Manual, Vol II,* 310

[180] HQ Eighth AF Tactical Mission Report-514, Weather, 4 Aug 1944, 1

to fly on what appeared to be a set course, "while still burning, before diving to earth." Moments later, he spotted eight other deployed parachutes scattered beneath him, which meant that the entire crew had safely exited the aircraft. Don also noticed "two P-51 Mustangs circling in the general vicinity to provide protective suppressing fire if necessary, as the crew descended and stayed with us until we [landed]."

Under canopy and descending to earth, Don recalled "It was very quiet in the air, and all I could think about was my mother's worrying . . . fearing I've been killed, and this bothered me." Don also started to consider how he would execute his evasion plan, and thinking, "What I am going to do when it hit the ground as I want to get out of there if I can. We had been taught evasion [procedures] by our Intelligence Service, and we were well-prepared." Months earlier, in February 1944, the War Department's Military Intelligence Service-X (MIS-X) branch had published an extensive manual on "Evasion, Escape, and Survival" to assist US Army Air Force personnel in evading capture.[181] The manual presented a wealth of information collected after two years of assisting airmen to successfully return to Allied control. Airmen shot down in northern Germany were specifically advised to head for one of four large ports on the Baltic–Danzig, Gdynig, Stettin, and Lübeck– and stow away on Swedish ships bound for their port of origin. The manual provided information on color schemes to identify Swedish vessels and advice on how to gain access. The MIS-X Manual also provided extensive information pertaining to several underground evasion networks established in Europe to move downed airmen back to England.* "We all had escape kits and the rest of it," Don said, "which included a small compass, maps, and local currency," in addition to a black and white photograph, taken while dressed in civilian clothing, to authentic false identification papers.

"After what felt like an eternity," Don continued, "[I] was fortunate to land on solid ground, yet I hit pretty hard. I think these 'chutes' were [made] for an average-size man of 160 pounds. I weighed 200 lbs. then, and probably came down pretty fast . . . although it seemed like it took

* A total of 4,658 Allied airmen successfully evaded capture after being shot down during the war. The majority of these airmen, 2,692, belonged to the US Army Air Force.[182]

[181] WD, MIS-X Manual on Evasion, Escape, and Survival (Feb 1944)
[182] Doyle, *A Prisoners Duty*, 286

an hour." Some of his perception was accurate. The rate of descent for a 150-pound man under a 24-foot diameter canopy was slightly less than 19 feet per second. The rate of descent for a heavier man of Don's weight would have exceeded 24 feet per second, which suggests he spent approximately six and one-half minutes in the air prior to landing, and did, in fact, "hit pretty hard."*

Before Don could recover from his parachute landing fall, "a kid around 15-years-old showed up, [in uniform] with a gun, and speaking German, ordered me to put up my hands. I was plenty scared as this kid was also scared to death. Here [I am], a guy [who has] dropped out of the heavens [after] bombing his [country], and German newspapers had been reporting that American airmen were 'terror fliegers' and 'luft gangsters.' Yet, this kid didn't know that [wasn't true]. And the look in his eye didn't make me feel very much at ease."

Any airman shot down over Germany had good reason to be anxious upon capture. A substantial number of women and children had been killed during the Allied bombing campaign. Most of these deaths were directly attributable to the policy of the British government to bomb German cities at night, with the specific intent to inflict mass causalities. Early in the war, the RAF lacked the technological capability to conduct precision bombing. Moreover, they could not afford the loss of aircraft or personnel resulting from a daylight campaign. Almost by default the government adopted a policy of conducting mass area bombings, in which the civilian population of Germany was intentionally targeted. Conversely, the US Army Air Force possessed the capability to conduct a more precise bombing campaign against primarily military targets, although these bombings also resulted in civilian casualties. The US policy to intentionally inflict mass casualties on the German population would not change for another six months, until the 3 February 1945 raid on Berlin.

In response to the increasing frequency and intensity of the Allied

---

* Calculations for the rates of descent were made in consultation with Dan Poynter, author of *The Parachute Manual*. Later, post war protocol examinations of former POWs found the "prevalence of back injuries was highest for aircrew members who parachuted from or landed with their disabled aircraft."[183]

[183] Williams, *Post-Traumatic Stress Disorder*, 137

bombing campaign, German Reich Minister, Dr. Joseph Goebbels, and other state functionaries had urged harsh and severe treatment of captured airmen. In late November 1943, Goebbels was able to exploit this theme more fully, following the capture of Lieutenant Kenneth Williams and two crew members of the 351st Bomb Group. All three airmen were wearing their leather flight jackets at capture with their aircraft's name, "Murder, Inc.," lettered across the back. A photograph of Williams appeared in a number of newspapers across Germany, along with an article that claimed "all [bomb] crews were composed of gangsters paid $50,000 per mission."[184] Goebbels further denounced the captives as murderers in his attempt "to incite the general public to take revenge against the American gangsters."[185]

The possibility of capture was a reality for all airmen participating in the air war over Europe. Still, few Americans could "foresee the hostile reception that often awaited them on the ground."[186] Anecdotal accounts alone, from American and British POWs who were later liberated, suggest that German civilians killed many Allied airmen shortly after they were apprehended. Moreover, author David Foy also noted that while considerate treatment was extended to some injured flyers upon capture, this was the "exception rather than the rule" and that most aircrew were mistreated by both German civilians and members of the armed forces. For these men, their first hours and days following capture were the most threatening and "the most dangerous period of their entire captivity."[187] Some members of Don's crew experienced this hostility once apprehended, although most, except for Staff Sergeant Richard Kukulian, were captured without incident.

Later that afternoon, as Don and the other members of his crew were moving to a central collection point in northern Germany, the returning aircraft of 398th Bomb Group crossed over the English coast, inbound for Nuthampstead. The group had successfully dropped 178 of a total 911, 1,000-lbs. high explosive bombs, in addition to other ordnance, on their target.[188] Assessment photographs taken later that afternoon indicated that "the electrolytic hydrogen peroxide plant,"

---

[184] Foy, *For You the War is Over*, 22
[185] Toliver, *The Interrogator*, 156
[186] Carlson, *We Were Each Other's Prisoners*, xviii
[187] Foy, *For You the War is Over*, 45
[188] HQ Eighth AF Tactical Mission Report-514, 4 August 1944, 8

long with other structures at the target site, was damaged.[189] The group
lost two Fortresses over Peenemünde, while a number of other aircraft
assigned to the 398th sustained significant battle damage. A total of
sixty-nine of the 221 participating aircraft had been hit by flak. A later
postwar chronology of USAAF missions during WWII would simply
note, on "4 Aug 1944, the Eighth Air Force launched 2,072 aircraft
on their 714th day of sustained operations, losing 14 heavy bombers,
15 fighters, and 153 aircrew." Another 325 aircraft reported varying
degrees of battle damage, of which four were beyond repair and noted
as Category E (salvage).[190]

That evening, after the crews at Nuthampstead had been debriefed,
John Bell inventoried Don's possessions, still under the mistaken
impression his friend had been killed on the day's mission. Over the
next week he would also return letters to Don's girlfriend, and transport
other personal items to the appropriate base facility for shipment back
to the United States. Years later, in a conversation with the author, John
would cite this experience "as one of his most painful memories of the
war." Other airmen released from the 4 August afternoon debriefings
went out drinking, yet the majority of these men simply ate at the
combat mess and went to bed. The following morning the Eighth Air
Force would launch another 1,062 plane raid into Germany, flown by
many of the same aircrew that had participated in the previous day's
operation, all hoping to complete another mission and return safely
home.

[189] HQ Eighth AF Tactical Mission Report-514, Summary, 4 August 1944, 15
[190] Carter & Mueller, *AFF in WWII: Combat Chronology, 1941–1945*, 414

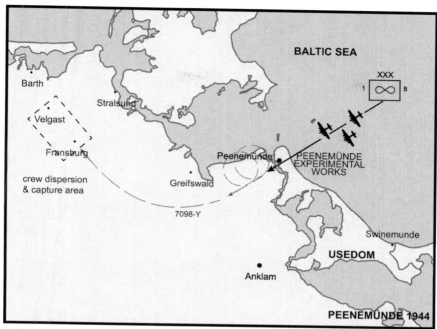

Mission 514 to Peenemünde   Author's collection

The US Army Eighth Air Force sent 221 B-17s of the First Bombardment Division to strike the electrolytic hydrogen peroxide plant at Peenemünde on 4 August 1944. The high group had just finished their bomb run when Carter's aircraft, 7098-Y, left the formation.

7

INTERROGATION

Few Allied airmen anticipated that their greatest danger in captivity would occur shortly after being apprehended. This was especially true during the last two years of the war when the German population was "strongly encouraged to kill" these airmen as soon as they were captured.[191] However, once Allied flyers were in the custody of the German military, especially the Luftwaffe, they were usually protected from hostile, threatening crowds. Still, this initial and often protracted first phase of detention represented a period during which time the German government did not formally recognize an airman's status as a prisoner of war. Formal recognition only occurred after the captured airman had been interrogated by military personnel and interned in a permanent prisoner of war camp.[192]

Recently apprehended airmen usually sustained varying degrees of physical injury from wounds received during aerial combat, exiting damaged aircraft or landing. All of these experiences were disorienting. Yet, the very act of being captured was equally traumatic, resulting in a loss of identity and control over one's environment. The experience, forced most combatants to assume, at least initially, a passive role, characterized by Winston Churchill, a former Boer War POW, as a "melancholy state," where one had to "possess [their] soul in patience."[193] Guilt further affected the emotional state of many airmen, who experienced "an element of shame" pertaining to the circumstances of their capture. This was especially true following some harrowing event in the air that forced them to abandon their aircraft, if not fellow crew members. Once in captivity, the protracted fear associated with possible execution further eroded an airman's psychological resilience.[194]

[191] Foy, *For You the War is Over*, 37
[192] Ibid., 45
[193] Williams, *Post Traumatic Stress Disorder*, 132
[194] Carlson, *We Were Each Other's Prisoner*, 29

Don experienced both types of disorientation following his jarring impact with the ground on landing, and immediate confrontation with the German soldier who threatened his life. Now, standing in a clearing, with both hands held in the air, the downed airman recalled how he tried desperately to make some type of personal connection with the youth. "I tried to make him think I'm his pal," Don continued, "because, brother, I felt like being his pal about that time. I wasn't mad at anybody. Here I am standing there looking at this guy. He's got blue eyes and just a few years younger than me. Made me wonder what it's all about."

"Fortunately, about 15 or 20 other guys showed up," Don said, "and I discovered this kid is from a flak unit nearby. An older man, [presumably an NCO] now took charge and told me to lay down flat on my face, and I thought I'd had it. He asked me if I had a pistol, which I did not, and for awhile I lay there as they all talked and I said my prayers, figur[ing] this was it! But pretty soon they said to get up and put my hands over my head, as we walked some distance to the nearest town."

German documents originating from the local air base at Parow, then later forwarded to the International Red Cross, reported that Don was captured mid-afternoon on 4 August 1944 near Velgast, 18 kilometers west of Stralsund. Similar documents drafted at the Pütnitz airfield cited that fellow crew members, Nigel Carter and Edward Castro, were captured around 1600 hours near Fransburg, 10–12 kilometers southeast of Don's location. The distance between these two capture sites suggests a broad dispersion of the aircrew after parachuting from their burning aircraft. Such an extended dispersal pattern is usually caused by the separation in time between each crew member's exit from their plane, the altitude at which they activated their parachute, and their respective rates of descent in the air. Don's early deployment of his parachute at or above 9,000 feet exposed him to yet another variable: the protracted influences of the winds aloft, which further increased his separation from the rest of his crew.

Corporal Bob Carr was also apprehended some distance from the rest of his crew. His landing wasn't as jarring as Don's experience, yet his reception was far worse. The first of three persons to approach Bob as he struggled to unfasten his parachute harness was a 45-year-old

German male. Advancing with a drawn pistol, the older man ordered Carr to move to a nearby farmhouse. Following their arrival, the man's "wife and two daughters [started to cut up the canopy of his parachute] for the silk material." Suddenly, and without warning, the unsuspecting gunner was "grabbed . . . from behind and thrown out into the yard." The town Burgomaster had arrived, enraged, and proceeded to repeatedly hit the startled airman, all the while asking him questions he could not understand or answer. The beating continued for some time while the town's mayor tore at Carr's clothing. A subsequent discovery of an escape kit incited further wrath and attack. Bob was then forced by his tormentor into town, where he was stripped of all his clothing, except for his shorts. At this point, the exposed airman was left standing in the middle of the road, surrounded by angry women, when another male arrived and proceeded to engage the Burgomaster in a heated argument. This dispute ended with the return of Carr's clothing, and after dressing, he was "led to another town," where his escort became embroiled in yet another altercation with a local resident. Continuing on, Bob was further beaten by "people who would come out [of their farmhouses] and take turns hitting [him] with their fists." The bruised and pummeled airman eventually arrived at a house where he was placed in a cellar that served as a holding locker. To his surprise, several members of his crew were already inside.

Sometime later, Don and his security detail arrived at the same farmhouse, where he was ushered inside the modified cellar to join the rest of his crew. At that point, Don recognized Carr sitting in the dim light. Embarrassed, yet apologetic, he cried, "My God, I'm sorry Bob, I was going to get you out of that ball but I didn't even think of anything [other] than how to get out myself." Carr was reportedly very good-natured about the oversight, and said, "Don't worry about it, Dorf—I was out of that thing before the rest of you."

The next day, the German Luftwaffe sent a vehicle from the local airfield at Pütnitz to retrieve Don and the other members of Carter's crew, now held some sixteen hours in the make-shift locker. En route to the airfield, they passed a recent crash site where the body of the pilot lay dead in the field. Circling the dead airman were a number of vengeful German civilians, kicking the lifeless body to vent their frustration and anger. Carr was later told by one of the survivors of the downed Fortress that the pilot had sacrificed himself by remaining at the controls of his plane so that his crew could get out safely.

Don and his crew arrived at the airfield and were united with other recently captured airmen, some of whom had untreated shrapnel wounds. All of the apprehended combatants were then stripped of their clothing, which was searched for useful information. The airmen were also "asked a lot of questions," and relieved of their service issued identification tags. This violation was very disturbing for the airmen, and surrendering their last remaining form of official identification only increased their apprehension. However, they were somewhat relieved to learn that information stamped on their dog tags was required when notifying the International Red Cross of their captive status. "While we were scared," Don recalled, "we still got a laugh out of the [antics] of this one lieutenant," who, when first questioned, tried to assert his authority, demanding a wide range of privileges 'because he was an officer in the US Air Force.' Well, the German official in charge could have cared less and so informed the lieutenant, who, moments later, became almost hysterical when they took his identification tags."

The lieutenant's protests, in recognition of his lost status and authority, amused Don and the other enlisted airmen of the group. The source of their entertainment was based on an earlier recognition of their own loss of status and autonomy after joining the service, whereas officers still enjoyed some privileges. Now, officers and enlisted men alike shared a similar sense of powerlessness and lack of control. The lieutenant would soon discover his rank as an officer in captivity would provide him with few, if any, advantages.

Don and the other airmen completed an initial, brief questioning at the Pütnitz airfield and were put on a train the next morning to the Luftwaffe's Intelligence and Evaluation Center near Frankfurt/Main. Once in transit, the men soon realized they were on a passenger train carrying German soldier's home on leave. According to fellow crew member, Bob Carr, "the soldiers showed little interest in the Americans" and the trip was uneventful until their train pulled into the Berlin *Hauptbahnhof*, the city's main train station. Once in the terminal, the airmen were transferred to another line that required they move through an angry crowd of German civilians who had gathered to jeer and assault the American airmen with rocks. To the credit of the German Luftwaffe, the captives were protected, for the most part, from any serious harm or physical injury.

Bob Carr recalled two incidents occurring during the transfer that characterized the animosity of the German crowd in the rail station and the defiant spirit of the transient airmen. In the first instance, the Americans were starting to board their train when a German officer unexpectedly approached one of the pilots in their group and hit him in the face. Startled and angry, the struck pilot told his assailant, "You son of a bitch, if I get lose I'll come back and bomb you again!" This occurrence was followed by a verbal taunting from another man standing on an adjacent platform, who, speaking perfect English, shouted "You bastards, you dirty bastards!" Sergeant Robert Doll, the crew radio operator, responded to this epithet by telling the bilingual German, "Blow it out your ass!"

Arriving in Frankfurt hours later, the airmen were again moved through a gauntlet of angry German civilians. Marching through the city, Don recalled, "I'll never forget the experience of having old women and young kids throw rocks at me, spit at me and hit me with sticks, and everything else. But I could not blame them. I'd do the same thing. You would too if they bombed your [country] and then dropped into your backyard. In fact, I guess a lot of [flyers] were killed [by German civilians] and never made it to a prisoners of war camp, although the German authorities and the Luftwaffe in particular, treated [me] every bit as well as I ever expected to be treated by an [enemy] power." Still, he continued, "it was another harrowing experience to be beaten, even though I wasn't beaten that much. I was just [shocked] that people could hate so much!"

The captive airmen eventually arrived at the *Auswertestelle West* late in the afternoon of 6 August 1944. The facility, located in the Taunus Mountain community of Oberursel, 12 kilometers northwest of Frankfurt was the Luftwaffe's primary Intelligence and Evaluation Center. The facility, also known as the *Durchgangslager,* or "Dulag Luft," consisted of three separate sections: the interrogation center at Oberursel, an adjacent hospital at Hohemark (for seriously wounded airmen), and the recently relocated transit camp at Wetzlar, 52 kilometers north of Frankfurt. The Center had first opened in December 1939 and initially interrogated only a small number of British and French airmen. Two years later, the Auswertestelle West was evaluating all personnel assigned to the air forces of the western powers, while Russian airmen, captured after the June 1941 invasion of the Soviet Union, were sent to another location.[195] The Center's primary focus was to gather strategic information pertaining to the strength, disposition, and capabilities of their adversaries through the use of various debriefing techniques.

These interrogation procedures improved markedly following the 1941 visit of Luftwaffe pilot, Franz von Werra. The dashing pilot had become a national celebrity following his successful escape from British captivity and subsequent return to Germany. Forced down over England during the Battle of Britain in early September 1940, von Werra escaped twice before he was sent to a POW camp in Canada. While crossing the US-Canadian border, the tenacious officer escaped again and made his way by train to Mexico. From there, he sailed back to Spain, returning to Germany 18 April 1941. Once back in uniform, von Werra was asked to tour the Evaluation Center in Oberursel and provide recommendations for improvement. While visiting the new facility, von Werra discovered the current practice at the Auswertestelle West was "superficial" and failed to appreciate "the immense importance of interrogation as a source" for gathering military intelligence. These deficiencies were noted during his departure briefing and cited in a later report to Herman Goering, who insisted the superior and more thorough British techniques be implemented by the Center's staff.

Over the next three years the Intelligence and Evaluation Center expanded in size and function as the air war over Europe intensified. "In 1942, 3,000 Allied POWs passed through the camp."[196] The following year, after American bomb groups starting attacking targets inside Germany, another 8,000 American and British airmen were interrogated at the center. That number increased dramatically to "2,000 a month" in the first half of the New Year, then peaked at 3,000 per month in July 1944.[197]

At the time of Don's passage through Auswertestelle West, some 300 Luftwaffe personnel, under the command of Oberstleutnant Erich Killinger, were assigned to the compound staff at Oberursel. In this group, approximately fifty-five officers and enlisted men conducted

---

[195] Foy, *For You the War is Over*, 53
[196] Foy, *For You the War is Over*, 53
[197] Ibid., 53

the interrogations.[198] These individuals were carefully selected native Germans who had spent part of their lives in either the United States or Britain. Further, all interrogators were "qualified interpreters, [who possessed] an excellent knowledge of the enemy's language and culture, and who were generally well educated."[199] Later in the war, the Gestapo and SS asserted their presence at Oberursel following the 20 July 1944 plot to assassinate Adolph Hitler. However, the Luftwaffe was adamant in their determination to retain control of all captured Allied airmen, and the camp commandant, Erick Killinger, resisted the intrusion of these two agencies. Killinger was ultimately forced to accept their access to only captives returned, as well as prisoners who had been assisted by the underground before capture.

The US War Department's Military Intelligence Division (MID) was well aware of Luftwaffe's efforts to extract military information from American airmen shot down over Europe. The Division's Military Intelligence Service-X (MIS-X) directorate, based on Britain's M19, was established shortly after America's entry into the war to assist evaders and those likely to be captured. In February 1944, the War Department published the "MIS-X Manual on Evasion, Escape, and Survival" to "assist aircrew, and other service personnel who were liable to be taken prisoner [or] evade capture."[200] The manual emphasized the importance of general security; cited prohibitions against carrying any "personal letters, documents, mess bills, theatre ticket stubs, photographs or laundry bills" during missions; and stressed the "importance of [the crew's responsibility for] destroying [their] plane, equipment and documents in enemy occupied or enemy territory."[201] The US Air Force was furthered identified as "an increasing important factor in the war, so the enemy continually tries to ascertain its strength, disposition, and capabilities."[202] The Army manual specifically identified the Evaluation Center at Oberursel as an interrogation center for "extracting information from personnel believed to possess military knowledge of particular value."[203]

---

[198] Barker, *Prisoners of War*, 64
[199] Ibid., 64
[200] WD, MIS-X Manual on Evasion, . . . ; Security (Feb 1944) 7
[201] Ibid., 7
[202] WD, MIS-X Manual on Evasion, . . . ; Interrogation (Feb 1944) 3
[203] Ibid., 6

While the MIS-X Manual identified procedures for safeguarding sensitive information, and techniques for evading capture, the publication's primary focus was meant to familiarize captured airmen with the protocols of the Geneva Convention, their rights as POWs, and how to successfully resist interrogation. These sections provided an overview of the Articles of the 1929 Geneva Convention, which was "the first formal codification of International Law concerning itself solely with the treatment and status of prisoners of war." The manual also acknowledged that all captured airmen would be sent to the Durchgangslager for interrogation where they could expect to be kept as long as a week in solitary confinement while being interrogated, although aircrew were known to have been confined for 15 to 30 days to obtain technical or operational information. To be kept longer, according to the briefing manual, "implied that you were useful to the enemy."

The chapter titled "Resisting Interrogation" further acknowledged that all captured airmen, following their arrival at the Durchgangslager, would be psychologically evaluated . . . and "an assessment made of each individual's perceived vulnerability. The strain of being a POW," according to the text, "will accentuate your [personality] type; [whether] sullen, vain, comedian, tough, meek, careless, etc. Aircrews are interrogated separately, commencing with the highest rank, in hopes of exploiting their weakness. [Yet], lately, the tendency has been to by-pass [officers] and concentrate more thoroughly on the NCO's of the crew."[204] The airmen were informed they would "encounter skilled interrogators, men and women, with perfect command of our language and a surprising amount of information on our service and equipment. The methods of questioning will vary with the type of person you exhibit yourself to be."[205] Last, potential detainees were advised they would be exposed to various types of direct or indirect questioning methods, employing one or more of 16 different interrogation techniques that ranged from empathic recognition of the captive's 'despair,' to 'appealing to one's vanity,' and sense of self-importance."[206]

The MIS-X Manual also offered practical suggestions for resisting interrogation, to " . . . avoid being classified into a specific sucker

[204] WD, MIS-X Manual on Evasion, . . . ; Interrogation (Feb 1944) 8
[205] Ibid., 8
[206] Ibid., 9

category." The airmen were advised " . . . to maintain a strict, polite, military bearing. The Germans are, "according to the intelligence handbook, "a military people, even in defeat . . . and they will respect you if you are as military as they. A correct military bearing makes psychological 'typing' difficult, if not impossible."[207] The airmen were further advised to "be courteous, salute all ranking enemy personnel, and stand at attention during interrogation."[208] Lastly, the US airmen were admonished to not outsmart the interrogation officer . . . [as] he'll trip you up every time to your astonished embarrassment."[209]

After Don and the other airmen in his crew arrived at the Auswertestelle, the officers and enlisted men were separated at the reception office, individually stripped of their clothing, and searched again. These searches, which included rectal exams, usually yielded various maps, mess hall chits, and tramcar tickets, in spite of earlier briefings admonishing airmen to refrain from carrying such contraband.[210] The collection of just the smallest amount of information provided a wealth of data to identify one's unit of assignment and added to the Luftwaffe's assessment of the Eighth Air Force order of battle.* The airmen were then photographed and fingerprinted at the transportation office to create an individual *Kriegsgefangenenkartel.*** After completing a preliminary in-processing the airmen were placed in solitary confinement.

The new airmen were assigned to one of more than 200 cells located in the "cooler," which was the largest of some 14 buildings at the Evaluation Center.[211] Each room in the building was initially designed for solitary confinement, yet by the summer of 1944 as many as four or five men might occupy a single cell, with a low ceiling that measured "10 × 13 [feet], and simply furnished with a bed, a wooden

* See pages 57–58
** These rose-colored cards, which measured approximately 8 × 11 inches, contained general information, a description of one's physical characteristics, and were later annotated with an assigned POW number and camp placement.

[207] Ibid., 8
[208] Ibid., 17
[209] Ibid., 17
[210] Durand, *Stalag Luft III*, 60
[211] Barker, *Prisoners of War*, 64

stool, and two blankets."[212] The wooden cells were kept intentionally "grimy and . . . evil smelling . . . to lower morale,"[213] The airmen were "cajoled, threatened . . . starved, or left to suffer nicotine [withdrawal] and ponder their fate."[214] This intentional deprivation was designed to promote psychological vulnerabilities and increase the likelihood a captive would cooperate in the interrogation process. Don and the other airmen would stay in these cells throughout the period of their interrogation. Their only diversions from the oppressive monotony were inadequate meals of bread, jam, and foul-tasting *ersatz* (substitute) coffee in the morning; soup for lunch; and bread and water at night. A member of the staff would eventually visit each cell, or have the service member escorted to an interrogation room, to initiate the assessment and questioning process.[215]

Now separated from the other crew members, Don was placed in a cell with five other airmen, "one of whom," he recalled, "had been wounded in the leg and [infection] had set in. [Eventually]," he continued, "we were all taken out of our cells, and the [Germans] did exactly what our Intelligence [Service] told us they would do. First, they asked us to fill out [fraudulent] Red Cross forms, designed to elicit sensitive military information, with questions pertaining to [their] aircraft, destination, and bomb loads, etc. Then, politely informed [us] . . . that because we did not have our identification tags we could be labeled as a spy [and shot] if we did not cooperate. Well, this shook up quite a few of us, but our orders were to limit our [disclosure] to name, rank, and service number. The interrogator then asked me to fill out some other forms, at which point I refused further cooperation." Don was then returned to his cell. His interrogation would continue over the next two days.

A prisoner's second exposure to an interrogator "usually began in a friendly manner," characterized with offers of "cigarettes or chocolate, and . . . light conversation about the war's unfortunate effects."[216] German interrogators also attempted to promote a sense of camaraderie with the captured flyers asserting "that there was honor among

---

[212] Ibid., 62
[213] Barker, *Prisoners of War*, 64
[214] Durand, *Stalag Luft III*, 62
[215] Toliver, *The Interrogator*, 14
[216] Durand, *Stalag Luft III*, 65

airmen."[217] If this initial approach proved to be unproductive in eliciting information, "threats of violence abruptly followed."[218]* Yet, as a general policy, the Luftwaffe personnel at Oberursel did not use force to coerce information from their detainees, although some of their procedures were abusive. Rather, most interrogators employed various psychological manipulations–in addition to very sophisticated techniques and forms of questioning–to elicit information pertaining to tactical innovations, radio frequencies, and call signs.

The most successful and seductive approach of any interrogator at the Evaluation Center was to present themselves as an advocate for the captive. One form of this approach was to profess a desire to help the captive establish his identity as a member of a uniformed military service, as opposed to commandos and saboteurs who were turned over to the Gestapo and shot. The captive was informed that the surest procedure for establishing his identity as a serviceman was to provide detailed information of a military nature. This would require the disclosure of information known to only a member of a uniformed military service. The interrogator would facilitate this process by employing a hierarchy of rewards for cooperation, while refusal to provide information beyond name, rank, and serial number resulted in the captive's return to their cell.

Should an airman accept the argument of having to prove their identity, the interrogator would slowly ask questions in ascending order of importance. Individuals who cooperated were usually allowed some "privileges," such as an opportunity to wash or shave. If someone "showed promise," he was held until he revealed all the general information considered significant. Then he would be transferred to a specialist who would focus on the captive's technical expertise. This procedure usually lasted from one to four weeks for American officers, and a much shorter duration for the enlisted crew members who were perceived to have limited access to both general and technical information.

---

* Following the war, Erich Killinger and four other Luftwaffe interrogators at the Evaluation Center were tried by a British military court, charged with committing war crimes between 1 November 1941 and 15 April 1945.

[217] Carlson, *We Were Each Other's Prisoners*, x
[218] Durand, *Stalag Luft III*, 65–66

One of the most successful interrogators at the Evaluation Center during the last two years of the war was Obergefreiter Hanns Scharff. Scharff had resided in Johannesburg, South Africa for eleven years prior to returning to Germany in 1939. Following the initiation of hostilities in Europe, Scharff's exit visa was revoked. Two years later, at age 32, he was drafted into the German Wehrmacht. Through good fortune, the senior lance corporal was reassigned to the Luftwaffe as an interrogation officer for the USAAF Fighter Section. He served in this capacity throughout the last part of the war and emerged as one of Germany's master interrogators. What was particularly unique about Scharff was that he never reverted to the use of force, or was ever known to raise his voice in working with Allied POWs.[219] Rather, Scharff was most successful in continuing to act in a friendly manner to a captive after their initial fears of interrogation had calmed. Fluent in English and knowledgeable of British and American customs, Scharff was able to gain the trust and confidence of many allied airmen, who often, unknowingly, volunteered information useful to the Luftwaffe.

Bob Carr recalled having similar experiences to Don's while at the Evaluation Center in Oberursel. "We arrived in the late afternoon," Carr said. "I got my picture taken, then was interrogated briefly, after which they promised some food, yet I didn't get any [thing to eat] that night. Over the next two days they assumed I was a [P-51] pilot as several were shot down in the area [where I was apprehended] and because I was separated from my crew." This insinuation was terminated during his last session, according to Carr, when the "interrogator provided the name and duty position of his entire crew," creating the impression that "the German officer knew full well that I was the ball turret gunner."

While Don and the other airmen were being interrogated at the Evaluation Center, Staff Sergeant Richard Kukulian, the crew's Flight Engineer, was captured near Damgarten, 25 kilometers from where the other crew members had been caught. The resourceful airman had successfully evaded human contact for almost three days, moving in a westward direction across mostly open country. On the fourth day, he was apprehended in early morning and sent to the Luftwaffe's Evaluation Center at Oberursel, where German interrogators attempted to learn how the lone airman had managed to elude capture.

---

[219] Toliver, *Master Interrogator*, 14

Don's last session of interrogation was memorable, if for no other reason than his encounter with an escort who came walking down the hall calling out, "Sergeant Dorfmeier! Sergeant Dorfmeier! Where in the hell is Sergeant Dorfmeier?" Although listed as a corporal on the crew manifest for the 4 August 1944 mission to Peenemünde, Don apparently identified himself upon capture as a noncommissioned officer (NCO) in hopes of receiving better treatment. "Then," according to Don, "my cell door opened, and I looked up from my cot, and in walked the perfect movie [stereotype] of a German flyer. He was tall and handsome, had pearl white teeth, steel blue eyes, and spoke perfect English. I was then escorted to one final session with the corporal, then allowed to see the 'Colonel'," who, in all likelihood was Major Waldschmidt, a former professor at Gottingen University before the war and renowned as a competent bomb crew interrogator at Oberursel.

Don characterized his last session and " . . . conversation with [his] interrogator [as] most interesting. He was a nice fellow and a very fatherly type guy. I imagined he was not an [ardent] supporter of Adolph Hitler. Once inside his office, he just sat down [and] opened a book which contained my name, where I was born, where I took my preflight, gunnery, what our mission was, identified our bomb load–everything. And I was impressed. But then I sat back and thought that most of this information was printed in the press in the States and not so hard to get hold of, and our security at the base wasn't the greatest.* People could get into those mission briefings. But it didn't make too much of a difference, because [the Germans] knew we were coming, and there wasn't anything they could do about it anyway."

Don's interrogator then commented, "'If you think our intelligence is good, you should see your own.' This statement made me feel pretty proud of my country. He informed me he was familiar with California, having studied at the University of California at Los Angeles." He had also spent some time at Stanford and knew the San Francisco Peninsula. So maybe this was a gimmick to [elicit information], although I don't think I said anything more, other than to ask, 'When do you think the

---

* The press department at the Evaluation Center was able to collect considerable amounts of information on individual servicemen and their units from stateside newspapers passed through a German clearinghouse in Lisbon, Portugal.[220]

[220] Kaplan & Smith, *One Last Look*, 170

war will be over?' He then got up and walked over to a big map [on the wall] and pointed to the Rhine River, and said, 'When the Americans reach here.' Well, that's about the way it went, but unfortunately it took almost a year to get that done." However, during that long year, from the summer 1944 through spring 1945, Don, the members of his crew, and thousands of other airmen in his camp would experience the harsh realities of a collapsing nation, a scarcity of adequate rations, and an epic event no one could have imagined.

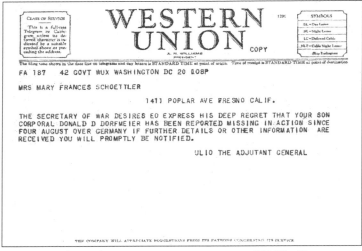

Western Union Telegram   US War Department

US War Department telegram sent to Don's mother in late August 1944. Hundreds of thousands of families across the United States received this type of notification during WWII prior to any further clarification of status.

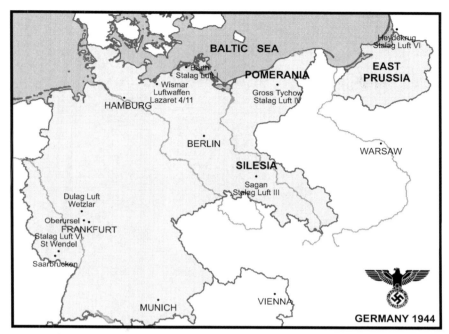

German interrogation and transit centers   Author's collection

Captured American and British airmen were sent for interrogation to Oberursel, 12 kilometers northwest of Frankfurt. Following three to five days of examination and questioning these airmen were transferred to the Dulag Luft transit camp at Wetzlar. New arrivals were then allowed to shower, issued Red Cross rations, and a small postcard to write their families. The airmen were later separated and transported by rail to a POW camp administered by the German Luftwaffe.

8

FIRST CAMP

The telegram arrived while Don's mother was out of the house, yet, upon her return, she could see the ocher colored envelope protruding from the top of her front porch mailbox. "She had expected the notification," Marie would recall years later, "because of a dream she had several nights previously." Now, two and a half weeks after her son, Corporal Donald Dorfmeier, had been shot down over Peenemünde, his mother was confronting one of the worst fears of any parent during a time of war–that of a son or daughter declared "Missing in Action."* Yet, the Western Union cable concluded on a hopeful note, promising, "If further details or other information are received you will be promptly notified."

An official letter from the War Department was usually sent to the serviceman's family residence within a month or so from the date of their initial notification. These letters attempted to bolster the hopes of the families, clarifying the term "missing in action," and answering anticipated questions pertaining to the servicemen's pay and other allowances. The letters were personally signed by Major General J. A. Ulio, Adjutant General of the Army, who, according to a wartime editorial, "received 40,000 daily requests for information pertaining to servicemen killed, wounded, or missing in action."

In spite of the government's official consolation, Marie ached for the answer to the one question she so desperately sought: the clarification of her son's status. Gratefully, her immediate concern and anxiety were alleviated, days later, after receiving unofficial contact from the spouse of former crew member, John Bell. Bell's wife, Gincie, had been working in the Pentagon that summer when, by chance, she learned of Don's capture through documents provided to the War Department by

---

* The term Missing in Action (MIA) was used to categorize any service member on active duty who had been killed, wounded, or become a prisoner of war. Hundreds of thousands of families across the United States received such notification during the war.

the International Red Cross. She then contacted Marie to inform her of Don's capture and current status as a prisoner of war.

Some time later, Marie received her son's first correspondence following his last mission. The postcard, dated 8 August 1944, just four days after Don's capture, was received with mixed emotions. She was, most assuredly, relieved to know that her son was still alive, yet she also worried about his safety as a captive of an enemy power. Still, the tone of Don's message was confident and optimistic. From the Durchgangslager's transit camp at Wetzlar, he wrote;

> "Dearest Loved Ones, I am well and healthy. I am a POW and doing OK. Don't write this address, but wait for another. Tell Frances, also tell her to wait but not sacrifice any fun but to remember I love her. See the Hopwoods or the Red Cross for instructions. Thoughts of all of you are very dear to me. Love to you all, Donald"

Don, along with the enlisted members of his crew and an unknown number of other POWs, had been transported by train from the Dulag Luft's interrogation center at Oberursel to the transit camp at Wetzlar.* The camp had been previously situated in central Frankfurt, then relocated 52 kilometers north of Frankfurt after Allied bombing of the city in March 1944. On arrival, the airmen were given their first opportunity to shower, shave, and discard old clothing for Red Cross issues. Some of the clothing was distinctively marked, identifying them as German POWs. The airmen were also given their first substantial food rations since capture: a Red Cross food parcel containing 8-ounce cans of corned beef, pork, and salmon, in addition to biscuits, processed cheese, and other condiments. Later on, each man was issued a postcard and allowed to write a brief message to their family. At the Dulag Luft's transit center, Don and the other new arrivals were separated into groups of officers and NCOs in preparation for transit to a permanent camp. In the summer of 1944, seven separate internment sites

---

* The same day Don departed Oberursel, Wallace Blackwell and his crew were shot down on their fourth mission to support the US Army Ground Forces moving out of the Normandy bridgehead. Blackwell's aircraft had been hit in the tail section by flak, killing the gunner assigned to that position. Except for the one casualty, the other crew members successfully exited, evaded capture, and were quickly recovered by Allied forces.

administered by the German Air Force held an estimated 32,000 Allied airmen. However, the majority of these prisoners were detained in four primary compounds, officially designated as "Stammlager der Luftwaffe," yet commonly referred to as "Stalag Luft," followed by the camp's numerical designation. All four primary camps administered by the Luftwaffe were established in eastern Germany to discourage thoughts of escape. Stalag Luft I, near Barth on the north Baltic coast, held Allied air force officers; Stalag Luft III, near Sagan in central Germany, held both officers and enlisted airmen. The two other compounds, Stalag Luft IV, near Gross Tychow in northeast Germany, and Stalag Luft VI, located at Heydekrug in East Prussia, were used exclusively for interned NCOs.

In mid-summer, 1944, several thousand American and British airmen held at Stalag Luft VI were evacuated to other camps as the Russians advanced into eastern Poland. The stammlager, which retained its designation as Stalag Luft VI, was relocated the following month on the West German border at St. Wendel, 35 kilometers northeast of Saarbrucken. Days later, Sergeant Don Dorfmeier, the enlisted members of his crew, and approximately 100 other Americans were the first group of Allied POWs sent to the new compound. Each airman arrived with a perforated, rectangular identification tag stamped with their lager placement, "Stalag Luft VI," and assigned *gefangenennumber.* The metal tags, beginning with the number series "4,000" were issued to the men while processing through Wetzlar and waiting transit to a permanent camp. Crew member, Bob Carr, was issued number 4030 while Don's identification tag was stamped number 4054, suggesting that the ever-methodical Germans processed the new arrivals at the Dulag Luft in alphabetical order.

From Wetzlar, Don and the others traveled back through the Frankfurt/Main rail station by third class civilian coach, where they witnessed another bombing of the city. Two days later, 16 August 1944, the group detrained at St. Wendel and marched through town to the newly relocated Stalag Luft VI, on high ground just outside of town. The compound, situated within a designated Luftwaffe security zone, was still under construction. Arriving at the new stammlager, Don and the other transit airmen were officially recognized by the German government as legitimate prisoners of war. The former Weimar Republic, established at the end of WWI, was a signatory to the 1929

Geneva Convention and had endorsed ninety-seven specific articles pertaining to the treatment of prisoners of war. These articles stipulated the manner in which enemy prisoners would be treated by a captive power, and regulated the size of prison camps, the arrangements of quarters, sanitary measures, discipline, punishment, activities, and access to mail. Moreover, POWs were not to be subjected to public display, indignities or acts of violence, although this had already happened to most of the men in Don's group.

Allied airmen departing Wetzlar   German Federal Achieves

The treatment of enemy prisoners of war detained by Germany during WWII varied according to rank and nationality. Generally, captives of Western Allied nations were afforded protection in accordance with the Geneva Convention.[221] However, prisoners from other countries, such as the Soviet Union, were horribly abused. Soviet Commissars and Russian officers were shot upon capture, while enlisted soldiers were subjected to starvation and exposure, and allowed to die in captivity. Such inhumane treatment reflected the "brutal, ideological nature of [the Russo-German war],"[222] and was responsible for the deaths of millions of Soviet POWs.[223]

The supreme command of the German Armed Forces, Oberkommando der Wehrmacht (OKW), had administrative oversight

---

[221] Foy, *For You the War is Over*, 21

[222] Ibid., 25

[223] Ibid., 25

of all enemy POWs. However, the respective services within the armed forces were responsible for the physical internment of personnel captured from similar services of foreign powers. This arrangement was "uniquely beneficial to the captured airmen of the western nations," especially in 1942–1943. American and British airmen captured during this period were, according to most authorities, afforded the best treatment when interned in camps administered by the German Luftwaffe.[224]

Preferential treatment extended to Allied airmen captured during the early phase of the war was directly attributable to the sentiment of the Reichsmarschall, Hermann Goering. Goering's attitudes toward warfare were shaped by his own experiences as a fighter pilot during WWI. Allied airmen shot down behind German lines frequently dined in the Officers Mess of the victorious squadron, prior to being sent off to a prisoner of war camp. Although a strict disciplinarian, "Iron Hermann" viewed war as romantic and, as Chief of the Luftwaffe, expected his men to be chivalrous in combat and magnanimous in victory.[225]

However, Goering had lost much of his personal influence during the later phase of the war as the Luftwaffe had been incapable of supporting the ambitious strategic and tactical requirements of the German war effort. Hitler, as well as other top political and military leaders, was furious with Goering for the Luftwaffe's failure to subdue England in 1941, and its inability to sustain the beleaguered Sixth Army at Stalingrad in 1942–1943. More recently, the Reichsmarschall was publicly criticized for failing to stop the onslaught of the American and British bombing campaign against industrial and military targets in Germany, 1943–1944. Humiliated, Goering ceded both personal and political power and had withdrawn from active participation in the war by summer 1944.

As Goering's authority waned with Adolph Hitler and the Wehrmacht, Heinrich Himmler, Reichsfuhrer of the SS, assumed additional responsibilities and expanded powers within the political and military hierarchy of the Third Reich. His influence became even more pronounced after the 20 July 1944 plot to assassinate Hitler. One

[224] Foy, *For You the War is Over,* 21
[225] Hoyt, *Angels of Death,* 40

of the new responsibilities delegated to Himmler that summer included assuming administrative control of all 4.75 million enemy POWs. This was "a position [Himmler] had long desired because he believed that treatment of Allied POWs had been too lenient."[226]

As the fortunes of war turned against Germany in late 1943, American and British airmen "were the first to [experience] the consequences of shortages of food, clothing, and fuel for warmth."[227] The following year they also suffered increasingly harsher punishment for failure to comply with camp regulations. The most notable of these reprisals, and a flagrant violation of Geneva Convention protocols, was the execution of 50 Allied prisoners of war caught after they had escaped from Stalag Luft III in March 1944.[228] This shocking incident was followed several months later, on 17 July 1944, when the German government announced that enemy POWs would be shot if they tried to escape.[229]

The harsher policies advocated by Himmler were being implemented as Sergeant Don Dorfmeier and the first group of American POWs arrived at St. Wendel in mid-August 1944. Yet, the airmen's immediate concerns were focused on the stark realities of their new environment. Most of these men recalled the physical structure of the camp, located outside of the designated compound, as very primitive. Some characterized their building as "a large garage with a dirt floor, accessed through an oversized door." Other prisoners remembered that the structure was surrounded by a 3-meter high barbed wire fence, some 4–5 meters from the building, and that adjacent buildings of similar size and shape were used by the Luftwaffe to service their motor vehicles. The camp latrine was as primitive as the common sleeping area. An open pit was used during the day, while half wine barrels were kept inside the building for nighttime needs. Food rations were also limited, and of poor quality, according to individual diary entries. However, "some of the airmen," noted Technical Sergeant John Anderson, "received their first Red Cross parcels on 24 August," and German issued rations became "plentiful" several days later.

---

[226] Foy, *For You the War is Over*, 27
[227] Ibid., 22
[228] Doyle, *A Prisoner's Duty*, 137
[229] Foy, *For You the War is Over*, 27

Twenty-one-year-old John H. Anderson of the 388th Bomb Group, was one of two senior-ranking NCOs in the initial group of POWs to arrive at Stalag Luft VI. A true Renaissance man, Anderson had completed a four-year college education from the Conservatory of Music in Kansas City prior to being drafted into the Army in January 1943. Shortly after his induction, he was transferred to the Air Force and trained as a radio operator after an officer recognized that his background in music would enable him to learn Morse code. Anderson was subsequently shot down over Berlin while conducting his 24th mission on 6 August 1944. After arriving at St. Wendel, he started a diary on a sheet of paper, hidden in the binding of his New Testament Bible.

The other, more senior ranking NCO among the first group of airmen to arrive at St. Wendel, was 24-year-old Master Sergeant Martin C. Chavis. Chavis joined the Air Corps in 1940, and clearly benefited from the service's rapid expansion, being promoted to the highest enlisted rank at a very young age. Chavis was also a competent NCO who could have served throughout the duration of the war in an administrative or supervisory position. Instead, he chose to volunteer for gunnery school and fly combat missions. Martin was then assigned to the 398th Bomb Group and deployed to Nuthampstead with the group's advance party in late April 1944. Over the next three months he flew 24 combat missions as one of only three Master Sergeants on flight status in the European Theater of Operations. Chavis was shot down over Berlin the same day as John Anderson.

Rank and experience provided Anderson and Chavis with a more confident and self-assured demeanor than many of the other airmen in their camp. Such qualities allowed both men to emerge as persons of influence and leadership as the airmen started to organize and establish an internal structure during their confinement. Men with less composure, understandably, sought out individuals with these characteristics in times of stress and great anxiety.

A second, larger group of American POWs arrived at St. Wendel on 18 August 1944. One of the airmen in this group was 22-year-old Staff Sergeant Karl Haeuser, a confident and assertive youth, who had a history similar to Don. Born in the central coast region of California, just 100 miles west of Fresno, Karl enlisted in the Air Corps Enlisted

Reserve in summer 1942. Like many airmen, Haeuser possessed a life-long interest in flying, and a later aversion to marching after observing thousands of recruits move across the nation's largest training center at Camp Roberts, 18 miles north of Paso Robles, California. Called to active service early the following year, Haeuser completed his preflight training in Santa Ana, California before being arbitrarily dismissed from the program. He, along with many other cadets, was terminated under the pretext of "the service having too many student pilots in training."

After completing gunner school, Haeuser was sent overseas and assigned to the 410th Bomb Group in July 1944. The group, comprised of twin engine Douglas A-20 Havocs, was subordinate to the Ninth US Army Air Force that provided close air support for the Army's Ground Forces in Europe. The bomb group was also trained to conduct night bombing, and Karl served as part of a three-man crew targeting roadways, bridges, and enemy troop concentrations. By 4 August 1944, the same day Don was shot down over Peenemünde, Karl Haeuser and the other two members of his crew had completed 10 combat missions and were allowed to "stand down" for the night. That afternoon, waiting in the base chow line and wondering how he might spend his free time that evening, Karl's contemplation was interrupted by a call for a volunteer. Almost reflexively, the ever-confident youth responded to the request, ignoring the prophetic comment from a friend, John Deary, who said "he would be sorry." Hours later, while flying south of Rouen, France, heavy flak sheared off the tail section of Karl's aircraft initiating an arching dive to earth. Miraculously, all three crew members managed to exit the ill-fated Havoc, although the pilot's parachute failed to open.

Captured immediately on landing, Haeuser was taken to a local villa and stripped naked before being presented to a Luftwaffe officer for interrogation. However, the officer, who was seated at his desk, was distracted from his official duty, and showed more interest in attempting to disassemble the airman's .45 caliber pistol. This demonstration of arrogance further aggravated Karl's already heighten sense of indignation and alarm, causing him to think—"I could still get killed if this guy isn't careful." Moments later, the airmen's anxiety overruled his passive composure, shouting, "For God sakes, quit playing with that thing. It's loaded; no use in killing both of us." Sufficiently embarrassed, the officer returned the weapon to Haeuser, who disdainfully pulled the receiver slide to the rear, "extracting the live round from the weapon's chamber." Days later, he and another group of airmen arrived at St. Wendel, via the Luftwaffe's transit camp at Wetzlar.

The following day, Don was allowed to write his first letter home. The German *kriegsgefangenenpost*, issued for such occasions, was a small, 6 × 10 inch, single sheet of paper with only 24 lines to express one's personal thoughts. The post was then passed through both German and American censors prior to being forwarded to its intended recipient. Don's first letter home was sentimental, reflecting a mood of loneliness and a desire to connect with his family.

"My Darling Mother, I know that you have been worrying, but pray this letter will stop some of it. I'm well and happy as can be under the present circumstances. I welcome nightfall because I dream of you & home quite regularly. I love to daydream of a new life at home with you, Chris, and school all being foremost. The day will come when we'll all be together again–It will be a day when our dreams and plans shall be realized. I'm allowed two letters a month and four postcards so you and Chris will get all my mail. Please tell the family & friends I'm OK and write Chris once in a while. Your loving son, Donald"

Most airmen interned at St. Wendel remember long days with little structure. Yet, according to John Anderson, "The prisoners were divided into work details shortly after their arrival. Some men were assigned to assist in the off-loading of beds that had recently arrived by truck, while others performed more strenuous manual labor, a violation of the Geneva Convention." The following week, a number of airmen assigned to the more physically demanding work details started to protest, arguing that according to the Geneva protocols, NCOs did not have to work. The Germans trumped their protest by informing the airmen that if they did not work, they would not be fed. The practical-minded Americans then reassessed their position and collectively decided that they would work, or "at least give the appearance of working."

During the last week of August, a third group of American airmen arrived at the St. Wendel compound. One of these prisoners was

22-year-old waist gunner, Paul E. McNally, assigned to the 385th Bomb Group stationed at Great Ashfield, 35 kilometers northeast of London. McNally and his crew were forced to abandon their damaged Fortress on 15 August 1944 after bombing an airfield near Handorf, Germany, and sustaining flak damage to the number one and two engines. Witness statements cited in the Missing Aircrew Report indicated "[their aircraft] fell out of formation, losing altitude while en route to the group's rally point," prior to returning to home station. The aircraft "was last seen at 1300 [hours] [in the afternoon], flying at 15,000 feet altitude, with smoke trailing from both engines." Shortly after this sighting, the crew's pilot, Lieutenant Robert K. Harrington, ordered everyone out of the aircraft, rather than attempting a crossing over the North Sea.[230] German reports later noted all crew members, except for Staff Sergeant James Moulton, landed safely and were subsequently captured around Meppel, Holland. Four days later, Mouton's fate was still listed as "unknown" on German documents transferring the recently captured airmen to an "Air Force Prisoner Concentration Point, located in Rear Area Holland." Harrington's crew arrived at the Luftwaffe's Intelligence and Evaluation Center in Oberursel on 21 August 1944. Following interrogation, the airmen were sent to the transit camp at Wetzlar, north of Frankfurt, where the officers and NCOs were separated and sent to different camps. Paul and the other enlisted members of his crew arrived at St. Wendel several days later.

Paul McNally possessed the type of confident, brash temperament that Don found attractive. However, what solidified their developing friendship was discovering they were both from Fresno. The revelation caused considerable excitement and elation for the two men. A personal connection with someone from home validated their geographic frame of reference and earlier identities. However, their sense of familiarity must have felt all the more extraordinary following the discovery that they both knew Jean Lamoure. Paul and Jean had known each other through their family's involvement in the French community of Fresno. Paul's father, Walter, had served in France during WWI as a pilot with the French Air Force. Following his discharge from active service, he met Clarisse Reynaud, and the couple later married in Boston. Two sons, Raymond and Paul, were born there in 1920 and 1922. The family later immigrated to France, where the boys attended school for eight years and learned to speak fluent French, imbuing Paul with a

[230] WD, HQ AAF, Missing Air Crew Report-7907, 15 Aug 1944

worldliness possessed by few other men his age. The family returned to the United States in the early 1930s and moved to Fresno in 1936. Once settled, Clarisse made social contact with members of the French community and ultimately developed an acquaintanceship with the Lamoure family.

The younger McNally attended Roosevelt High School in Fresno. After graduation, he worked as an inspector for Remington Rand, Inc. On 8 September 1942, Paul enlisted in the US Army Air Force and trained as an engine mechanic. He later volunteered for aerial gunnery duty and, after 14 months of additional training, received his combat crew wings at Tyndall Field, Florida. The following year, the Fresno gunner deployed to England, where he was assigned to the 385th Bomb Group and completed fifteen combat missions prior to his capture.

Following Paul's arrival at St. Wendel, these two Fresno airmen had ample time to converse. New prisoners in camp were always a novelty and often possessed much sought-after information pertaining to the war and other current events. Moreover, the small size of the camp's population, the large open communal area in which they lived, and the lack of a formal structure with which to regulate activities led to several opportunities for the two men to talk with one another and establish a friendship.

Before the first contingent of American POWs arrived at St. Wendel, US Ground Forces in Normandy had breached German defensive positions at St. Lo, and passed south through Nantes. Shortly thereafter, a German counterattack was launched in an effort to stop the American advance. In early August 1944, six under-strength panzer divisions, lacking air support, moved against Mortain and attacked the rear of the US First Army streaming southward toward Brittany. Although the German armored thrust was initially successful, their drive was slowed by "strong resistance, including devastating air attack."[231] The following day, the first of several Allied counterattacks trapped most of the German armored units in a killing field around Falaise. The ensuing confusion and slaughter destroyed the last mobile reserves of the Wehrmacht in Western Europe, resulting in the collapse

---

[231] Cooper, *The German Army*, 508

of any meaningful German resistance in France.* Veteran units, such as the 12th SS Panzer Division, Hitlerjugend, retired from the fighting, having suffered almost 8,000 casualties during the last three months of combat. During this same period, the German Army fighting in Normandy had lost "almost twice as many men as it had at Stalingrad" in 1942–1943.[232]

After destroying some 32 German divisions during the fighting in and around Normandy, victorious Allied armies advanced east and liberated Paris on 25 August 1944. Five days later, lead elements of the US Third Army had reached the Moselle River, 125 kilometers from the German border, but stalled for lack of fuel. Maintaining the forward momentum of these forward units had become increasingly more difficult owing to the success of the Allied air campaign in France prior to the invasion. The virtual destruction of nearly all French rail lines, rolling stock, and bridges, meant that supplies for Patton's army could only be moved by truck, which significantly slowed delivery.

Toward the end of August, the airmen at St. Wendel were beginning to believe that the war might be ending soon. Their reasoning was based on individual observations, limited conversations with Italian workers, and pervasive camp rumors. However, the most noticeable indication that the war was moving into Germany was the increased number of bombings conducted by the American and British Air Forces within the general region of their camp. "The first of many such raids," according to John Anderson, "started on 26 August 1944." In total, 15–19 raids were conducted over the next 10 days; six of which occurred on the first day of September. Some of these bombings were close enough to require the men to seek shelter for their protection. Other indications that the Germans were in full retreat was drawn from the noticeable increase, visible from the elevated location of their camp, of motor vehicle traffic, moving on a major roadway through Saarland into Germany. Small, single-engine aircraft were also dropping large quantities of leaflets within the region, with specific instructions urging German soldiers to surrender. Soon, individual wagers were offered

* The German Army had lost over 2,200 tanks in Normandy as of early September 1944, and possessed only 100 such vehicles for current operations.[233]

[232] Ibid., 511
[233] Ibid., 512

throughout the camp as to when the war might end. Speculations were based on one's best guess, as well as a sense of urgency for liberation. Most estimates, according to Anderson, were that the war would end in late September or October 1944.

The optimism circulating throughout the camp might have inspired the tone of Don's next correspondence, sent during the last week of the month. On a postcard dated 27 August 1944, he has a clear future focus. Brief and direct, Don wrote:

"Dear Family, Well kids, I've plenty of time to plan for the future and my plans all center around going back to school.* I think of you constantly. Tell Jacky and Tommy to be good boys. Sending all my love, Donald"

The speculation of pending freedom generated a heightened tension in the camp that motivated Staff Sergeants Francis E. Dyer and Charles W. Hartney to attempt an escape in early September. Both men had experienced great trauma during their capture, and were perhaps more anxious for their freedom than many of the other prisoners at St. Wendel. Dyer was one of only three men in his crew to survive the downing of their bomber by ME-109 and FW-190 fighters. Hartney had survived an "unmerciful" beating by enraged German civilians, who also killed his pilot after they bailed out of their stricken aircraft south of Hamburg.

Both men had also been among the first group of POWs sent to St. Wendel. Their familiarity with the environment and the routine of the limited security force assigned to the camp, bolstered their assessment that they could make a successful escape. Acting on Dyer's suggestion, both men attempted to hide in a latrine stall within the Luftwaffe compound, prior to executing the next phase of their plan. However, the two airmen were discovered in short order and placed in solitary confinement as a disciplinary action. Interestingly, each man recalled the duration of his period of confinement differently. Dyer, who had maintained a diary, thought they spent three days in isolation, a claim supported by another prisoner, Sergeant Jack Fischer. Conversely,

---

* In June 1944 President Roosevelt signed the Serviceman's Readjustment Act of 1944, also known as the "GI Bill," which would provide educational assistance to returning war veterans.

Hartney has told the author that the two men were released the following day as the stammlager was being evacuated.

The evacuation of the recently reactivated Stalag Luft VI was initiated on 5 September 1944, as elements of the US Third Army moved closer to the West German border. Early that morning, an estimated 450 American POWs were marched out of their small compound and down to the rail station at St. Wendel. Their hopes of liberation dashed, the disappointed airmen now contemplated where they might be sent and what experiences awaited them in the next phase of captivity.

"Test of Courage"   Keith Ferris

German FW-190s attacked the low squadron of the 303rd Bomb Group returning to England on 15 August 1944, shooting down nine Fortresses in only two minutes. Introduced three years earlier, the Focke-Wulf 190 proved to be a superior aircraft to the German Messerschmitt.

Balkenkreuz

Luftwaffe fuselage and
wing markings

9

FIVE DAYS IN "FORTY & EIGHTS"

The march to the rail station was disheartening, and the airmen's realization they were being moved again created intense anxiety. This was especially true for Sergeant Jack Fischer and the twenty POWs who had accompanied him to St. Wendel. Just two weeks earlier, Jack and the other men in his group came within moments of being seized by an angry mob of several hundred German civilians. In all likelihood, this unruly crowd would have overpowered the two security guards detailed to protect the prisoners and lynched or beaten the airmen to death. A small gathering of civilians had discovered the POWs sitting aboard a lone passenger coach on a siding near one of the rail stations in central Germany. Following their discovery, Fischer and the others watched apprehensively as the hostile assembly swelled in number. Over the next 30 minutes, the crowd became increasingly loud and intimidating as more men and women arrived with an assortment of weapons. Suddenly, the heightened agitation of the group propelled them to rush the railcar. Yet, as the approaching mob moved within a few meters of the airmen's coach, an attached locomotive was able to generate enough momentum to slowly pull the threatened men to safety.

Fischer's pervading sense of vulnerability, while exacerbated by the harrowing incident with the mob, was activated weeks earlier when he broke his right ankle and injured his back. On 15 August 1944, Fischer and other crew members assigned to the 303rd Bomb Group were returning to England after completing their 11th combat mission to Wiesbaden, Germany. En route to home station, Jack's squadron was caught by surprise and attacked by heavily armored Focke-Wulf 190 fighters from one of the Luftwaffe's elite "Sturm Groups."* Pilots of these fearsome units were, according to Fischer, "known for their

---

* Renowned aviation artist Keith Ferris captured the drama of this specific incident of aerial combat in a painting titled "Test of Courage," which depicts Sergeant Jack Fischer in the ball turret of his B-17 exchanging fire with a closing FW-190 fighter flown by Oberleutnant Bretschneider.

aggressive tactics, [and] would literally ram a heavy bomber in mid-air to knock it down if they could not shoot it out of the sky." In keeping with this reputation, several German fighters, each configured with new 30mm cannons, targeted Fischer's aircraft in a running gun battle that killed three of his crew members along with disabling their Fortress. Fischer's injuries, however, occurred after abandoning his aircraft. German cannon fire shot away approximately one-quarter of his parachute, causing him to fall at a much faster rate, sustaining a jarring impact with the ground. Initially able to crawl into a nearby forest, the injured and hobbled airman was apprehended four days later. He eventually arrived at St. Wendel with Paul McNally and the last group of airmen sent to Stalag Luft VI, immediately prior to the camp's evacuation

At the rail station, Fischer and the other POWs from St. Wendel were ordered to load onto the infamous "Forty & Eight" boxcars waiting their arrival. These rail wagons, named for their capacity to carry 40 soldiers or 8 horses, were first used for transport by the French Army during WWI.* The wagons were short and stubby in design, measuring 8.5 × 20.5 feet, and usually stenciled with the emblem "40/8" to denote the car's function. The Wehrmacht appropriated these boxcars to transport its own forces in Western Europe following France's defeat in 1940. The Germans also used these rail wagons to carry freight, POWs, and the *untermenschen*–various ethnic groups considered subhuman, to internment and concentration camps in central Europe.

Prior to loading, the airmen received a modest ration of bread and butter to supplement an earlier, yet limited distribution of Red Cross parcels. These packages were appreciated as a much-needed augmentation to the inadequate rations provided by the German authorities. Once entrained, the 40 to 50 airmen assigned to each boxcar were separated into two groups, pressed into either end of the wagon, and confined by barbed wire for the duration of the trip. This configuration limited the airmen's freedom of movement, yet allowed their guards to occupy the center section of each car, along with the

---

* After WWI, a group of American veterans formed "The Society of Forty Men and Eight Horses," to acknowledge the shared experience of miserable travel. However, this organization's efforts to affiliate on the basis of minor inconvenience shouldn't be confused with the horrific experiences suffered by countless others during WWII.

airmen's shoes and trouser belts. The POWs had been ordered to remove these personal items before loading to discourage thoughts of escape. "Your shoes and belts," they were told, "will be returned following the completion of the journey."

Sergeant Don Dorfmeier and the others were shocked to find themselves crowded into such a limited space in these boxcars. Earlier transit on third class passenger coaches, while not desirable, had certainly been preferable to this arrangement. Perhaps the decision to use these particular wagons to move a large group of POWs was based on what was most economical or expedient, given the Allies' increased efforts to target German rolling stock over the past couple months. Regardless of the reason, the experience, which limited each individual to less than three square feet of floor space, would be the first of many deprivations the airmen would endure in the coming months.

For most airmen, the crowding in the small boxcars was extraordinarily distressing. The two possible exceptions were Staff Sergeants Frank Dyer and Chuck Hartney. Prior to this evacuation, both men had been placed in solitary confinement as punishment for an earlier attempt to escape. Given a choice, both men would have preferred the company of their fellow airmen. Still, the confinement within the boxcars was, according to Don, "so crowded that most guys . . . could only alternate positions of standing, sitting, or lying down by requesting the cooperation of the other men in their immediate vicinity." The impact of this distressful experience would affect most men for the rest of their lives. Some developed life-long fears and aversions characteristic of agoraphobia.

Although individual recollections of the evacuation from St. Wendel and the rail movement across Germany vary, all the airmen remembered the degrading experience of having to using the wooden, 5-gallon buckets allocated to each car for urination and defecation. Many men remember this experience as very humiliating, given their total lack of privacy. Technical Sergeant Bob L. Cash of the 492nd Bomb Group recalled that "most everyone had dysentery and we were not allowed off the train to take care of ourselves, which meant we did [so] in the face of [the other men]. The stench," according to Cash, "was unbearable." Gratefully, many of the rail cars traveled during daylight hours with their doors open. This at least allowed for ventilation and a glimpse at the truly magnificent countryside, noted for its picturesque order of villages, farmland, and forests.

A rail movement across Germany under these conditions was taxing enough, yet the changing nature of the air war in Europe added an increased element of danger. That summer, Allied staff planners unleashed an intense bombing campaign on the German border. In July and August 1944, the Allied air forces started actively attacking German rail targets in Western Germany. The initial and most noticeable concentrations of these strikes occurred in the Saarland region in mid-August 1944, and are cited in the early diary entries of John Anderson and others. A later postwar chronology of USAAF missions conducted during World War II also noted, "On 27 August 1944 . . . a total of eleven fighter groups of P-51s strafed ground targets in Germany, destroying 24 locomotives, [while other] groups attacked rail transportation in eastern France and the Saarland, claiming over 100 locomotives and 200 railcars destroyed."[234] Another 150 locomotives were destroyed the following day in the vicinity of Strasburg, Trier, and Bad Kreuznach. A week later, . . . "five fighter-bomber groups strafed and bombed rail transportation east of the Rhine River" in an effort to further degrade Germany's "complex, dense, and well equipped transportation system."[235]

This increased Allied air activity was coordinated to support the advance of their armies in Europe. "Attacks on marshalling yards and interdiction efforts [targeting rolling stock] moved [further] eastward" toward the German interior as American and British ground forces moved across France toward the Rhineland.[236] Yet, not all the men evacuated from Stalag Luft VI were unaware of the evolving nature of the air war when the 10–12 boxcars of POWs departed St. Wendel on the morning of 5 September 1944. Prior to evacuation, Bob Cash noticed that "their train was proceeding without benefit of either a Red Cross, or other special markings to allow for proper identification." This omission would subject the airmen in the unmarked rail cars to being targeted and strafed during their five-day transit across Germany, initially traveling south for Saarbrucken, then turning northeast toward Frankfurt.

---

[234] Craven, *The USAAF in WWII*, 435
[235] Levine, *The Strategic Bombing of Germany*, 163
[236] Levine, *The Strategic Bombing of Germany*, 164

The POW's first experience with Allied air attacks occurred in the marshalling yards of Saarbrucken. Here, the prisoners were intentionally left in the locked cars as their guards found shelter during transfer operations to another rail line. However, the airmen's initial anxiety and fear subsided after they were exposed to the serenity of the German countryside. Don was particularly impressed with the magnificent panorama as they crossed the Rhine River, "wishing that we were there just enjoying ourselves, [as] it was rather pleasant when there was nothing going on." The spirits of the men in John Anderson's car were especially buoyant, according to the diary entries noted during that first day of travel. "Our morale was high," John recorded, then added, "[we] sang a lot that first day and evening," and felt that "nothing can beat us!" However, it was Anderson's last entry for the day–"How wonderful to be an American,"–that was most telling.

Frankfurt marshaling yard 1944   USAAF

The airmen's optimistic mood was short-lived. Traveling through the Taunus Mountains of central Germany, en route to Frankfurt, local air activity forced the train's engineer to seek shelter in a tunnel to avoid being strafed by Allied fighters. The ensuing wait in the dark tunnel generated much anxiety. Many recalled difficulty breathing as their prolonged stay consumed oxygen in their cars. Feeling faint and on the verge of suffocating, the airmen struggled to control their sense of panic. The incident was especially difficult for Staff Sergeant Karl Haeuser, who was feeling none of the earlier confidence or self-assuredness exhibited when first captured and questioned by the Luftwaffe officer who had almost shot him. "I was feeling scared, and [was] crying uncontrollably," Haeuser admitted in a later interview with the author. Jack Fischer also provided a poignant description of this incident: "The available oxygen in my car, [just prior to the resuming their travel], was insufficient for burning a [single] candle."

Days later, the airmen spent their last evening in transit, parked in the marshalling yard of the Berlin rail station. Around midnight, the Royal Air Force arrived, and Don recalled, with customary self-deprecating humor, the terror and chagrin of the men in his car who were caught in the air raid. Following the air raid siren, the airmen were once again left in their locked cars while the guards found shelter. However, on this occasion, a man in Don's car refused to cower, opting instead "to provide some comic relief for the amusement of the group. Standing and looking out through a small window of the boxcar," the airman assumed the role of a moderator, parroting "the commands of a bombardier during an actual bombing run, shouting, 'Bomb bay doors open. Smoke bombs away. Bombs away!' And there we were," Don continued, "all sitting down, [enjoying the humor of the moment], when before you knew it, all hell broke loose, with antiaircraft guns going off and debris landing all on top of our car.* Once that happened, you couldn't pass that bucket around fast enough. In fact, some guys never got the chance to use the bucket. Well, we didn't know it at the time, but we were pulled up next to a German railway flat car with mounted antiaircraft guns; their ejected shell casings were hitting our car. After the air raid sirens shut off, the guards returned and opened our doors [so] . . . we could see what was making all the noise, and then we all had a big laugh. But we weren't laughing when we first heard all the noise outside."**

On their last day of transit, the train carrying the American airmen

---

* Antiaircraft guns mounted on railroad wagons were an integral part of the Luftwaffe's air defense of the Third Reich. These Eisenbahn flak units consisted of special railway wagons that were designed to accommodate a variety of antiaircraft guns and their crews.[237]
** The airmen focused on the humorous aspects of their experiences, according to former POW, Philip Miller, to "retain their sanity."[238]

[237] Gander & Chamberlain, *Weapons of the Third Reich*, 248
[238] Carlson, *We Were Each others Prisoners*, 81–82

to their final destination in Pomerania attracted the attention of at least one US fighter pilot operating east of Berlin. As the pilot banked his aircraft to attack this target of opportunity, Don recalled, "There is nothing as terrifying as a strafing. All you hear is the whine of the diving plane, the firing of the [guns], and the crashing of the bullets hitting metal and wood. And you don't know whether they're within 100 yards of you or they're right over your head. And this goes on until it's over. Well, we were hit. Fortunately, I wasn't. But some people were."

German train under attack   USAAF

Around mid-day, 9 September 1944, the train carrying the 450 airmen from St. Wendel finally arrived at the Kiefheide rail station in Pomerania. During the past five days the men had traveled some 885 kilometers in overcrowded conditions, cited by Bob Carr, as "terrible, with little food . . . no water [and] on several occasions [left] in marshalling yards [during] bombing raids." Bob Cash, reflecting on his experiences years later, asserted, that "the train trip was one of the most inhumane acts perpetrated on us up to that time. Thank God [none of the] bombs hit us, but the last day of the trip a P-51 [fighter] strafed the train, not knowing who was aboard, and unfortunately, killed several [prisoners] in the last car."

Bob Cash was especially outraged by the conditions to which he and the others were subjected after having received compassionate care, months earlier, for wounds he received on the day of his capture. A native of Okmulgee, Oklahoma, 19-year-old Cash was serving as a radio operator assigned to the 492nd Bomb Group en route to Politz, Germany when he was shot down 20 June 1944. His group was flying over the Baltic Sea, midway between the islands of Rugen and Bornholm at the time of the attack. During the encounter, Bob sustained second and third degree burns to his hands and face, in addition to being wounded in the right thigh, just above his knee. Following capture, the injured airman was treated for two months in a Luftwaffe hospital in Greifswald, Germany prior to being sent to Oberursel for interrogation. Cash characterized his care and treatment during his hospitalization as "good" and acknowledged, that while bedridden, "He was carried by two German orderlies down four flights of stairs to a basement shelter on several occasions as the Eighth Air Force flew in to attack local and nearby targets in the area." Quite possibly, one of those raids was Don Dorfmeier's 4 August 1944 mission to Peenemünde, just 24 kilometers east of Greifswald. Both men eventually arrived at the Dulag Luft transit camp at Wetzlar, presumably on the same day, given the numbering of their respective German issued identification tags.

The airmen from St. Wendel now started to detrain; their belts and shoes were also returned for the three and a half kilometer march from the train station to the camp, later noted in John Anderson's diary as "a 40 minute activity". Don was "quite happy to have [finally] arrived, "thinking [to himself], thank God I'm off that car." The surrounding woods presented an initial sense of freedom and tranquility. For a moment Don thought "this might [even] be pleasant"–until he heard the shrill ranting of Hauptman Walther Pickhardt. The German captain, known as the "Beast of Berlin",[239] had been enraged the past several weeks, forcing new arrivals at Stalag Luft IV to run a gauntlet of abuse and brutality from the train station to the camp.[240] During these earlier incidents, airmen were clubbed, bayoneted by excited guards, or bitten by dogs that hounded the airmen the entire length of their run. Fortunately, Don and the others would not be forced to run this gauntlet as had been the case with earlier arrivals. The senior medical officer at the camp, Captain Henry Wynsen, among others, had protested

[239] O'Donnell, *A History of Stalag Luft IV*, 49
[240] Ibid., 72

this abuse to the International Red Cross, which somewhat curtailed Pickhardt's cruel and abusive activity.[241] However, the German captain still retained a position of authority at Stalag Luft IV and continued to make life miserable for all Allied prisoners of war held at the new compound.

[241] O'Donnell, *A History of Stalag Luft IV*, 72

10

STALAG LUFT IV

The airmen were shocked as they approached the clearing in the forest and caught sight of the barbed wire fences and the uniformly spaced guard towers of the new compound. These initial impressions suggested that internment in this camp would be a more austere and impoverished existence than their previous confinement at St. Wendel. The contrast between the two facilities and surrounding environments could not have been more pronounced. The compound at St. Wendel had been located within a densely populated urban area, which presented a range of visual and auditory stimulation to provoke interest and a momentary distraction. The physical environment of the new camp, constructed in the middle of a small clearing surrounded by woodland, would offer few such diversions. For the majority of these new prisoners, this stark and isolated site, and the stillness of the forest, would only accentuate an increasingly oppressive boredom.

The camp, Stalag Luft IV, was located near the village of Gross Tychow, 20 kilometers south of Belgard in the northern East German province of Pomerania. The area had been first cleared for an airfield, yet never used for that purpose. Later, an internment camp was built for Russian POWs following Germany's attack on the Soviet Union in June 1941. In early 1944, the compound was acquired by the Luftwaffe and designated as Kriegsgefangenen Stammlager Luft IV.[242] This newly acquired facility was intended to hold the increasing number of American and British enlisted air force personnel who were being captured at a rate of 2,000 airmen a month. Ultimately, this new camp would become the largest and most notorious of the four largest compounds administered by the German Air Force.[243]

Stalag Luft IV officially opened, prior to completion, on 14 May 1944, with the arrival of 64 American POWs from the Dulag Luft at Wetzlar. Staff Sergeant Jack L. Browder, 92nd Bomb Group, arrived

---

[242] O'Donnell, *A History of Stalag Luft IV*, 59
[243] *Behind the Wire*, Al Zimmerman, DVD, Eighth AF Historic Site 1994

one week later and recalled that "there were almost no food rations available for an entire month." The first Red Cross parcels were not distributed in the new camp until 15 June 1944. In mid-July and early August, another 3,200 American and British airmen arrived at the compound following the evacuation of Stalag Luft VI at Heydekrug, East Prussia.[244] On 22 June 1944, a Russia summer offensive had engulfed two German armies, and, for a time, threatened the entire Eastern Front. Weeks later, following the destruction of these armies, and the loss of all Belo-Russia, the Soviet advance stopped on the 1939 border of East Prussia and the Vistula River in central Poland.[245]

Stalag Luft IV 1944   German Federal Achieves

Over 2,000 of the new prisoners arriving at Stalag Luft IV that summer were American airmen recently evacuated from East Prussia. This long-suffering group of POWs departed the port city of Memel, "crowded into the hold of an old Russian coal ship, which then sailed for 72 hours to the German naval based near [Swinemünde]."[246] The conditions aboard ship during this passage were horrific. The prisoners were packed into the ship's hold, afforded standing room only, and denied access to food, water, and other supplies that were readily available. Lacking ventilation and sanitary facilities, a number of men became dehydrated; others became crazed from the heat as the ship's storage was quickly fouled by dozens of men who urinated, defecated,

[244] O'Donnell, *A History of Stalag Luft IV*, 77–78
[245] Keegan, *The Second World War*, 391
[246] Kaplan & Smith, *One Last Look*, 174

and/or vomited where they stood. At least one airman went mad. Bolting from the ship, he dove into the Baltic Sea, and was shot and killed by a German guard.[247]

Once removed from the foul-smelling ship, the dazed airmen were shackled (in violation of the Geneva Convention) and forced into crowded "40 & 8" boxcars. They were then transported to the Kiefheide rail station. On arrival, they remained confined to their locked cars for the night. The following morning they woke to the shrill screaming "of a voice that sounded wild . . . insane," accusing the airmen of being the "murderers of women and children."[248] Their car doors were then thrust open and guards with fixed bayonets grabbed, pulled, and shoved the prisoners on the ground and into ranks, where they faced a ranting and incoherent German officer.[249]

The ranting "mad bastard" standing in front of the disoriented airmen was Hauptman Walther Pickhardt, the captain in charge of the camp guards at Stalag Luft IV. The junior officer had arrived with a "detachment of 16-year-old Kriegsmarines," assigned to march the Allied prisoners to the internment camp, some three and a half kilometers from the station.[250] However, this would be no ordinary march. After finishing his tirade, the deranged Pickhardt ordered the airmen to run the entire distance to the camp. Panicked and fearing for their lives, the shackled POWs managed to run as best they could. "Vicious dogs" were "unleashed [to] bite the legs and heels of those who fell or lagged behind."[251] The young German cadets showed no mercy and bayoneted prisoners who stumbled and fell.

Some of the stronger and healthier airmen attempted to assist those who were injured and unable to fend for themselves. One participant who witnessed such an act of compassion during this traumatic incident was 21-year-old Staff Sergeant Glen Jostad, of the 452nd Bomb Group. He was running 12 feet behind Sergeant Don Kirby, who had stopped to aid wounded and fellow crew member, Clyde Tinker. A guard, outraged by this airman's audacity and defiance, clubbed him

---

[247] O'Donnell, *A History of Stalag Luft IV*, 130
[248] Kaplan & Smith, *One Last Look*, 175
[249] Ibid., 176
[250] Ibid., 176
[251] Ibid., 176

across his shoulders with the butt of his rifle, which broke the stock of the weapon. Although stunned by the blow, the athletic Kirby was able to maintain his balance and hold onto his friend, in addition to aiding another man, prior to reaching the end of their run. Kirby, and others in his immediate vicinity, were able to assist those who were hobbled because they had not been shackled during their transit from Swinemünde. Their good fortune was to due to a reciprocal gesture of kindness extended to them by their guards when first entrained. Asking for water, the airmen shared part of their Red Cross ration of coffee with their captors, who then ignored the order to chain the POWs in their car.

The harassed and extended column of airmen eventually reached the camp and were released from their shackles. Although exhausted, some of the more enraged POWs threw their restraints to the ground in reaction to their abusive treatment. Pickhardt's responded to this defiant gesture by ordering those prisoners shot, although his directive was then countermanded by a senior Luftwaffe Major who had witnessed the demonstration.[252] Later, this frantic dash from the rail station at Kiefheide to the Stalag Luft IV would be known among the participants and other airmen in the camp, as the "Heydekrug Run." Other POWs sent to the Gross Tychow compound were also subjected to the same abuse on at least five separate occasions in July and August 1944. In a sworn deposition, taken 20 July 1945, Captain Henry J. Wynsen stated that he and fellow medical officer, Captain Wilber E. McKee, "treated injured American and British [airmen] . . . on 17, 18, 19 July and 5 and 6 August . . . who had been bayoneted, clubbed, and bitten by dogs while en route from the railroad station to Stalag Luft IV."[253] Wynsen further stated that "over 100 American and British [airmen] were bayoneted during the course of these runs," with at least "one American airman bayoneted as many as sixty times." The total number of men wounded during these road march incidents was later revised to 340 following an early October 1944 camp visit by a delegate from the Protecting Powers.[254]*

---

* A Protecting Power is a state that represents the interests of another when two sovereign governments do not have diplomatic relations.

[252] Kaplan & Smith, *One Last Look*, 176
[253] O'Donnell, *A History of Stalag Luft IV*, 72
[254] Ibid., 85

Don and the other airmen transiting from St. Wendel drew closer to the new compound and began to notice that hundreds of men had gathered near the closest exterior fence line. The arrival of a large group of new prisoners was a notable event, and offered an opportunity for those men interned in the camp to look for a friend or acquaintance. These reunions were emotionally uplifting for both parties, especially for those who had been POWs for some time and yearned for information about the war and what was happening on the home front in the United States. In mid-July 1944, Jack Browder, along with other airmen interned in the camp, was watching a group of new prisoners being marched into the Vorlager.* To his surprise and disbelief, he recognized his older brother, Norwood. His brother, who was assigned to the 445th Bomb Group, had declined an opportunity to return to the United States after Jack had first arrived in England. However, weeks later, flying his 35th and final mission, mechanical problems forced Norwood's Liberator to crash land in Belgium, where he was subsequently captured.

Allied POWs arriving at Stalag Luft IV   German Federal Achieves

Once Don's group arrived at the camp's Vorlager, located in front

* The Vorlager was a collection of administrative and other ancillary structures located in front of the main internment camp. This collection of buildings contained the offices of the camp's command staff, barracks for several hundred guards and Russian prisoners of war, in addition to an infirmary for the POWs. Smaller lockers and storage buildings contained clothing, mail, and parcels sent by the International Red Cross to augment the prisoner's meager rations.

of the main compound, they were taken to a large building and, again strip-searched. "This search," according to Staff Sergeant George W. Guderley, who was exposed to the same procedure several weeks later, "included [another] rectal exam in search of the small compasses issued to every airman as part of their escape kit." In addition to this personal indignity, every article of the men's clothing was examined for any item that could assist in an escape. During this initial search, new arrivals to the camp were exposed to Feldwebel Hans Schmidt, a senior Luftwaffe NCO, who was one of the camp's more sadistic and reviled personalities. This NCO was known for his large size, hostile disposition, and tendency to randomly strike any POW for the slightest provocation. Many airmen remember Schmidt confiscating letters and photographs of wives or girlfriends, making lurid gestures and crude remarks to provoke an emotional reaction. Understandably, the airmen at Stalag Luft IV hated Schmidt with a visceral intensity and derisively referred to him as "Big Stoops," in mocking reference to an oafish cartoon character featured in "Terry and the Pirates." As he inspected the men's clothing in Don's group, he singled out Sergeant Jack Fischer for not responding appropriately to one of his commands. Fischer acknowledged as much years later, characterizing his encounter with the German NCO with the terse remark, "I got stomped real good!"[255]

Staff Sergeant Athel V. Arnew provided a more sobering account of Hans Schmidt's treatment of Allied POWs in a sworn deposition provided to the Judge Advocate General's Department after the war. According to Arnew's statement, he arrived at Stalag Luft IV with a new group of POWs on 23 September 1944. Following a strip search and the confiscation of their Red Cross parcels, the airmen were allowed to dress. Retrieving his clothing, another prisoner next to Arnew placed his foot on an adjacent bench to tie his shoe, provoking an outraged response from Schmidt. The prisoner, however, did not understand the directive or the intent of the unintelligible ranting. The German NCO then charged this unaware individual, and hit him with a stick "one and a half inches in diameter and three and a half feet long. Schmidt struck the man on the back and neck with the stick, [in addition] to [striking him] with his fist. The airman was knocked to his knees, and tried to crawl away [as Schmidt] followed him, kicking him in the back and sides with his hobnailed boots. [The beating continued for a full] minute or so, [before] I was ordered out of the room, but I heard the blows and

---

[255] Jack Fischer, video, Andersonville National Historical Site, 1994

cries stop a few seconds later. "[256]*

After dressing, Don and the other new arrivals were assigned to one of two functional lagers, now markedly overcrowded. The evacuation of Stalag Luft VI in East Prussia caused an immediate influx in the camp's population. Moreover, the almost daily arrival of recently captured POWs soon filled the compound to excess capacity. By early September, the camp held some 5,643 American and 865 British airmen.** New arrivals, such as Don's group, were placed in tents or other makeshift structures called "Dog Houses" while they waited for the completion of new lagers under construction.

The two occupied lagers at Stalag Luft IV, in addition to four others under construction, were similar in size and structural design.*** All six lagers occupied approximately a quarter square mile and contained two rows of five barracks for 1,600 POWs. The barracks measured 40 × 130 feet, and were partitioned into ten rooms, each designed for 16 prisoners. Individual barracks also had a washroom and a two-hole latrine for nighttime use. The two rows of barracks in each lager were separated by a large open field used for mandatory morning and evening formations to conduct a head count. The parade field also served as an area where POWs gathered for sports activities, concerts, or other services, weather permitting. Each lager had two larger outside latrines and washrooms, positioned at the mid-way point, between the two rows of barracks. Every lager also had its own outside kitchen and adjoining activity room, a potato cellar and coal shed to function as an independent and autonomous camp. Accordingly, all six compounds were separated by double rows of barbed wire fences, eight to ten feet high . . . with loosely coiled barbed wire lying between the two parallel fences. Uniformly spaced watchtowers were located along the perimeter

* Staff Sergeant Joseph O'Donnell, author of *A History of Stalag Luft IV*, cites numerous testimonies and depositions from POWs who were abused by Schmidt during their internment.
** The contingent of British airmen included Australians, Canadians, and Poles, in addition to other nationalities that also served in the Royal Air Force.[257]
*** Lagers B, C, and D were built upon three-foot high piers to prevent prisoners from constructing tunnels for escape.

[256] O'Donnell, *A History of Stalag Luft IV*, 66
[257] O'Donnell, *A History of Stalag Luft IV*, 16

fence lines so that sentries, armed with mounted machine guns and strong search lights, could survey the entire camp and surrounding area.

After being assigned a place to sleep and store their possessions, Don and his group had their first opportunity to socialize with other POWs in the camp. "We were warmly greeted," Don recalled "by the other prisoners who were interested in hearing the stories pertaining to our capture and treatment. Well, I told my story, and I talked to those fellows who had been on the Schweinfurt raids, and some of their tales were fantastic. I learned that one fellow was blown out of his aircraft unconscious, and woke up with his parachute in his hands. Another guy whose parachute failed, fell all the way [to earth] into a snow bank and lived to tell about it."

Allied airmen shot down in 1942–1943 faced a more formidable German Luftwaffe than most other men who were captured during the last year of the war. Yet, those interned later in the conflict also experienced traumatic events in the air. On 18 July 1944, Mel W. Wylie, of the 483rd Bomb Group, was a crew member on one of 14 heavy bombers lost on the "infamous Memingen raid, all shot down by German ME-109 and FW-190 fighters of the 'non-existent German Air Force.'"[258]* Four members of Wylie's crew were also killed or wounded.[259] Staff Sergeant Herman Steck, one of the airmen who marched into Stalag Luft IV with Don, also survived a similar, harrowing experience of being shot out of the sky. On 9 August 1944, Steck was flying his 22nd mission across central Germany with the 305th Bomb Group to strike Munich. However, excessive cloud cover over the city caused all three bomb divisions in the approaching formation to be redirected to their secondary target at Karlsruhe. This decision required the entire formation to make a complicated and dangerous 150-degree turn, which tragically, left all three Bomb

---

* The Luftwaffe could still mass hundreds of aircraft to protect specific targets throughout most of 1944. On 11 September 1944, the German Air Force put some 350 fighters in the air to confront the Eighth Air Force over Czechoslovakia, resulting in the loss of over 50 aircraft on each side "in only a few minutes of combat."[260]

[258] O'Donnell, Luftgangsters *Marching across Germany*, 31
[259] Ibid., 31
[260] Zdiarsky, Jan, "Bloody Encounter," *Flak News* 22.4 (Oct 2007) : 6

Divisions flying for 30 minutes without protective fighter escort. Equally problematic, Herman's squadron, the trailing element of his bomb group, could not maintain the protective integrity of their formation while executing this maneuver, nor could the individual aircraft of his squadron provide protective fire for each other.

During this period of vulnerability, German FW-190 fighters emerged from the heavy vapor trails of the American bomb groups in pursuit of the isolated Fortresses in the larger formation. "Attacking in waves," Steck recalled, "the stalking FWs slaughtered us, shooting down six out of the 12 aircraft of our squadron, leaving a trail of burning B-17s across Germany." Herman's aircraft was the second bomber of the squadron to be shot down. After being hit, Steck moved to a forward position in the fuselage where he became trapped by centrifugal force as his Fortress spun out of control. He then blacked out, and when he regained consciousness, Herman was free falling. "Our plane had exploded in flight," Steck continued. "The tail section was [separated] from the plane at the trailing edge of the wings . . . and the navigator and I were blown clear [of the aircraft]." Five of the other seven crew members were killed in the explosion. Twenty-six of the 54 airmen lost in the squadron were killed in action.

On the ground, Steck and the navigator successfully evaded capture for several days, moving only at night to avoid detection. However, on the evening of 12 August, the two airmen were caught and taken to a home in the small village of Lichtenau. Fortunately, the woman of the house provided each captive with a glass of water and an apple when she learned that the two captured Americans were fliers. She then showed them a picture of her son, wearing the flight uniform of the German Luftwaffe.*

The invitation extended to Don and others to "tell their story" was motivated by more than just good will and cordiality on the part of the

----

* In 1998, Herman returned to the village of his capture where he met the granddaughter of the woman who had befriended him the night he was apprehended. During their meeting, Herman learned that if he and the navigator had been taken to any other house in the village they most likely would have been killed. The woman's kindness, however, was resented by others in the community, resulting in self-imposed confinement as "her neighbors would have done her bodily harm."

other airmen in the camp. Eliciting information from new arrivals was a necessary screening requirement conducted by the POW leadership within the stammlager. The questioning was necessary to establish the identity and creditability of every new POW as German agents frequently attempted to infiltrate the camp's population posing as Allied airmen. Don recalled that his initial encounter with the older prisoners as being "very direct." After recounting his story, he was abruptly told, "Okay, we've heard [your story] once, however, we don't care to hear it again!" This terse statement was intended to acknowledge that each airman had a unique experience or rite of passage in becoming a POW. However, greater concerns now demanded their focus and full attention.

New arrivals to the camp were also informed of the consequences for knowingly or inadvertently violating strict camp regulations. The most grievous infraction was that of entering the restricted area between the "warning wire" and the interior fence lines surrounding each lager. This restricted area, defined by a two-foot high wooden rail, was a twenty meter set-back from all four fence lines. POWs who violated this restricted area, usually in pursuit of a ball, were subject to being shot, unless they first received permission from a tower guard to cross the wire.* The German guards at Stalag Luft IV would also shoot to kill for less serious infractions. One such incident occurred midday on 21 June 1944. Technical Sergeant Aubrey J. Teague was arbitrarily shot and killed by a German guard after exiting his room through an open window,[261] rather than using the designated doors of his barracks.

The shooting of Teague was an act of wanton murder, committed by a German guard who was most likely irritated by the casual indifference to formality and social convention exhibited by most Americans. Less threatening, yet equally invasive, was the presence of German intelligence agents who posed as guards in the lagers. These agents attempted to position themselves in non-obtrusive ways throughout the compound to gather information pertaining to the prisoner's activities. Most agents, referred to as "ferrets," spoke very fluent English, having

* German Prisoner of War Regulations did not provide for any warning shots to halt errant behavior. Rather, service personnel were instructed that if the occasion for the use of firearms arises, they must shoot with the intent to kill.

[261] O'Donnell, *A History of Stalag Luft IV*, 5

lived and worked in the United States before the war.

After the airmen's informal screening, and advised of the most significant camp regulations, the new men began assimilating the attitudes, norms, and expected behaviors that governed the culture of the camp. This collection of attitudes and passivity evolved, in part, from the standards of conduct stipulated by the Geneva Convention. They were also based on what airmen considered to be acceptable among themselves and their interaction with their German captors. Not surprisingly, the dominant attitudes within the camp were those shaped by the 3,200 American and British airmen evacuated from Stalag Luft VI. These POWs had justifiable reasons to remain bitter toward the German authorities. They had been subjected to the traumatic Baltic passage from Memel to Swinemünde, and the subsequent gauntlet run from the Kiefheide railroad station to the camp. This group of prisoners had also witnessed the unprovoked shooting deaths of several airmen at Stalag Luft VI prior to their evacuation.[262]

The man most of the Allied POWs held responsible for their inhumane treatment was Oberstleutnant Otto Bombach, former Deputy Commandant of Stalag Luft VI, and now the commandant of the new stammlager at Gross Tychow. Bombach, according to sworn testimony of Technical Sergeant Francis S. Paules, the elected Man of Confidence for Stalag Luft VI, knowingly tolerated acts of "persecution . . . and physical violence" perpetrated by members of his staff.[263] Hauptman Walther Pickhardt and Oberfeldwebel Reinhard Fahnert were also reviled for committing atrocities and mistreating American and British POWs at Heydekrug, and during the evacuation of the camp. The assignment of Bombach and his staff to administer the new compound in Pomerania further antagonized the already resentful prisoners and perpetuated a discernible hostility among the airmen at Stalag Luft IV.[264]

Francis Paules's role as the senior representative for the enlisted POWs at Stalag Luft VI was a designated position sanctioned by the Geneva Convention. Paules, and other similarly elected spokesmen, were afforded the privilege and responsibility "to negotiate [grievances]

---

[262] O'Donnell, *A History of Stalag Luft IV,* 30

[263] Ibid., 51

[264] O'Donnell, *A History of Stalag Luft IV,* 21

with the camp commandant ". . . representatives of the Protecting Powers and delegates of the International Red Cross and Young Men's Christian Association (YMCA). It was an extremely demanding position, usually assigned to the most senior NCO of the group and "required substantial tact" in order to maintain credibility with all parties and "cope with the diversity of problems."[265] On arrival at Stalag Luft IV, Francis Paules was again elected Man of Confidence for the new compound. Yet, Bombach would not recognize Paules' election. The new commandant was enraged that the senior airman had filed an earlier accusation of mistreatment with the Protecting Powers and accused him of attempting to incite a revolt. Moreover, Bombach had Paules beaten when he attempted to exercise his responsibilities, then threatened to turn him over to the Gestapo if he did not resign from his elected position.

Technical Sergeant Richard M. Chapman, who served as the first Man of Confidence at Stalag Luft IV prior to the arrival of the Heydekrug airmen, was willing to resign his position as a gesture of support for the more well-known Paules.[266] He was talked out of doing so by a delegate representing one of the Protecting Powers. During a camp visit on 5 and 6 October 1944, the delegate had requested that Chapman "remain in office . . . and uphold the prisoners' interest with placidity, prudence, and wisdom."[267]*

Chapman certainly had the physical courage and moral leadership to represent the airmen in the new compound, as demonstrated in an incident recalled by Technical Sergeant Jack Browder. In July 1944, the German authorities at Stalag Luft IV were transferring POWs at the camp into the recently constructed B-lager. After several hundred

---

* Following the war, prosecutors from the War Crimes Tribunal collected 58 volumes of testimony against Bombach, Rickhardt, and Fahnert for committing war crimes against Allied prisoners of war interned at Stalag Luft VI and IV. However, all three individuals were released without going to trial due to the "highly contradictory and confusing nature of the [POW] statements"[268] and, in the author's opinion, for reasons of political expediency following the war.

[265] Christiansen, *Seven Years among Prisoners of War*, 31
[266] O'Donnell, *A History of Stalag Luft IV*, 21
[267] Ibid., 84
[268] Foy, *For You the War is Over*, 122

names had been identified for reassignment, some members of the group noticed that prisoners assigned with Jewish surnames were not being called. This caused Chapman to confront the German staff, to state his concern that Jewish prisoners were being isolated, and to protest the transfer unless they were moved as an integrated unit. The process was then halted. Eventually, after a very long period of negotiations, the German staff relented, and some 2,000 American airmen, including Browder, moved into the new lager.

By summer 1944, harsh treatment and the wanton killing of Allied POWs accentuated the tension that existed at Stalag Luft IV and other German internment camps. The fortunes of war had turned decidedly against the Third Reich during the past two years, and the Allied bombing campaign was now systematically destroying large cities, manufacturing and industrial facilities, and the national transportation system. The intensity of the Allied bombing also resulted in a significant increase in the number of airmen captured by the German Armed Forces, which changed the demographics within the internment camps. This was especially true of the POW camps administered by the Luftwaffe, which swelled with numbers of young, physically fit airmen. Conversely, these camps were manned with older and often disabled German soldiers as the Third Reich sought to find the necessary manpower to sustain an increasingly costly war.* The guards at Stalag Luft IV were, according to a February 1945 US Army Air Force intelligence report, "all disabled veterans forty to sixty years old."[269]

The differences in age and physical health between the airmen and the German guards at Stalag Luft IV and other internment camps in Europe, created continual tension between these two populations. The primary theme of this tension was a mutual fear of being harmed as both groups possessed differing forms of power to threaten one another. The Germans used harsh enforcement of seemingly arbitrary

---

* This policy was implemented in late 1943, after the German Army had suffered 2,077,000 permanent losses, in addition to a 500,000-man decline in troop strength on the Eastern Front. To find a required one million replacements, subordinate commands were ordered to reduce their staffs and "no men under thirty years of age and no able-bodied men were allowed to remain in rear area assignments."[270]

[269] Foy, *For You the War is Over*, 122
[270] Ziemke, *Stalingrad to Berlin*, 214–15

rules to maintain order, which included withholding food and using deadly force to control the camp population. The airmen hated the rigid, obsessive camp regulations and exercised a passive compliance that was equally resented by the German guards. The camp authorities also feared a possible revolt, which threatened their personal safety. Such incidents had already occurred in other camps.

Civilian internees in Eastern Europe staged successful revolts and escapes from the Auschwitz, Struthof-Natzweiler, and Sobibör concentrations camps, while Allied POWs made two large-scale breakouts in 1943 and 1944. In the latter instances, sixty-five RAF officers escaped from Oflag VIIB in Eichstatt, Bavaria on 3 June 1943.[271] The following year another group of seventy-six British airmen escaped from Stalag Luft III on 24 March 1944.* These revolts and mass escapes triggered brutal retaliatory responses, the most heinous being the execution of fifty RAF POWs who were re-captured following their escape from Stalag Luft III. These executions were reprehensible and in clear violation of the Geneva Convention, which sanctioned escapes.[272] The murder of the British airmen by the German Gestapo also initiated the implementation of a much harsher policy pertaining to the treatment of POWs. This change was announced in July 1944 with notification posted in all POW camps proclaiming that, henceforth, all escapees "faced a death sentence."[273]**

In mid-September 1944, an incident occurred at Stalag Luft IV that captured the immense tension that existed within the camp between Allied airmen and German guards. According to multiple witnesses, pilots of the German Luftwaffe used the airspace over the compound and the sparsely populated providence of Pomerania to conduct tactical

---

* The commandant of Stalag Luft III was jailed for a year by an angry Adolph Hitler following the escape of RAF airmen in March 1944.[274]
** The 1929 Geneva Convention stipulated the appropriate and specific application of penalties for POWs who attempt or execute a successful escape. In both instances, "corporal punishment is forbidden" while "escaped POWs who are retaken . . . shall be liable only to disciplinary punishment . . . not [to] exceed 30 days solitary confinement."

[271] Doyle, *A Prisoner's Duty*, 134
[272] Doyle, *A Prisoner's Duty*, 137
[273] Ibid., 137
[274] O'Donnell, *A History of Stalag Luft IV*, 21

maneuvers. In all likelihood, some of these pilots enjoyed conducting their training in this location, hoping that their aerial performance would intimidate the prisoners and produce a demoralizing effect on the confined Allied POWs.

On 17 September 1944, three German FW-190 fighter pilots were performing tactical maneuvers over the camp, flying above what many observers remember as a "low cloud ceiling." The airmen who watched these demonstrations probably did so with ambivalent feelings. Some may have admired the aerodynamic characteristics of the German Focke-Wulf 190 or the performance of the pilots. Yet, these same men also feared this aircraft and the aggressive pilots who had shot down many of the prisoners in the compound. After several minutes of overhead activity, most of which was concealed from direct observation, all three fighters dove through the low cloud ceiling as if in pursuit of one another. The last aircraft, however, failed to pull out of its dive and crashed in the forest a short distance from the west fence line of the compound. Almost immediately, a spontaneous and thunderous cheer arose from the camp as observant airmen grasped the opportunity to vent their resentment and anger toward the German pilot and their camp guards. The spontaneity and the intensity of the prisoner's response provoked an equally dramatic reaction from the Germans. Guards stationed in the towers along the outer fence line quickly turned their mounted machine guns toward the interior of the camp and commenced firing. The sound of rapid and sustained gunfire rang out over the compound, passing intentionally over the heads of the stunned POWs. Other guards then rushed into the lagers and herded the now subdued and compliant airmen back into their barracks. Don's only acknowledgment of this and other incidents of defiance, which I heard on several occasions during my youth, yet without reference to context, was a terse comment, "that the Germans would occasionally fire their machine guns over our heads to get our attention [and] to remind us who was in charge."*

This tension between the Allied airmen and German authorities at Stalag Luft IV was noticeable to the various representatives of the

---

* Airman Clair Miller made a similar acknowledgment, noting, "During daylight hours, the Germans would order all men out [of their rooms], barricade the barracks, then test-fire their machine guns over our heads."[275]

[275] Ibid., 19

Protecting Powers and other humanitarian agencies who made periodic inspections to monitor the conditions of German POW camps.[276] Following one such visit on 5 and 6 October 1944, Mister Biner characterized Stalag Luft IV as a "bad camp, although the situation, the accommodations, and the food do not differ from those in other camps."[277] Mister Albert A. Kadler, a member of the American Legation in Bern, Switzerland, was more specific. Following his 10 October 1944 inspection, he filed a report with his office, noting the POWs as "very bitter" and mentioned that "continuous friction [existed] between the [prisoners and the Germans]." The American representative further characterized Bombach and his staff as totally consumed with "the fear . . . of an escape" and "not the least interested in the welfare of the prisoners."[278]

By late September 1944, a sense of disappointment and frustration had settled over Don and the other airmen who accompanied him to Stalag Luft IV. Just weeks earlier these men were at St. Wendel where they were they had hoped that the war would soon end. Now they found themselves in a remote location in eastern Germany, almost a thousand kilometers from advancing Allied forces, stalled on their approach to the West German border. Similarly, the violent Russian summer offensive in the east had lost momentum and halted at the Vistula River. Both developments allowed the battered Wehrmacht a brief respite, with an opportunity to regroup, replace some of their losses, and establish fortified positions along the borders of their homeland. The war in Europe, contrary to Walter Winchell's earlier prediction, would not end by Christmas.

---

[276] O'Donnell, *A History of Stalag Luft IV*, 83
[277] Ibid., 21
[278] O'Donnell, *A History of Stalag Luft IV,* 21

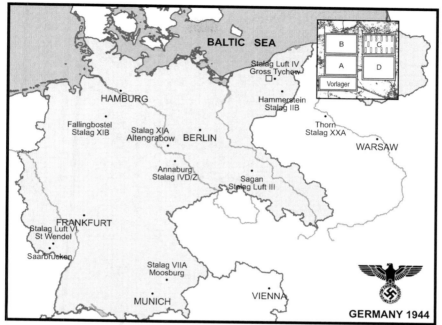

Stalag Luft IV   Author's collection

Stalag Luft IV officially opened 14 May 1944 with the arrival of 64 American POWs from the Dulag Luft at Wetzler. The new camp, located near the village of Gross Tychow and 20 kilometers south of Belgard, was necessary to hold the increasing number of Allied airmen who were captured at a rate of over 2,000 men a month. Ultimately, this new camp became the largest and most notorious of the four primary POW camps administered by the German Air Force.

11

C-LAGER

In late September 1944, some 1,850 Americans POWs, including Sergeant Don Dorfmeier and the other airmen from St Wendel, were transferred to another section of Stalag Luft IV. The new enclosure, known as C-lager, was one of two units constructed to alleviate the tremendous overcrowding in the main camp. However, the move only allowed the airmen to occupy more spacious quarters. Most of the wooded barracks in the new lagers were not completed, nor were any of the rooms furnished.

The barracks in the new lagers were all similar in design and construction. Each contained ten, 16×23 foot rooms, accessible through an interior door adjoining a central hallway. Each room had one shuttered window for natural sunlight, and a single, low watt electric bulb provided minimal illumination at night. The interior of each room, an area no larger than 368 square feet, was designed for 8 double-tiered beds, one or two tables, and stools to accommodate 16 prisoners. However, in summer 1944, the Germans were capturing more Allied airmen than they could adequately house, and the majority of rooms in C-lager were overcrowded on the first day they were occupied.

Don, along with Frank Dyer, Jack Fischer, and Chuck Hartney, were four of 21 airmen assigned to room 10 in barracks IV. All but one of these young men had been interned at St Wendel and endured the five-day rail transit across Germany to Stalag Luft IV. The lone exception was Technical Sergeant Clement F. Leone. The 19-year-old radio operator, assigned to the 445th Bomb Group, was shot down on 24 February 1944 during his sixth mission over Holland. Leone's experience prior to being apprehended was also uniquely different from the others. Months earlier, he had been in hiding with the Dutch Resistance in German-occupied Holland. Dazed and injured after parachuting from his burning aircraft, Leone was rescued from capture and received local treatment for his wounds before being moved to Amsterdam. In the Dutch capital, the recovering airman was given sanctuary, civilian clothing, and false identity papers in preparation for his passage through one of the established escape and evasion networks operating throughout Western Europe. These networks, known as rat lines, were established by the British intelligence service and run by civilian auxiliaries of the resistance movement in Europe. These volunteers accepted great personal risk to assist thousands of British, Commonwealth, and US airmen to return to Allied control.[279]* "More than five hundred were arrested and shot—or died in concentrations camps."[280]

In late 1943, the Abwehr, working in concert with the Gestapo, successfully infiltrated the Dutch Resistance movement and hundreds of downed airmen and other evaders were betrayed to the German authorities. One of those individuals was Clement Leone, apprehended in Belgium and sent to Oberursel for interrogation. At the Evaluation Center, Clement was held in solitary confinement for one week as interrogators tried unsuccessfully to obtain information pertaining to the underground that sheltered him for almost four months.**

Weeks later, Leone and hundreds of other airmen interned at Stalag Luft IV were transferred to C-lager and assigned rooms that lacked furniture. Most men slept on the floor on top of their German issued "mattress" bags, which were simple, corrugated sacks filled with wood shavings and straw. Those who were not so fortunate were forced to use one of two issued blankets to make their own bedding. Eventually, most of the rooms were furnished with double, wooden bed frames, and plain, open-face shelving that provided a minimal level of physical comfort.

Assigned to their new quarters, the airmen elected representatives

* Some 1,966 British and Commonwealth airmen, in addition to 2,693 officers and enlisted crewmen of the US Army Air Forces, successfully evaded capture in Western Europe during WWII.[281]
** "Robert" Rene van Muylen, the man who betrayed Clement Leone, was apprehended after the war and charged with delivering 177 evaders to the Gestapo. The Belgian collaborator was subsequently tried, condemned to death, and executed by firing squad.

[279] Doyle, *A Prisoner's Duty,* 144
[280] Ibid., 144
[281] Ibid., 286

as stipulated by the 1929 Geneva Convention's treatment of enlisted prisoners of war. The prime responsibility of these room and barrack's leaders was to maintain order and discipline within the compound, and represent the airmen to the German authorities. The men in Don's room elected Master Sergeant Martin Chavez as their room leader. "The position," according to the senior NCO, "required the arbitration of petty interpersonal conflicts and assignment of minor housekeeping duties and other tasks." Chavez further characterized his responsibility as "not very taxing. The men were all very cooperative . . . as they really didn't have any [options]."

A typical room in most lagers   USAAF

The men in each barrack then elected a group representative. These individuals assumed the same responsibilities as room leaders, yet they functioned at a higher level within the leadership hierarchy. The airmen in Don's quarters selected him for this position, although he was one of the youngest POWs in the lager and outranked by almost everyone in the compound. Regardless, the majority of the 200 or so airmen assigned to Don's barrack recognized that he possessed the physical attributes and personal traits so critical for effective leadership. The most salient of these qualities was his robust and imposing physical presence, which conveyed a sense of strength and authority. Technical Sergeant Robert Cash, fondly recalled, "Don was about 50 pounds heavier than the rest of us, and we sure appreciated standing behind him in formation [every day]," where he stood, front and center, accountable for the men he represented.

Sergeant Don Dorfmeier's physical presence was complemented by a good-natured, agreeable disposition, and a direct and effective style of personal communication. Martin Chevas further noted that he had a "wonderful, quick and a disarming smile." Collectively, these qualities conveyed the sense of confidence Don had acquired in school sports, public speaking, and as a cadet in the Army Air Force Flight Training Program, all of which provided multiple opportunities for him to function well in a variety of formal and informal leadership roles.

While Don and the others began adjusting to their new quarters, recently captured POWs continued to arrive at Stalag Luft IV. New arrivals assigned to C-lager were billeted in the barracks' laundries or forced to sleep on tables and available floor space in other rooms. However, the holding capacity of the lager's two outside latrines was overwhelmed by this influx of new prisoners, causing both facilities to overflow and foul the ground. The increase in the camp's population also coincided with the onset of autumn and cooler temperatures. Barracks' windows were soon closed during the day to conserve heat. By late October, small, single coal burning stoves were installed in most rooms, which provided the only warmth against the cold winter temperatures. But now, inadequate ventilation, in addition to the overcrowding, increased the likelihood of transmitting communicable diseases.

Don's greatest concern for the men in his barrack was one of maintaining high standards of personal hygiene. His worry was all the more pronounced because no shower or delousing facilities were in operation at Stalag Luft IV when the compound first opened five months earlier–in May 1944. These deficiencies were noted in a number of reports filed by various representatives of the Protecting Powers.[282] In the absence of showers, Don required that each man in his barrack bathe at least once a week with whatever water could be heated, a requirement more easily accomplished once the coal burning stoves were placed in the rooms. "I set up rules," Don said assertively, "that once a week, no matter what the weather; each man had a turn at a bucket of hot water that we kept on top of the coal stove. There was a rule, that when it was a man's turn to bathe, he'd bathe. And I saw to it that every one of the men in [the rooms] bathed to keep our barrack from being loused. I [was willing to] enforce this physically, yet it didn't take long for the fellows to realize that we had the cleanest and

---

[282] O'Donnell, *A History of Stalag Luft IV*, 78

best barrack in the lager."*

The airmen's senior elected representative, the honorific Man of Confidence, was awarded to 29-year-old Staff Sergeant Francis Troy, 375th Bomb Group. Troy had been a POW since 23 February 1944, initially interned at Stalag Luft VI and had experienced the traumatic Baltic passage during the camp's evacuation in July 1944. A former boxer, Francis projected the quiet confidence of someone who knew his own physical and emotional strengths. Fellow crew member, Staff Sergeant Leonard Deranleau, characterized the senior representative as, "Older, more mature and a father figure who inspired confidence. One who would immediately intercede to settle a dispute to restore order." In a later conversation with the author, Troy acknowledged his role in the lager, citing his primary responsibility as " . . . the maintenance of good order in the camp." He performed these duties, he continued, "while engaged in daily interactions with the German officer designated to supervise all POW activities within our compound."

The leadership hierarchy within the lager formalized an organizational structure for the airmen that replicated a military chain of command. Effective leadership within that chain was critical for the POWs to maintain military discipline and perform daily tasks and responsibilities. This was an important psychological function as most prisoners were separated from their former crew members and familiar relationships. Don characterized the organization in his lager as "complete, down to the squad level." This degree of organization was also noticeable to the representatives from the Protecting Powers, prompting one delegate to note, "The prisoners were making an effort to maintain excellent discipline."[283]

Other airmen held key positions in covert activities in the lager that were unknown to the delegates of the Protecting Powers or the German authorities. Chuck Hartney acknowledged his involvement in one such

---

* My father never mentioned that he held a leadership role while a prisoner of war. I first learned of this information through written correspondence with Chuck Hartney. Another roommate, Frank Dyer, further corroborated Hartney's assertion during a taped video interview, acknowledging Don, by name, as "our barrack's leader."[284]

[283] O'Donnell, *A History of Stalag Luft IV*, 85
[284] Frank Dyer, video, Andersonville National Historic Site, 1992

activity, noting that " . . . their room was tasked with the planning and leading a camp uprising. [We] were designated," he continued, "as a 'takeover room,'" if, as Don clarified, we were "ordered to breakout," or other circumstances required them to revolt.

Another covert activity organized within the lager included the formation of an escape committee to assist airmen willing to initiate such a dangerous undertaking. One of the committee's more creditable planners, Staff Sergeant George W. Guderley, of the 463rd Bomb Group, had successfully evaded capture for eight days after being shot down 12 September 1944. Guderley, a 22-year-old Illinois native, was participating in his 13th mission to bomb the Lechfeld airfield, 50 kilometers west of Munich. Extensive flak damage killed three crew members and started a fuel cell fire, forcing an immediate evacuation of his aircraft.[285] Although wounded by shrapnel in the right foot, Guderley managed to elude an initial search effort conducted by a squad of soldiers and their dogs. During the following week, the determined airman moved some 135 kilometers through the Bavarian Alps, prior to being apprehended in the Austrian village of Steeg, near the Swiss border. In addition to demonstrating skill and determination in eluding capture, Guderley had also received special instructions as a radio operator to contact fictitious addresses in the event of capture, to pass and receive intelligence and/or special instructions.* However, Guderley's expertise would provide little benefit to the airmen in his lager after they had been told to "stand fast" in their camps. The end of the war was perceived as imminent, and escape was now considered "too dangerous" an undertaking. Recent publication of German orders authorized a "shoot-to-kill" policy in response to any escape attempt.

C-lager's Man of Confidence, Francis Troy, assembled a small staff of airmen to assist him in the organization and management of his duties. One member of Troy's staff, Technical Sergeant Norwood Browder, was tasked to make a roster of the room assignments for all ten barracks in the lager. These rosters provided Troy with a detailed accounting of the location of key personnel and the total number of airmen assigned to each barrack. The recorded list of men assigned to

---

* Some 7,724 US aircrew personnel were trained in the use of this special code.[286]

[285] Guderley, "The Thirteenth Mission," *Friends Journal* 27.2 (Sum 2004) : 10
[286] Dear, *Escape and Evasion*, 73

Don's room, compiled in later September or early October, is an accurate and detailed account of the name, rank, and serial numbers of all 21 airmen initially assigned to the new quarters. Of particular note is that Don identified his rank as Staff Sergeant, which he apparently assumed weeks earlier when posting a letter sent to his mother in late September 1944. Don had been a POW for just six weeks at that time, and it's unreasonable to think there was an official basis for his first, much less second, "promotion." A more rational interpretation suggests Don changed his rank on 26 September, the day of their move into C-lager, to fit his new role as barracks leader. Such thinking would have been supported by the airmen's emphasis on a structured hierarchy of senior NCOs, and the need to enhance his status with the camp authorities.

The barracks' rosters also provided a basis for the requisition and distribution of food rations and other supplies. The men received two hot meals a day, which were prepared in the lager's kitchen. Representatives from each room were sent to the kitchen to draw their allocation of rations for the men assigned to their room. Don recalled receiving "hot water in the morning, and a quarter [loaf] of black bread a week, of which 20 percent was sawdust."[287] George Guderley, a room leader in barrack X, provided a harsher assessment of their bread allotment, noting its consistency as having a high content of "sawdust and ground leaves, oats, and only enough rye flour to make the entire mass stick together. One of the better ways to make it almost palatable was to cut it about a quarter inch thick, and slap it on to the side of the small heating stove. When it was toast, it fell to the floor and could be eaten." The airmen, according to Don, also received a bucket of potatoes at night, "with dirt and all, which we mixed with our own canned rations of corned beef." The meager provisions distributed by the German authorities in the camp were supposed to be augmented by a weekly distribution of a full Red Cross food parcel to each airman. However, in autumn 1944, these supplemental rations were restricted to one-half, or less, parcels per man per week. Heinrich Himmler, the Reichsfuhrer SS, and an advocate for harsher treatment of POWs, initiated this new ration policy following his appointment to administer the activities of all enemy POWs.[288]

Aside from withholding their supplemental rations, the Germans

[287] O'Donnell, *A History of Stalag Luft IV*, 18
[288] O'Donnell, *A History of Stalag Luft IV*, 18

authorities in the camp also pilfered individual, as well as the bulk parcels of cigarettes sent to POWs by the International Red Cross. However, it was the practice of puncturing all canned goods contained in the food parcels, prior to issue, that really irritated the airmen. The Germans perceived this as a necessary precaution to prevent the hoarding of food which could be used to escape. Don would "protest these abuses to the German authorities, but to no avail."

The limited, low-quality rations available at Stalag Luft IV were occasionally rancid or infested with maggots, according to reports written by delegates representing the Protecting Powers. Yet, while these reports characterized the quality of these rations as "poor," they were also recognized as consistent with rations provided in other camps. The senior medical officer of Stalag Luft IV, Captain Henry Wynsen, provided a more detailed description of the German issued rations in a memorandum written in July 1945. In his report, Wynsen stated: "Food [at Stalag Luft IV] consisted of daily rations of bread (approximately 300 grams/20 ounces), margarine, (30 grams/2 ounces), and plain boiled potatoes or a soup mixture made of potatoes, other vegetables, or dehydrated sauerkraut." The airmen also received "a meat allowance of 15 grams (1/2 ounce)."[289] Captain Wynsen further estimated that the limited rations provided by the Germans, when augmented by the contents of the Red Cross parcels, provided each prisoner with no more than "1,200 calories of food daily." The ranking physician further speculated that these dietary restrictions resulted in an "average loss of weight per man [of] approximately fifteen pounds." Wynsen's estimate was in keeping with Don's assessment that he had lost "about 20 pounds during his first four months of captivity."

Precise and exacting rules governed the division and distribution of rations within the lager and every man received his fair share of nourishment. Technical Sergeant John Anderson, assigned to barrack I, characterized these procedures as a "model of social democracy." There was "intense interest, and active participation of all parties." However, Martin Chavez could not recall what procedures were used in his room. Rather, his primary recollection was " . . . how little food they received, rather than how it was distributed." "The only airmen who did not lose weight on this limited diet," according to Don, "were those members of Troy's staff, who slept in the kitchen." These men

---

[289] Ibid., 71

referred to as "arbiters," served as cooks and were responsible for receiving, preparing, and supervising the distribution of the rations to the other airmen in the lager. Don's characterization of these men may not have been accurate, although it did capture the sentiment and common perception that persons who have access to resources will abuse the privilege.

In addition to supplemental food rations, cigarettes were another commodity provided to all prisoners of war by the International Red Cross. Four packs of cigarettes were included in every food parcel, while bulk shipments of this supplement were also sent to all German POW camps. Cigarettes were considered essential for those men who smoked at Stalag Luft IV and they served as the primary medium of exchange among the servicemen in the camp. The trading and exchange of cigarettes allowed prisoners to augment their food rations, acquire articles of clothing, or purchase other sought after items of material comfort. Although bulk shipments of cigarettes were sent to Stalag Luft IV on a regular basis, these shipments were frequently pilfered or stolen by the German guards, whose own government ration was limited to "only sixty cigarettes per month."[290]

Following the breakfast and noon meals, the Germans conducted mandatory morning and afternoon formation at 0900 and 1730 to count the number of POWs assigned to each barrack. The intent of these roll-call formations was to maintain accountability of the POWs assigned to the lager, and thwart any possible escape from the compound. Staff Sergeant Herman Steck recalled, "The airmen would align themselves in front of their assigned barrack," on the center parade field, "in ranks of five files deep. Once formed, one guard would count the front rank while another guard would verify the number of aligned files and multiple by five to determine the 'head count' for each barrack." The entire procedure could be conducted within a short period, usually ten to fifteen minutes, if the prisoners were cooperative. However, this activity provided an occasional opportunity for the airmen, if so inclined, to passively defy the authority of their German captors by "fouling the count." This was just one of many forms of harassment conducted by the POWs, which they referred to as "goon bating." Elaborating further, Don said, "Morning formations allowed us the opportunity to really bother them. They'd line us up and start down

---

[290] Foy, *For You the War is Over*, 105

the line, counting, *'ein, zwei, dri'* . . . and we would have intentionally left one or two guys in the rooms just to harass the 'Krauts' and foul their count. On some occasions we would do this until the commandant ordered a search of all the barracks. We knew then that we had gone far enough, and had to get everyone out."

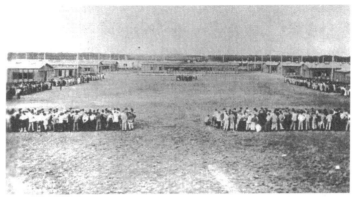

Stalag Luft IV roll call   German Federal Achieves

Shortly after the last meal of the day, the airmen were locked up in their barracks for the evening. In spring and summer months, they enjoyed the luxury of longer daylight and "lock-up occurred around 2130 hours." However, by early October 1944, the prisoners were forced back into their rooms from "1600 hours in the afternoon until 0700 hours" the following morning. During lock-up, the two doors on opposite ends of the barrack were barred, and outside shutters of all the barrack windows were closed to prevent prisoners from observing the activities of the posted sentries. Menacing guard dogs were then let loose to detect any unauthorized activity on the part of the airmen. Ever more threatening were the German sentries, who would shoot to kill any airman who stepped out of their barrack prior to the appointed time the next morning.

The airmen interned by the Luftwaffe had little structure in their day other than morning and afternoon distributions of rations and roll-call formations. The NCOs of the Allied air forces were treated by the Germans with the same deference extended to officers of other Western countries, in that neither group was required to work and most days were notably void of any organized activities.[291] The most

---

[291] Christiansen, *My Seven Years Among POWs*, 34

salient challenges, therefore, were boredom and the propensity to give into despair.[292] To combat this hopelessness, a phenomenon referred to in the camps as "barbed wire psychosis," many men attempted to remain engaged in previously developed interests or activities. Airmen at Stalag Luft IV and other POW camps, were assisted in their efforts to engage in meaningful activity by the World Alliance of the YMCA, whose mission was to provide for the physical, mental, and spiritual welfare of prisoners of war of all nationalities. The organization accomplished this daunting task by negotiating with the German authorities for permission to deliver books, sports equipment, and religious paraphernalia for worship services. Field delegates would also visit the camps as frequently as possible to monitor the distribution of these materials, and observe Germany's compliance with the articles of the Geneva Convention.

Christian Christiansen, a Danish theology graduate who worked for the YMCA as a field delegate, supervised the northeastern part of Germany that included the provinces of "Pomerania, Mecklenburg, and Brandenburg."[293] This region of the country "contained 24 Prisoner of War camps, [including Stalag Luft I and Stalag Luft IV], and six field hospitals that housed thousands of prisoners from all the Allied nations."[294] Commenting on the character of these men, Christiansen noted " . . . the POW camps afforded countless examples of altruistic and unselfish men who spent their time and abilities making life more tolerable and pleasant for their comrades."[295]

In September 1944, over 300 prisoners assigned to D-lager at Stalag Luft IV starting attending classes in English literature, physiology, and a variety of foreign languages that were taught by other airmen. The students gathered in the laundries of various barracks for two hours in the morning and afternoon, until overcrowding required that these rooms be assigned as actual living areas. Lacking paper, the men used the wrapping material from packs of cigarettes and other available scraps of paper for notations.[296]

---

[292] Ibid., 35
[293] O'Donnell, *A History of Stalag Luft IV*, 88
[294] Christiansen, *My Seven Years Among Prisoners of War*, 15
[295] Christiansen, *My Seven Years Among Prisoners of War*, 38
[296] O'Donnell, *A History of Stalag Luft IV*, 81

Other airmen, like Don, were athletically inclined and interested in sports. This early life focus served him well as a POW, where the primary concern was to keep himself healthy and physically fit. Fellow roommate, Sergeant John R. Fetteroff, 460th Bomb Group, recalled Don as someone "who was always doing push-ups, sit-ups, and other isotonic exercises to keep toned." In high school, Don's primary social interests had been athletic competition, and his participation in sports had provided a sense of identity. Not surprisingly, Don's efforts in the camp were directed toward organizing a touch football league in the lager, with each barrack fielding a six-man team to play a round-robin tournament on a 40 × 80-yard field. "The games," according to John Anderson, "were played on a weekly basis in October 1944, and served to unite the men of the barracks. Some men even voluntarily shared part of their limited food rations with the players who represented them on the field." The competition among the barracks also allowed others to engage in speculative betting, and the "bookies" in the lager accommodated all wagers.

Technical Sergeant Carl Moss from Dearborn, Michigan, was one who played with Don on their barrack football team. Moss had joined the US Army Air Force in February 1943, and completed 15 missions prior to being transferred to serve as lead radio operator in a command ship of the 389th Bomb Group. Two missions later, on 11 July 1944, he and his crew were forced to abandon their stricken Liberator over Lille, France after sustaining flak damage during their early morning raid on Munich. Unfortunately, one crew member's parachute failed to open.

Moss became entangled in wires at landing and was apprehended immediately with four other airmen. The remaining seven crew members successfully evaded capture and returned to England. Several weeks later, Moss, and approximately 120–140 other airmen, arrived at Stalag Luft IV after being subjected to one of the infamous runs from the rail station at Kiefheide. Yet, Moss considered himself fortunate for not having been shackled, and not occupying a position in the middle of the formation where he could have tripped over other men. Rather, he found himself in the farthest right file of the formation and "near a guard armed with only a machine gun, and therefore unable to use a bayonet or deliver a severe blow" while harassing him or the others in the column.

In addition to playing football, Don boxed with other airmen while interned at Stalag Luft IV. On one occasion, his men had bet heavily on his winning a forthcoming match. To his chagrin, he lost two of a three-round match, citing, "I was initially scared of this guy, who was probably five years older than me, and I stayed away from him for the first two rounds. But I went after him in the third round, and discovered he wasn't that good. Unfortunately, it was too late, I had lost, and a lot of my guys lost their shirts."

Don also walked the interior fence line of the rectangular-shaped compound twice a day to keep himself focused and in shape. "I made it a practice," he said, "to make two trips around the compound, mornings and afternoons, because so many fellows would let themselves go, physically and mentally. Regardless of the weather, I walked the compound every day." The exercise also gave Don the opportunity to visit with his friend Paul McNally, who, along with Herman Steck and Jim Skarles, were assigned to barracks VIII located across the parade field on the north side of the lager. On one such walk, Don recalled, "I went to see a pal of mine, a kid from Macon, Georgia. He was a good guy, but he let himself go. His barrack was one that wasn't kept clean. Well, I found this kid in the back corner of his room, just like an animal. He looked just like an animal and just about ready to 'go around the bend.'* Well, I got him outside and we walked that perimeter until he sobered up. He wasn't drunk, he'd just let himself go. That's what happens when people give up. Mentally, they literally give up. And he'd given up. Well, we walked and talked for along time. Then we went back to his room, got all his gear and took it outside and washed it all. Then we got some hot water from my barrack and we gave him a bath and shave so that he regained some of his self-respect again. That's the only thing we were really interested in doing."

Other airmen at Stalag Luft IV assumed leadership roles that were as important as any position held within their elected chain of command. These individuals provided religious and spiritual comfort to countless other prisoners. Three chaplains in the compound performed religious services in the utility rooms located in the kitchens of each lager. John Anderson, assigned to barracks I in C-lager, recalled, "Approximately 240 men would normally attend religious services

---

* British slag for a psychological break

in their camp." However, the utility rooms were neither large enough
nor always available to meets the needs of all POWs who wished to
attend these services. These rooms were frequently used for other
purposes. The chaplains' freedom of movement was also restricted,
requiring guard accompaniment when moving from one compound
to another.[297] Moreover, the chaplains could only hold their services
after their "sermons had [been] officially censored by the German
security [officer]" of the camp.[298] Fortunately for the men of C-lager,
John Anderson was willing to lead morning devotions, in addition to
organizing and directing a camp choir. Drawing upon his education and
training in music, John provided an opportunity for the men to express
themselves on a spiritual dimension.

In mid-November 1944, another airman of exceptional character
and inspiring leadership arrived at Stalag Luft IV. This individual was
Captain Leslie Caplan, a medical doctor and flight surgeon assigned
to the 449th Bomb Group of the 15th US Army Air Force. Caplan had
been captured on 13 October 1944, after the crew with whom he had
been flying was forced to abandon their flak-damaged B-24 Liberator
near Dernisch, Yugoslavia. The 36-year-old doctor served as an
observer on a mission to bomb the marshalling yard in Vienna, Austria.
A flight surgeon in the US Air Force, Caplan was required to fly a
minimal number of hours periodically to meet requirements of his duty
position and remain eligible for a monthly incentive flight pay. Yet, on
this specific day, Caplan was particularly interested in understanding
the physical and psychological stresses of the air war that affected the
crews in his squadron.

After arriving at Stalag Luft IV, Caplan was assigned to the camp's
medical team to provide care for the men in C-lager. Initially confined
to the 133-bed *lazaret* in the Vorlager,[299] Caplan's only contact with
the general population of the lager was limited to those individuals
referred to him following a morning sick call or those who required
hospitalization. Regardless of these constraints, Caplan's assignment
was a significant augmentation to Stalag Luft IV's small medical
staff. Graduating from medical school in 1936, Caplan completed
postgraduate work in Public Health and practiced four years of general

[297] O'Donnell, *A History of Stalag Luft IV*, 81
[298] Christiansen, *Seven Years Among Prisoners of War*, 44
[299] O'Donnell, *A History of Stalag Luft IV*, p. 72

medicine in Detroit, Michigan prior to enlisting in the US Army Air Force, July 1941. This experience in general practice and the study of communicable diseases would later prove to be immensely beneficial to the men in his care during the closing months of WWII.

Before he was captured, Caplan had been responsible for the medical care of five-hundred men assigned to the 719th Bomb Squadron stationed at Grottaglie, Italy. A flight surgeon at the squadron station, Caplan had the benefit of caring for physically healthy men, while being supported by a fully staffed station hospital and a well-stocked pharmacy. However, these resources were not available at Stalag Luft IV. Caplan and three other physicians, working under the direction of the Senior Medical Officer, Captain Henry J. Wynsen, attempted to provide medical care to a camp population that would exceed some 10,000 prisoners by early January 1945.[300] Moreover, the airmen of all four lagers were malnourished, and according to Wynsen's assessment, subsisting on less than 1,200 calories of food per day.[301] Describing the medical conditions of the camp's population, Caplan identified three separate groups of men who needed medical care. The first group, 15–20 percent of the population, consisted of "those who were wounded, burned or maimed in aerial combat."[302] Another group, which represented more than 50 percent of all airmen, suffered from general illness such as gastritis, diarrhea, and diphtheria, in addition to a variety of skin diseases resulting from poor sanitation. Last, he observed that "numerous casualties" suffered from psychological disturbances ranging "from irritability to outright insanity."[303]

In a brief article written after the war, Caplan characterized Stalag Luft IV and the airmen interned there as a "domain of heroes," who paid a high price for their acclaim. Caplan's tribute to these airmen was a validation of the US Army Air Force's exacting selection criteria that required individuals to meet high physical and psychological standards as conditions of enlistment. Equally important were the development of strong bonds of personal allegiance to one's crew formed during long hours of training and combat operations. These attributes, in addition to the indomitable character of the American spirit, sustained the airmen

---

[300] O'Donnell, *A History of Stalag Luft IV*, 72
[301] Ibid., 71
[302] Ibid., 73
[303] Skinner, *The Wild Blue*, 353

in the camp, and later during the more rigorous trials of a long, arduous evacuation.

PRISONERS OF WAR BULLETIN

Published by the American National Red Cross for the Relatives of American Prisoners of War and Civilian Internees

VOL. 3, NO. 2   WASHINGTON, D. C.   FEBRUARY 1945

A Report to Relatives of Prisoners

By Maurice Pate

POW Bulletin   American National Red Cross

The *Prisoners of War Bulletin* was a monthly newsletter published by the American National Red Cross, from mid-1943 to June 1945, for relatives of American prisoners of war and civilian internees.

12

CHRISTMAS '44

By November 1944, Don Dorfmeier, and the other airmen from St. Wendel were anxiously waiting for mail from home. American prisoners of war who had arrived at Stalag Luft IV earlier that spring speculated that a letter written from their compound would take a minimum of six to eight weeks to reach the United States, assuming the correspondence was not lost or destroyed in transit. Several considerations were accountable for this interminable delay. All outbound mail was first screened by a POW committee, then routed by rail through a German censorship office at Stalag Luft III in central Germany before being forwarded to its final destination. Similarly, incoming mail sent to Allied prisoners of war was also routed through German censorship prior to distribution.[304] This process had become all the more protracted after the Allied Air Forces started attacking the German rail transportation system months earlier.

Protecting Power delegates who visited Stalag Luft IV routinely noted that "incoming mail [was] very irregular" and "some of the American POWs who had been captured [over] five months ago had [received] no mail."[305] Technical Sergeant John Anderson's one and only letter received during captivity arrived on 27 December 1944. Yet, the 22-year-old radio operator was grateful for both the letter and the timing of its arrival. Sergeant John Fetterolf, one of the airmen to accompany Don from St. Wendel, recalled he "was one of the first to receive mail in January 1945. It was," he said, "like a book–every one in the room had a chance to read it. It was a great boost to . . . morale." Sadly, most of the men in the room never received any mail while interned as POWs.

Letters written by Don and Paul McNally, four to six weeks following their transfer into C-lager, indicated that neither man had received any correspondence from home. Yet, both men had written

---

[304] Foy, *For You the War is Over*, 85
[305] O'Donnell, *A History of Stalag Luft IV*, 20

and encouraged their families to send letters and packages with food. In a letter dated in early November 1944, Don noted that he had yet to receive a parcel from home, writing;

> "Dearest Mother & Family, Well, another month has rolled around & with it the opportunity to write you again. I hope you took it upon yourself to send a package as soon as you heard about my capture. Taking for granted you have, keep up the good work with candy, cigarettes, and canned goods. This letter should reach you all around Christmas time so Merry Christmas to all my brothers, sisters, relatives & friends. Let not your heart be troubled over my predicament. I am well and keep myself busy in the camp with my duties. When peace is again over the world we shall live in appreciation & humbleness, thankful we are together. I remain your adoring son, Donald"

Don and Paul requested packages from home, yet neither airman was probably aware that the United State's government restricted the number of parcels their families could mail overseas. Moreover, the shipment of packages was slow, and subject to multiple mishaps.[306] This awareness probably explains why Paul McNally's parents mailed him a package on 16 December 1944, containing an assortment of dried fruit, chocolate, and tobacco; nothing reflected a holiday theme, knowing that their parcel might take months to arrive, if at all. Regrettably, few packages ever reached POWs during the later phase of the war. Those parcels that did arrive from home were long delayed en route, frequently damaged, and most often pilfered.[307]

The conditions in all POW camps were depressing by any standard, and mail from home directly affected a prisoner's mental attitude. The receipt of mail and packages from home served as "tangible assurance of another world" which was vital to maintain an airman's emotional stability.[308] The airmen were also anxious to receive information about the war, although this type of news was readily forthcoming from the constant influx of recently captured airmen. The lack of mail inevitably increased a POW's primary sense of isolation, and caused most men to experience some degree of despair, frequently expressed as feelings of

---

[306] Foy, *For You the War is Over*, 85

[307] Ibid., 76

[308] Ibid., 84

sadness or emptiness. More serious symptoms, such as "a loss of hope, pervasive sense of guilt, and worthlessness," were indicative of a more threatening condition of clinical depression.[309] However, symptoms of depression in the camps could also be induced by the physiological effects of a general medical condition, such as excessive weight loss or hypothyroidism. Significantly, these symptoms became more prevalent "the longer a POW remained in captivity."[310]

Clinically depressed prisoners of war, once despondent, had difficulty concentrating, thinking clearly, or making sound decisions. This condition increased the incidence of rash or erratic behavior. Don identified one such incident occurring in late November or early December 1944. An airman in the camp succumbed to a sense of hopelessness, and made a fatal mid-day dash to climb the exterior fence line.*

The approach of winter in northern Germany further affected the psychological and physical health of the prisoners of war interned at Stalag Luft IV. With the change of seasons and the onset of longer nights, airmen in the compound were confined to their barracks for more extended periods of time. The evening lock-up now occurred at 1600 hours in the afternoon and remained enforced through 0700 hours the following morning. To enforce this curfew, the Germans unleashed aggressive guard dogs inside the lagers during the airmen's evening confinement to their barracks. Moreover, camp guards would shoot to kill any POW who left the confines of his barrack prior to the authorized hour. The American State Department officially protested this policy as early as mid-November 1943, yet the German order was never rescinded.[311]

The dogs released in the lagers were free to roam throughout the

_____

* Author Victor Frankel describes similar psychological processes and behaviors among the prisoners of the Auschwitz concentration camp. According to Frankel, some prisoners consciously chose to "run into the wire," opting to commit suicide rather than submit to a life of continuing degradation and hopelessness.[312]

[309] Frances, *The Diagnostic and Statistical Manual of Mental Disorders-IV*, 320
[310] Foy, *For You the War is Over*, 136
[311] Foy, *For You the War is Over*, 124
[312] Frankl, *Man's Search for Meaning*, 31

compound and underneath the elevated barracks. Lagers B, C, and D had been built on short three-foot posts to prevent any escape through underground tunneling. One evening, Staff Sergeant Herman Steck recalled, "noticing one of the dogs as he peered through a crack in the siding of his barrack. In an instant," Steck continued, "the dog lunged at the [startled airman], who was knocked back [from his interior position]" by the force of the 75-pound animal hitting the exterior siding of the building. The animal happened to be close enough to the structure to either sense or notice Herman, pressed against the inside of the barrack wall.

The airmen hated these dogs and enjoyed harassing them whenever possible. The animals were most vulnerable to being provoked as they roamed underneath the barracks where they could be heard and seen through the cracks in the flooring. In such instances, the men would form two separate groups and position themselves at opposite ends of their long hall way. One group would then start stomping on the floor, creating a disturbance that would attract the attention of the dog, who would start barking to raise an alarm. Once the animal became excited, the first group of airmen would cease their activity, while the second group at the other end of the barrack started making a similar commotion, causing the dog to run to the far end of the barrack to investigate. The intent and anticipated excitement of this provocation was to run the animal to exhaustion. The men were further amused listening to the frantic efforts of the German guards as they attempted to call off their canines amidst the barking and laughter emanating from inside the barrack.[313] On a less humorous note, some POWs would discard used razor blades through the cracks in the flooring, in hope that the animals would cut their paws while they wandered beneath the building.

The airmen's confinement for 15 hours a day coincided with an increasing number of new arrivals to Stalag Luft IV, creating demands on the prisoners that did not exist during late summer 1944. Overcrowding in all the barracks now caused increased personal irritability and a heightened degree of social friction that all but dissipated with the airmen's access to the parade field, and their participation in outside activities during the warmer months of the year. Fortunately, the daytime temperatures in mid-November were still warm enough to

---

[313] O'Donnell, *The Pangs of the Thorn*, 150

allow the airmen of C-lager to play a championship football game on 20 November 1944.

Playing their league tournament games, Don and his team members from barrack IV had made it to the championship playoffs. Still, they were considered underdogs in the forthcoming game. "The camp bookies favored the other team by six points," according to Don, "because they had a real quick kid who could run, and we had no one who could cover him. And they also had a kid who could throw. So I outlined a defense that was essentially a zone coverage on the pass, playing our two defensive backs very deep to cut off the long bomb. Then I suggested that we not play to win the game, [rather], we'll play to win the bet. So we voted and we agreed to go for the deal. So the next day," Don continued, "we went out and bet anything and everything of value, and the rest of the camp picked up the bet. On the day of the game we must have had 4,000–5,000 spectators; many prisoners in the [adjoining] lagers stood along the fence lines. Even the Commandant and his entire staff came out to watch it. And it was a hell of a ball game. It was tough. I was hit as hard playing that game as I've ever been hit since. It was for blood, because brother, the team that won, won everything. Well, the other team won the game, [although not by six points] but we won the bet. Needless to say, [other guys] were carrying stuff over to our barrack for a week."

During November and December 1944, temperatures in north-eastern Germany dropped to an average of 4.4 to minus 1.5 degrees Celsius (40 to 29 degrees Fahrenheit). Five-to-ten-mile an hour winds off the Baltic Sea, some 50 kilometers north of Stalag Luft IV, would further drive the temperature below freezing, creating a risk of frostbite or other exposed flesh injuries. The POWs in all fours lagers lacked adequate clothing to sustain them during the severe weather conditions. However, their protracted indoor confinement did protect them from overexposure to the cold, severe winter. The only warmth generated in the men's barracks, aside from overcrowding, was from the single coal-burning stove, fueled by a limited daily ration of poor quality peat bricks made of compressed coal dust. The weather temperatures became all the more unbearable in late December 1944 and January 1945, when daytime temperatures in central and Eastern Europe dropped below freezing for weeks.[314]

---

[314] Beevor, *The Fall of Berlin*, 27

Throughout the long evenings of their confinement, the airmen of C-lager participated in a variety of activities and antics familiar to college fraternities. The older veterans in the barracks would frequently "hold court" or initiate "bull sessions," entertaining the younger men with adventurous (and most likely exaggerated accounts) of flying, personal accomplishments, and sexual exploits. Staff Sergeant Jim Skarles of the 397th Bomb Group recalled that Paul McNally was very adept at holding the attention of his roommates with his engaging personality, varied life experiences, and his willingness to demonstrate some off-color gesture or behavior.

Don contributed to the evening entertainment in his barrack with periodic impersonations of various world political leaders, including mocking impressions of Adolph Hitler. He and the others also enjoyed harassing the German guards, stationed in the towers, and the sentries walking along the exterior fence line. Late in the evening, after the daytime temperatures had dropped 15 to 20 degrees, Don and his roommates would make catcalls to the German guards proclaiming "how warm they were inside their barrack and [speculating] how cold and miserable [the guards] must be outside. Then, everyone in the room would laugh about teasing the Germans because "there wasn't a thing they could do about it!"

Some POWs worked on small craft projects to either occupy time or to create an item of value for barter. Don was impressed by the men who invested time and energy mending their uniforms or, in some cases, making "new" uniforms all together. "These fellows were very clever," he said, "[making] Eisenhower battle jackets and fabulous uniforms for themselves," utilizing materials supplied from either the YMCA or items sent in packages from home. However, the most popular activity among the airmen in his barrack was playing cards, which, according to Chuck Hartney, "were homemade from thin cardboard cracker boxes received in our Red Cross parcels." To Don's disdain, most men engaged in endless hours of playing bridge, some of whom he said, "would get up very early every morning looking for a table and play bridge all day long. That drove me nuts. Some of these guys got to where they could make one play, and slam down their hand, then [brag all day long] about who could beat whom. Those guys could have rewritten the book of Hoyle. To this day I can't stand to play bridge for that reason."

In December 1944, the POWs of Stalag Luft IV were adjusting to their confinement and the monotony of the winter season. Then, one morning, the disposition of the German guards changed. The more astute men of the lager noticed this change when German NCOs conducted the day's first roll call and head count. Don sensed the difference in hearing the warm tone in the voices of the camp authorities as they greeted each other and some prisoners with salutations of "*Wie gehts*" and "*Gruss gott.*" By mid-day, even the most detached and apathetic prisoners had noticed the change in attitude of the German sentries. Their evaluated mood that morning was attributable to the initial success of a new German offensive operation in Belgium. Early morning, 16 December 1944, lead elements of three German armies had smashed an 84-kilometer length sector of the American lines in the extensive Ardennes Forrest. For the first time in three months, the Wehrmacht had seized the tactical initiative in Western Europe, with a major offensive operation involving 28 divisions.

For the past 12 weeks, the German OKW had concentrated the last of their strategic reserves of personnel, equipment, and fuel in assembly areas adjacent to American defense positions in the Ardennes, Belgium. Hitler was willing to risk these last reserves on the chance that his forces were strong enough to penetrate the Allied line, encircle the British Second and Canadian First armies, and reoccupy the port city of Antwerp. The primary objectives of the operations were to deprive the Allies of their forward supply base and fracture the Anglo-American Alliance. The German leader hoped that a victory of this magnitude would force England to sue for peace, and shift the political and military balance of power in Western Europe. "Veteran NCOs in the Wehrmacht exulted at the idea that history might now be corrected."[315]

The German assault achieved complete tactical surprise, routing 4 US infantry divisions and capturing "more than 23,000 [US soldiers], including 4,000 on one day."[316] Yet, the seizing of so many American POWs created logistical problems for advancing German units as they moved forward on the narrow forest roads. In some instances, the Germans shot their captives, rather than be inconvenienced by moving them to rear areas and further clog the restricted road network in the operational area of the Ardennes. The most infamous of these executions

---

[315] Beevor, *The Fall of Berlin*, 5
[316] Carlson, *We Were Each Others Prisoners*, xviii

occurred on 17 December 1944 at Malmedy, Belgium, when German soldiers of the 1st SS Panzer Division shot a group of 125 American soldiers of the 285th Field Artillery. Other American POWs were also executed at Honsfeld and Bullingen, yet these atrocities never received as much publicity as the incident at Malmedy.

The Ardennes, 1944   German Federal Archives

The first reaction of the airmen at Stalag Luft IV when they learned of the German offensive was one of shock and disbelief. Over the following days, these reactions turned to resignation, after reports from London acknowledged the continuing advance of the German operation. The reports, in addition to the increasingly arrogant attitude of the camp authorities, cast a further, disheartening pall over the POW population. Most airmen captured during the past year had started to accept the reality that they would be spending Christmas "behind barbed wire," while others prisoners captured earlier in the war were bitterly disappointed that they would spend yet "another Christmas in 'Goon land.'"[317] At this moment, the outcome of the war seemed to be in doubt.

News broadcasts from London were picked up by at least one radio hidden in the camp. Receivers were not terribly difficult to assemble given the broad range of individual talents and ingenuity possessed by the American and British NCOs in the various lagers, especially among those airmen trained as radio operators. Moreover, radio parts were smuggled into camp hidden inside baseballs provided by the YMCA POW Aid Program. Critical items necessary for the construction of a radio were contained in baseballs identified by their reverse stitching.[318]

"We were fairly well informed . . . while in the camp," Don said, "[lagging] only about three or four days behind the latest news." Receipt of new information was generally passed to the compounds by airmen who visited the lazaret in the Vorlager. A designated individual would feign symptoms of illness that required evaluation by the American or British doctors assigned to the camp's infirmary. There, the latest news was circulated among the airmen, who later disseminated it on their return from sick call. In C-lager, this was accomplished by one individual moving "from room to room, while other members of the barrack would watch for German guards;" or, more specifically, the "ferrets" who would position themselves around the camp to overhear personal conversations of the POWs and gather useful pieces of information. The German authorities at Stalag Luft IV had long suspected that their POWs had at least one radio hidden somewhere in the camp. The rooms of all the barracks in each lager were searched frequently, and on occasions, literally torn apart looking for this contraband. "One evening," Don recalled, "the Germans came in the middle of the night to search our room. Big Stoops, and a detail of other guards, came looking for what they thought was a small crystal receiver hidden in our room. They came around midnight, and turned [our entire] room upside down. We were forced to tear open our mattress bags, and empty the contents of our cans of jam and powdered milk out on the floor. Then they walked out and turned off the lights, leaving twenty some guys bare-ass naked. Well, that room was blue with swearing."

For the next ten days, the spirits of the airmen at Stalag Luft IV flagged as German forces continued to advance in the Ardennes. In contrast to the subdued mood of the POWs, the German guards were boastful and arrogant, taunting the men with insinuations that "the prisoners were going to rebuild Berlin because they were responsible for [the city's destruction]." This sentiment was captured by the refrain now circulating throughout the camp, "You'll carry bricks in '46 and back in the States in '48."

---

[318] O'Donnell, *Luftgangsters Marching Across Germany*, 67

Before Christmas, Don received a letter from his mother, Marie, informing her son that the family had recently gone to see entertainer Bing Crosby in the movie *Going My Way*. Don liked Crosby and had even written to the singer from a USO lounge prior to his overseas deployment, recalling, "I thought he was a wonderful guy, and represented everything that America stood for." Marie's letter most likely elicited a melancholy response in her youngest son. Crosby's signature record and movie, *White Christmas* had been released in mid-1942, and quickly become the best-selling popular recording in all history. The Irving Berlin song redefined the holiday for America and American servicemen, and captured their longing for home and family. Marie's reference to Crosby evoked similar emotional sentiments in her son as he now faced his first Christmas away from home, "behind barbed wire." However, Don refrained from expressing anything but a positive attitude in his letters home to not cause his mother any further worry. In a letter penned just before Christmas '44, Don expressed longing and resolution when he wrote;

"My Dearest Mother and Family, In a few days it shall be Christmastime again. Christmas here won't be like home, but we have worked hard and have made these holidays something extra special. I hope you won't worry too much. It is true that this is no bed of roses, but not as bad as you probably think. I dress warmly and the barrack is warm. This life is nothing but another phase of soldiering. [Don't forget] to send me plenty of candy and sweets. Also keep track of all your best recipes and plan on cooking plenty for me when I get home. Say hello to everyone for me. Tell Glen I'm still planning on going back to school. You and I will make up for this lost time, Mother dear. Your loving son, Donald"

In preparation for Christmas, a number of men in Don's room decided that they wanted a tree to celebrate the holiday. Chuck Hartney and "Pop" Eschback, at age 30, the oldest member of the room, were designated as representatives to negotiate with the Russians. The next day the two men approached several Slavic workers in the lager and offered them American cigarettes in exchange for bringing a tree into the camp. The following day, the Russians delivered on their agreement. From a distance, the pine, taken from the surrounding forest, looked to be the most perfect tree imaginable. Yet, when the two airmen approached the

Russians, they detected an increasingly offensive odor emanating from this prized possession. On further investigation, the two roommates learned that the Russians had smuggled the tree into the lager by placing it in the holding tank of their "honey wagon," humorously referred to by Hartney and others as the "super duper *scheizen* scooper." The Russian "wagon" was actually a truck configured with a large holding tank and motorized suction hose used to evacuate the human waste from the camp latrines. The contents were then spread as fertilizer on the adjacent fields just outside the stammlager. Undaunted, determined to salvage their investment, the airmen carried the tree to an outside water pump and tried to wash off the residue and offensive stench. The other airmen of their room were also willing to tolerate the residual pungent odor emanating from the Yuletide decoration for an overnight trial. The following morning, however, there was no denying the pine smelled god-awful. Later that day, the disheartened men traded the tree to another room whose occupants possessed less discriminating sensitivities.

On the morning of 23 December 1944, Chris Christiansen, one of six field delegates who worked for the YMCA in Germany, arrived at Stalag Luft IV for his third and final visit to the camp. Christiansen, a Danish theology graduate, had worked for the YMCA for the past four years and was assigned to the northeastern part of Germany that contained "twenty-four prison camps and six field hospitals that housed thousands of prisoners from all the Allied nations."[319] Two of the 24 camps located within Christiansen's area of responsibility were designated for Allied airmen, the largest being Stalag Luft IV at Gross Tychow. At the time of his visit, the camp's population had increased to over 10,000 American and British NCOs.

Christian was initially apprehensive in anticipation of his arrival at Stalag Luft IV. During previous visits, he "had encountered . . . unusual feelings of distrust, and sometimes even hostility, on the part of the German staff." More significantly, Christiansen perceived that the commandant, Otto Bombach, a "very mean and contemptible" man, delighted in harassing the prisoners and making them suffer.[320] An example of Bombach's harsh treatment of the Stalag Luft IV prisoner's was reportedly demonstrated after a bread ration had been stolen from

[319] Christiansen, *Seven Years among Prisoners of War*,15
[320] O'Donnell, *A History OF Stalag Luft IV*, 89

the German guards. Informed of the incident, Bombach ordered the airmen of the offending compound to fall out in ranks and stand out in inclement weather "until the guilty party confessed." When no one stepped forward, punitive reprisals were threatened. Only after ten men were selected for what might have been an execution, "was the guilty party forced out of ranks by the other prisoners and, according to author Robert Doyle, never seen again."[321]

Christiansen's fears, however, did not materialize. On the morning of 23 December 1944, he was greeted "with a few surprisingly kind remarks" from the commandant, who expressed his appreciation for "all of the things you have sent to my prisoners since your last visit." Bombach attributed this change of attitude to several repatriated German officers who told the commandant of "the valuable help the German POWs received in Canada and in Great Britain from the YMCA POW Aid program." It is more likely, however, that Bombach's good will was influenced by the recent success of the German Armed Forces. Regardless, Christiansen was informed that he would have complete freedom of movement within the lagers and that he could "speak freely and openly to everybody."[322]

The YMCA delegate spent the first day of his visit in routine discussions with the senior American and British representatives of the compound and the designated representatives from all four lagers. During this meeting, Christiansen was briefed by the various staff members who were responsible for all camp activities. Christiansen was impressed by the level of organization exhibited by the airmen, and characterized these discussions as "a very useful introduction to a camp visit." However, the YMCA delegate was most impressed by the spirits of the airmen, in particular the British POWs, many of whom had posted pictures of Winston Churchill in their rooms above the caption "Our Man of Confidence."[323]

Christiansen had always found the spirits of the airmen at Stalag Luft IV to be resilient and "usually very high." This was especially true this time of year after "everybody had received their Red Cross parcels prior to Christmas with real American and British Christmas food, with

---

[321] Ibid., 124
[322] Christiansen, *Seven Years among Prisoners of War*, 65
[323] Ibid., 65

turkey, plum pudding, coffee, chocolate, raisins, butter, wheat biscuits and lots of other [items]."[324] These specially designated parcels for each POW contained "one pound of plum pudding, three-quarter pound of boned-meat turkey and a quarter pound of small sausages, in addition to a variety of other food items."[325] Each parcel was specifically addressed to each POW by name, requiring a signature to confirm receipt.

On the afternoon of 24 December 1944, Christiansen toured the barracks of C-lager; all rooms had been decorated with candles and chains of fir provided by the YMCA. Later, he met with John Anderson in the lager's Red Cross room in the kitchen. The choir director requested "manuscript paper, a music text, and other supplies" for his program. Christiansen indicated that he would send the requested items after noting that their "camp had less equipment and supplies than any other camp he had visited."

Christmas Eve was made all the more special at Stalag Luft IV when the camp commandant gave his permission for the compound lights to remain on until 0100 hours the following morning. Furthermore, the gates of all four lagers were opened so that friends and acquaintances could visit throughout the compound. Brothers Jack and Norwood Browder, interned in different lagers, especially appreciated this gesture. At midnight, the POWs gathered in the center of the C-lager parade field. There, the Glee Club, under the direction of John Anderson and accompanied by four trumpeters, sang for almost 30 minutes. Christiansen noted that the weather was very cold, having fallen to "5 degrees Fahrenheit [with falling snow, yet no wind] muffled the well-known Christmas hymns that could be heard far away."[326] The entire camp was illuminated by powerful searchlights, while outside the wire fence German sentries patrolled the exterior perimeter with "rifles and [guard dogs] on leashes." At the conclusion of the religious hymns, the American and British Man of Confidence addressed the group, offering words of encouragement. In closing, the POWs sang "God Bless America," and "God Save the King" as a salute to the approximately 800 British airmen of the RAF held in D-lager. Then, slowly and silently, the men returned to their rooms.

---

[324] Ibid., 66

[325] Foy, *For You the War is Over*, 75

[326] Christiansen, *Seven Years Among Prisoners of War*, 68

During Christiansen's tour, other airmen were "brewing alcohol," according to Don, "with the intention of making Christmas 'merry' one way or another. So we got an oak bucket and [filled it] with all the fruit and sugar we were receiving from our Red Cross parcels and packages from home. Well, that [mixture] worked and worked, and very soon it [smelled] strong enough to almost knock you over whenever you entered the room. So Christmas night, we celebrated by getting drunk . . . , and had ourselves a ball. Later, we found out that the boys in the kitchen had done the same thing with potatoes, attempting to make vodka. Well, they made potato booze, but they never got a chance to drink it. When they attempted to move [their bucket], the bottom dropped out. Just as well, it probably would have killed them if they had drunk that stuff."

Seven hundred and seventy-five kilometers west of Stalag Luft IV, another group of American servicemen were also surrounded by German soldiers on Christmas Eve, 1944. These men were Army paratroopers of the 101st Airborne Division who, for the past five days, had stubbornly defended the vital road junction at Bastogne. Hitler's bold and audacious offensive in the Ardennes had achieved tactical success, yet the stubborn defense of Bastogne, along with other isolated positions held by ad hoc units of the US Army, prevented the Germans from achieving their strategic objectives.

The German operation had achieved its initial success, in part, due to the severe winter weather that enveloped all northern Europe, significantly curtailing Allied air operations. Freezing cold temperatures and overcast skies had restricted air support for the Allied ground operations during the first ten days of the German offensive. In spite of these hazardous weather conditions, the US Army Eighth Air Force conducted a "maximum effort" on 24 December, bombing the marshalling yards in Coblenz, Germany in an attempt to disrupt German supply lines to the operations area in Belgium. In support of this endeavor, the 398th Bomb Group at Nuthampstead, England lost two Fortresses when both aircraft crashed on takeoff due to foul weather conditions over the airfield.[327]

On 26 December 1944, the weather front over northern Europe cleared sufficiently to commit the full weight of the Allied Air Forces in

[327] Streitfeld, *Hell from Heaven*, 70

supporting ground combat operations in Europe. With air support, the vanguard of the German thrust toward Antwerp was blunted, allowing American armored forces to grasp the tactical initiative and relieve Bastogne. Three weeks later, the US Third Army under George Patton, whose photograph was featured on the front cover of the 15 January 1945 issue of *Life* magazine, was credited with the restoration of the American position in Belgium.

The defeat of the German offensive in the West exhausted the last strategic reserves of that nation. Many senior German officers now recognized they had clearly lost the war; the country could no longer provide the manpower or vast quantity of material necessary to continue the struggle. However, another six million persons would perish before the Wehrmacht ceased to function as a military organization and Adolph Hitler committed suicide in the ruins of Berlin, ending the long war in Europe.

13

EVACUATION

The forthcoming Russian Winter Offensive was planned and coordinated to exploit the Red Army's spectacular success of the previous summer. Preparations for a new Soviet campaign into central Europe were initiated that fall, and progressed through late December as German troops and equipment were transferred from the Eastern Front to support the now failed operation in the Ardennes. At the onset of the New Year the Soviets had assembled an overwhelming number of armies to begin their last offensive operation of the war. Joseph Stalin wanted the honor of capturing the German capital for its symbolic value. Equally significant, the Soviet tyrant also wanted to seize the seven tons of uranium oxide deposits thought to be held at the Kaiser William Institute for Physics, located in a southwestern suburb of Berlin.[328]

In early January 1945, 6,700,000 soldiers of the Red Army were deployed along a front line that stretched from the Baltic to the Adriatic.[329] In opposition to this over-whelming strength stood 1,500,000 German soldiers assigned to the Eastern Front, who knew they could not stop the Russian juggernaut. "We are lost," acknowledged one German sergeant, "but we will fight to the last man."[330] General Heinz Guderian, Chief of the General Staff of the Army, was similarly dismayed knowing that two army groups, with only 71 under-strength divisions, were assigned to defend East Prussia and central Poland. Despairingly, he characterized the Eastern Front as " . . . a house of cards. If the front is broken through at one point," Guderian reasoned, "all the rest will collapse."[331]

The first phase of the Russian Winter Offensive was launched 12 January 1945. Striking with unrelenting fury, the Soviet armies

---

[328] Beevor, *Fall of Berlin*, 139
[329] Ibid., 11
[330] Ibid., 11
[331] Ibid., 13

of the First Ukrainian Front breached German defensive positions 175 kilometers south of Warsaw. By nightfall, the lead elements of several Red armies had advanced some 35 kilometers toward Breslau, and threatened the industrial regions of Silesia. It was in this East German province where the all-important armament factories had been relocated to protect them from the destructive power of American and British air forces. Two days later, Soviet armies under Marshal Zhukov attacked north of Warsaw and, over the next two weeks, advanced an unprecedented 480 kilometers across western Poland to eastern Germany. On 31 January 1945, the Red Army reached the Oder River to capture Zehden, a town 58 kilometers northeast of Berlin.

Soviet T-34 tanks   State Archives Russian Federation

The Soviet breach of German defensive positions on the Vistula River destroyed Army Group A and most of its subordinate units.[332] Entire formations, losing half their assigned strength during the first day of fighting, "split into disconnected fragments" and were overwhelmed.[333] A few units managed to extract themselves from this maelstrom by abandoning all their vehicles and heavy equipment. Further north, the Second and Third Belorussian fronts advanced into East Prussia as other Soviet forces in Poland crossed the Vistula River, then moved into Pomerania. These combined operations threatened to encircle and destroy three overextended German armies defending the two northeastern provinces of the Third Reich.

Panic gripped the civilian populations of the two Baltic provinces as

[332] Duffy, *Red Storm on the Reich*, 78
[333] Ibid., 78

German defensive positions collapsed on the Eastern Front and Soviet forces penetrated into the ancestral homeland with "speed, frenzy, and savagery."[334] Months earlier, in mid-October 1944, the East Prussian village of Nemmersdorf was captured by Soviet forces, who "raped at will and wreaked an atavistic vengeance"[335] in retribution for German brutality committed in Russia. Three weeks later, German forces recaptured the Prussian village during a successful counter-assault, only to discover "a wholesale massacre of the population,"[336] which had been shot or butchered by the Russians in a murderous rampage that now spread throughout the country.

German infantry in retreat   German Federal Archives

By late January 1945, terror had swept through all East Prussia and the eastern provinces of Pomerania and Silesia. The savagery and barbarism unleashed by the arrival of the Red Army in East Prussia caused unspeakable "misery, terror, and degradation" for millions of Germans, and became appropriately known as the "East German Passion."[337] Within a matter of days, "800 years of German settlement in the East . . . ended as [millions of refugees] left . . . farms, villages, and towns in a frantic trek" of unprecedented tragedy.[338] Some refugees were able to flee the Soviet onslaught by securing passage on overcrowded trains heading west. Others embarked on ships departing

---

[334] Keegan, *The Second World War*, 512
[335] Ibid., 512
[336] Duffy, *Red Storm on the Reich*, 275–276
[337] Lucas, *The Third Reich,* 172
[338] Keegan, *The Second World War*, 512

from the Baltic ports of Konigsberg and Danzig; all hoping to find shelter in the interior provinces of their German homeland.[339]

The German *Kriegsmarine* "pressed all available naval and merchant shipping into service"[340] to start evacuating refugees from the various Baltic ports. The operations would continue for three months and eventually rescue some 1,900,000 persons. However, the undertaking was conducted at high cost with the loss of 223 out of 366 deployed ships. [341] One of the vessels lost early in the evacuation was the cruise liner, *Wilhelm Gustloff*. Sailing with 6,600 women, children, and wounded German soldiers, she was torpedoed by a Soviet submarine on the night of 30 January 1945. The ship sank in less than an hour, taking the lives of 5,300 on board.[342]* Other tragedies would follow with the sinking of the hospital ship, *General von Steuben*, carrying 2,680 wounded soldiers,[343] and the *Goya*, a modern freighter sailing with another 7,000 passengers.[344] The US Official Naval History of the WWII would later describe the German effort to evacuate these refugees as "perhaps the greatest rescue operation in the history of maritime war."[345]

German refugees   German Federal Archives

The vast majority of the German refugees were mostly women and

---

* Other sources cite this loss as exceeding 9,000 persons.

---

[339] Beevor, *The Fall of Berlin*, 48–49
[340] Duffy, *Red Storm on the Reich*, 289
[341] Lucas, *The Third Reich*, 172
[342] Beevor, *The Fall of Berlin*, 51*
[343] Duffy, *Red Storm on the Reich*, 291
[344] Duffy, *Red Storm on the Reich*, 291
[345] Lucas, *The Third Reich*, 172

children, as all able-bodied men had been drafted into the Volksstrum, or the Wehrmacht.* Forced to flee on foot during one of the worst winters in memory, they could only move a few kilometers a day on snow-packed roads. Many perished from hypothermia and starvation as a relentless east wind forced temperatures below zero for weeks at a time. In these extreme conditions, individual possessions were abandoned and dead children were left on the roadside as the refugees attempted to flee Russian battle tanks that deliberately crushed the slow-moving columns.[346] As many as "2.2 million Germans from Eastern Europe remain unaccounted for,"[347] and were thought to have perished in this largest forced migration in history.[348]

The sudden collapse of the Eastern Front and the rapid advance of the Red Army caused apprehension and anxiety among the German authorities at Stalag Luft IV. The airmen in the lagers first noticed this uneasiness with the abrupt change in the behavior of the camp guards, who congregated more frequently to exchange information, in hushed voices that conveyed their concern. The airmen also noted an increase in the number and frequency of German JU-52 transport aircraft flying to and from the northeastern province of East Prussia. These flights suggested the possible delivery of supplies, and evacuation of either key personnel or the seriously wounded. The airmen's observations were, in fact, correct. "Having made no plans for the disaster," German officials struggled to maintain their authority by using "[all available aircraft] from the Luftwaffe to drop supplies to snowbound and starving columns," yet senior officials privately resented the waste of fuel for such undertakings.[349] These observations, in addition to radio broadcasts from London reporting a major Soviet offensive, dramatically changed the dull and settled routine of camp life for both the German guards and their prisoners.

Shortly, the behaviors of many Germans in the compound became noticeably more agitated, arbitrary, and harsh. Incidents of guards

---

* The Volksstrum was a paramilitary organization of teenagers and elderly men, subordinate to the Nazi hierarchy, with limited significance or effectiveness as a military organization.

[346] Duffy, *Red Storm on the Reich*, 292
[347] Ibid., 277
[348] Beevor, *The Fall of Berlin*, 36
[349] Beevor, *The Fall of Berlin*, 49

shooting into the lagers and certain barracks occurred on a more frequent basis. Staff Sergeant Gerald J. Ralston, assigned to barrack number V in C-lager, noted in his dairy on 14 January 1945, "Six boys in the "limey" [D] lager were shot last night. There was an air raid . . . we heard the planes. During the blackout a British barrack was fired into because of a light [left unextinguished]." The account of the shooting into the compound may be accurate. However, Staff Sergeant Joseph O'Donnell, who was interned in B-lager, and later published a history of the Stalag Luft IV, refuted Ralston's claim that six airmen were killed, asserting "no such incident occurred." Still, Ralston's diary entry has merit, if not for factual detail, than for capturing the airman's perceived indifference of the guards and their willingness to use deadly force.

The frequency of room inspections also increased in C-lager during the last month of January 1945. The German authorities were insistent on enforcing continued compliance with camp regulations, in addition to thwarting any contingency planning for an escape or mass revolt. The airmen's food rations were further cut as another means of controlling the camp population. The most noticeable curtailment was the daily bread ration, although this might have been caused by disruptions in the local economy or the pressing need to feed refugees transiting through the region. According to numerous diaries, the distribution of Red Cross parcels, stored in abundance in the camp's Vorlager, were similarly reduced during the last two weeks of January 1945. In contrast to these harsher official policies, some German guards in C-lager adapted a more diplomatic posture anticipating Germany's pending collapse and a probable reversal of roles.

Awareness of the Russian advance stimulated most airmen's hopes for liberation, yet also provoked much apprehension and uncertainty. Weeks earlier, Staff Sergeant Charles Hartney recalled hearing rumors from Russians POWs, who performed menial tasks in the compound, of mass executions occurring in other camps located in Poland. These reports, in addition to the recent excavation of a large rectangular pit outside of the compound, ostensibly dug for "potato storage," generated rumors of a similar fate for the POWs at Stalag Luft IV.

Rumors related to mass executions and genocide in Poland were more than plausible. For the past four years, all of German-occupied

Poland had become a territory of 430 concentration and labor camps. Six of these sites were extermination camps built in 1941–1942 at Treblinka, Sobibör, Majodanek, Belzec, Auschwitz, and Chelmno. Over the next 18-month period, millions of persons, most notable Jews, in addition to hundreds of thousands of other untermenschen (undesirables) were murdered in these six locations. The closest of these sites to Stalag Luft IV was located at Chelmno, 225 kilometers southeast of Gross Tychow. The camp was opened in 1941 and, over the next two years, killed 152,000 Jews of the Lodz Ghetto, gypsies from Poland, and Russian POWs.* Another concentration camp at Stuthoff, 160 kilometers east of Stalag Luft IV, was designated for the extermination of Polish elites. The presence of these camps and the mass murder conducted at these sites was surely known by the area inhabitants. The awful stench of death emanating from these facilities extended for miles beyond their immediate location. Moreover, the use of burial details to dispose of hundreds of thousands in mass graves would have exposed the extermination programs at these sites. Word of the atrocities would have also circulated throughout the underground in Poland, if for no other reason than to provide motivation to resist the German occupation.**

Other airmen feared that the advance of the Red Army would result in indiscriminate casualties among the POWs. Soviet indifference had already resulted in the killing of "eighteen French prisoners of war . . . among the fifty-six people murdered by the Russians at Krenau in East Prussia at the onset of their rampage."[350] Later, according to author Robert Doyle, units of the Red Army overran Stalag IIIB at

---

* Author Richard Evans cites hundreds of thousands of murders were carried out by the army and the SS Security Service Task Forces by the end of 1941.[351] Moreover, a total of "662 sub-camps were established in the Third Reich and the incorporated territories by early 1945."[352]
** The Soviets intentionally suppressed all reference of the mass genocide in Poland until after the war to prevent any shift in focus from their self-serving agenda. Moreover, later reports released in May 1945, and printed in American and British newspapers, failed to acknowledge that the majority of the genocide victims were Jewish.[353]

[350] Duffy, *Red Storm on the Reich*, 278
[351] Evans, *The Third Reich at War*, 239
[352] Ibid., 690
[353] Gilbert, *The Day the War Ended*, 149

Furstenburg, "killing 50 American POWs and wounding hundreds," in the mistaken belief they were attacking Hungarian units fighting with the Wehrmacht.[354] The incident, in addition to other hasty attacks without proper reconnaissance, reflected Stalin's ruthlessness and obsession with capturing Berlin and subjugating Eastern Europe. For many Allied POWs interned in the East, "the prospect of liberation' by an [undisciplined Russia Army] became distinctively unappealing."[355]

Days later, rumors of a possible evacuation of Stalag Luft IV started circulating furiously throughout the lager as the airmen, in the absence of any definitive information, attempted to create or sustain some degree of predictability to their existence. However, the planning for such a contingency had begun shortly after the onset of the Soviet offensive. The precedent for an evacuation had already been established with the earlier transfer of the airmen from both Stalag Luft VI at Heydekrug and St. Wendel the previous year. Now, similar plans were being made to evacuate the Allied airmen held at Stalag Luft IV, along with tens of thousands of other prisoners of war held in numerous camps along the eastern border of the Third Reich.

For many POWs at Stalag Luft IV, speculation regarding an evacuation and forced departure from the relative safety and security of the camp, was distressing. Moreover, an evacuation would most likely require a forced march of some duration in the middle of a severe winter and under unimaginable conditions. The contemplation of such an ordeal was generally unsettling, most especially for the 3,000 airmen who had experienced the earlier evacuations from Heydekrug and St. Wendel. For some, such as Staff Sergeant Leonard Deranleau, previously interned at Heydekrug, thoughts of another evacuation were enough to elicit nightmares associated with the infamous Baltic Passage and the gauntlet run from the Kiefheide rail station to the camp.

Sergeant Deranleau's anxiety had been intensified by his recent diphtheria, an acute, highly infectious, and potentially fatal upper respiratory disease. The ailment had left him physically and psychologically exhausted. An outbreak of this contagious virus occurred in C-lager around Christmas 1944, afflicting Leonard several days later. Although admitted to the camp's lazaret, and treated almost

---

[354] Doyle, *A Prisoner's Duty*, 142
[355] Duffy, *Red Storm on the Reich*, 278

immediately, the 24-year-old airman became delirious and remained semiconscious for almost half of his ten-day admission.*

Regaining consciousness, Leonard heard one British medical officer state, "Oh! I see you have finally come around; we thought maybe we would lose you."[356] The physician's comment was as much an assessment of Deranleau's illness and physical stamina, as a reflection on the medical staff's ability to provide care and treatment. The camp's lazaret was small in size and consisted of only two buildings with 133 beds for all the Allied POWs at Stalag Luft IV. Delegates representing the Protecting Powers frequently noted the number of available beds in the infirmary as inadequate for the camp's population. In a written report dated 10 October 1944, the delegates noted "a minimum of 240 beds were required for the camp's [current] population of 8,000."[357] Yet, at the time of Deranleau's admission, the number of POWs at Stalag Luft IV had increased to almost 10,000. Medical supplies, such as "blankets, toilet requisites, and medication" provided by the International Red Cross, were also in short supply and frequently confiscated on arrival. Short of medications, the lazaret was forced to make an urgent request for "200,000 units of Diphtheria Antitoxin and 2,000 tubes of Sulfodiozol."[358] In a confidential report dated 2 December 1994, Colonel Albert D'Erlach, President of Mixed Medical Commission A for Germany, was cited for his unofficial comment, that "[the lazaret at Stalag Luft IV] is the worst [facility] I visited during the recent . . . tour of my [committee]."[359]

The anticipation of evacuation caused significant concern and presented a dilemma for the Allied medical officers assigned to the lazaret. These officers knew that a significant number of POWs were invalid and ailing men lacking the physical stamina to sustain the rigors of a forced march of any duration, much less one conducted in severe weather. The majority of men were malnourished and vulnerable to disease. Moreover, the lazaret's limited medical supplies could not

---

* Diphtheria is an illness that requires prompt administration of antibiotics to prevent pneumonia, possible inflammation of the heart, and damage to the nervous system.

[356] Deranleau, *Memories of an Aerial Gunner*, 121
[357] O'Donnell, *A History of Stalag Luft IV*, 80
[358] Ibid., 80
[359] Ibid., 24

be transported, much less dispensed, on a road march under such conditions. Pondering this predicament, Leslie Caplan elected to dispense his entire allocation of Typhus vaccines, a meager 300 doses for 2,400 plus airmen of C-lager in hope of providing some protection to at least a portion of the lager's population. Caplan was unsure if anyone would be willing to wait in line in subzero weather for an inoculation, but a limited distribution was preferable to abandoning the vaccines altogether. The day of the planned vaccination, Caplan was pleasantly surprised to discover hundreds of POWs assembled outside the lazaret, "in such bitter cold [weather] just to get the needle." In fact, so many men stood in the "minus 10 degree temperatures"[360] in hope of receiving a vaccination that a decision was quickly made to dispense half-doses, which allowed the medical staff to inoculate 600 men. Regrettably, not enough vaccinations were available for all those who wanted the inoculation. Many, such as Chuck Hartney, were refused and turned away.

Rumors and speculation of a pending evacuation were soon followed by several significant developments initiated by the German authorities. Heavy coats were distributed to the POWs, along with other confiscated articles of clothing, now necessary to protect them from subzero temperatures that blanketed north central and Eastern Europe. This act alone reinforced the general perception that evacuation was imminent. Later, on 26 January 1945, the first of some 3,000 disabled Allied prisoners of war were evacuated by rail to other camps in central Germany. One group was sent to Stalag Luft I at Barth, while a second group entrained to Stalag VIIA at Moosburg. These non-ambulatory airmen had to first negotiate, on foot, the three and one-half kilometers from the stammlager to the rail station at Kiefheide. However, an insufficient number of rail wagons was available to accommodate all of the POWs on the first day of this phase of the evacuation. The men left at the station were forced to return to the camp and depart the following day or later in the week.*

One of the truly injured airmen evacuated on 26 January 1945 was 27-year-old Technical Sergeant Patrick D. Benker of the 384th

---

* Not all the evacuees were invalids. Staff Sergeant Joseph O'Donnell told the author in a later interview, "Several members of my crew feigned injury in the hope of not having to evacuate the camp on foot."

[360] O'Donnell, *The Evacuation . . . ,* 60

Bomb Group. Benker had been shot down nine months earlier, on 9 April 1944, breaking the femur in his left leg on impact. The airman's injury was severe enough to require surgery to set the broken femur with a titanium pin. Following surgery, Benker was hospitalized for six months in two separate facilities, prior to being sent south to Oberursel for interrogation and arriving at Stalag Luft IV on 18 October 1944. Now entrained, and moving west out of Pomerania, Benker and the other airmen were thankful they were spared from the uncertain fate of the others who remained at the stammlager at Gross Tychow.

The *kriesgefangenenlarger* at Barth was originally designated as a British camp when it opened in late 1942. By September 1944, the majority of the approximately 6,000 Allied airmen held at Stalag Luft I was American Air Force officers. All these POWs were held in five separate compounds that followed the natural contours of the bay on which the camp was situated. Most of the barracks within the compounds were completely lacking in maintenance, and provided little protection from the cold northern climate of the Baltic coast. Yet, the airmen from Stalag Luft IV were grateful for just surviving their eight-day ordeal and the horrid conditions in the boxcars. "There were so many of us . . . ," said one of the occupants, "that if you fell asleep, people fell asleep on top of you." Moreover, the men "were seldom let out of [their confinement]," even during a four-day period when they were stranded on a siding or during their frequent stops. One airman recalled, "We [bribed] the guards with a few cigarettes . . . to push some snow through the crack of the door so we could let it melt for drinking water." This allowed the airmen to "save our two buckets for the POWs with dysentery, [which] most of us had."[361]

Another airman evacuated out of Pomerania by rail, yet heading south to Nüremberg was Milton O. Price, Sr. of the 487th Bomb Group. Although Price would later characterize his seven-day journey as "the single worst experience in my life," he was possibly one of the luckiest airmen on that train. Drafted in 1940, Price completed basic training in Maryland and was assigned to the 29th Infantry Division. Following the division's deployment and another year's training as an infantryman "on the . . . Salisbury Plains of England," he was "invited to transfer to the Air Force." Price then returned to the United States to train as a gunner at the time of the Allied invasion of Normandy and the 29th

---

[361] O'Donnell, *The Evacuation. . . ,* 34

Infantry landed on Omaha Beach. "Of the eleven men in my former squad," Price reflected, "six were killed and the other five wounded on D-Day plus one."[362]

The decision by the German authorities to provide rail transportation for the disabled POWs in Stalag Luft IV represented a sincere effort to execute a planned and coordinated evacuation of the camp. Although the conditions under which the airmen were transported were deplorable, the assembly alone of the required number of boxcars to transport them was a significant logistical accomplishment for the German *Reichbahn* in 1945. During the preceding six months, the national railroad had lost more than 108,000 wagons as a result of the deliberate targeting by Allied air forces. As a result of these losses, the Third Reich possessed fewer than 28,000 rail wagons in early 1945, and was no longer even capable of sustaining the civil and economic requirements of the nation.[363]

Following the evacuation of the disabled POWs from Stalag Luft IV, airmen remaining in A and B-lagers were moved to the other two compounds. The largest transfer involved moving approximately 500 airmen still interned in B-lager. One of these airmen forced to relocate to a new barrack in C-lager was Staff Sergeant Joseph O'Donnell, a ball turret gunner assigned to the 483rd Bomb Group.[364] O'Donnell, shot down on his 13th mission over Weiner Neustadt, Austria, had been assigned to a permanent barrack in B-lager shortly after his arrival at Stalag Luft IV on 21 May 1944. The move to another compound was upsetting for the 21-year-old New Jersey native. He had spent "more than eight months in one place," and felt comfortable "in my little niche." Yet, the physical and psychological discomfort Joe experienced transferring into C-lager, while disruptive and inconvenient, was only a mild foreshadowing of what the airmen would experience in the weeks to come.

The movement of the remaining ambulatory POWs into C and D-lager allowed German authorities to accommodate the transit of thousands of Allied POWs arriving from Stalag XXA at Tourn and Stalag IIB at Hammerstein. Both camps, located 175 and 58 kilometers,

---

[362] Rutkowski, *"We Regret to Inform You . . . ,"* 92

[363] Duffy, *Red Storm on the Reich,* 49

[364] O'Donnell, *The Evacuation . . . ,* 5

respectively southeast of Stalag Luft IV, were evacuated shortly after the Red Army breached German defensive positions in central Poland. The sight of these gaunt and emaciated English, French, and Polish POWs, some with "wooden shoes, no socks, and hardly able to walk," shocked many of the airmen at Stalag Luft IV. "These prisoners looked in pretty bad shape and worse for the wear," noted Staff Sergeant Gerald Ralston in late January 1945. "It's rumored that they were on the march for 21 days." The physical presence of the POWs also provided the airmen with their first tangible evidence of a German retreat in the East and generated further speculation that an evacuation of Stalag Luft IV was imminent. Some men remember being told, "The camp would not be evacuated," although all indications now seemed to suggest otherwise.

In response to the increasing likelihood of an evacuation, the airmen initiated their own preparations by mending articles of clothing that were ripped, torn, or otherwise unserviceable. The more creative individuals modified army-issued scarves for use as balaclavas, to protect their face and heads, and fashioning long-sleeve shirts to serve as improvised rucksacks for carrying their limited personal possessions. Apprehensive groups of airmen also started walking the fence lines of their lager in futile attempts to condition their feet and increase their endurance in anticipation of a forced march under demanding conditions.

The last anxious, frantic days of January 1945 provided a dramatic context for two incidents that happened to the men assigned to Sergeant Don Dorfmeier's room, yet could have characterized the lives of many POWs at Stalag Luft IV. The first incident, recalled by John Fetterolf, involved the roommate's behavior following a mistaken issue of a second breakfast ration prior to the camp's evacuation. The famished airmen "were elated with their good fortune," Fetterolf said, as all food rations had been curtailed for the past several weeks and the present allotment was insufficient to sustain them during the severe winter. Yet, when Don returned to the room, after a brief absence, he was shocked by what he discovered. Immediately he "objected to the group's acceptance of the second, unauthorized allocation," telling those who were willing to listen, "If you eat this food, other men will go hungry!" The other airmen thought differently, however, and, according to Fetterolf, "they all looked at Don as if he were full of shit." Then, he continued, "Every one in the room ate their portion of the extra ration *except your father.*"

Don was, undoubtedly, just as hungry as the other men in his room on the morning they received the extra ration of food. However, his attitude and behavior were constrained by his role as the elected representative for the entire barrack. This position required him to consider the needs of other prisoners who might not have been fed that morning. As a leader, the young airman was compelled to act in the best interest of all men assigned to his barrack, and not to be influenced by the dynamics of the smaller group with whom he lived. For Don to have acted otherwise would have compromised his integrity and moral authority to lead.

Another second distressing event occurred sometime later, which affected everyone in Don's room, yet did not cause the same intergroup conflict. The incident happened after the completion of the long-awaited shower facility in the Vorlager. The construction of a shower point had lagged for some eight months, ostensibly for lack of materials, and many POWs in the lager had not showered since moving into the compound four months earlier. However, the completion of the project created apprehension, rather than anticipation. The airmen's anxiety was caused by earlier rumors of murder and extermination in other camps in Poland. Thus many of the men became highly suspicious when, according to Chuck Hartney, "a formal detail of German guards marched into their lager and headed directly for their barrack, then escorted everyone in their room to the Vorlager." Once in the showers, the airmen's anxiety mounted further as they waited, "stripped naked in the locked facility for 30 minutes," contemplating their fate. Eventually, a fine spray of warm water broke the tension of the group, calmed their fears, and allowed them to relax for the moment, knowing they would live another day. The incident, however, was stressful enough for Jack Fischer to "totally block the experience" from his mind "until someone recounted the incident at a POW convention years later."

Over the next few days, new groups of Allied POWs continued to arrive and transit through Stalag Luft IV as the Red Army continued to move into Pomerania. On 1 February 1945, advancing Soviet forces captured the town of Ratzebuhr, 54 kilometers southwest of the Allied camp. Airmen who kept diaries noted that "flashes of bright light" penetrated the wooden shutters used to secure the prisoners and enforce the camp's blackout restrictions. The penetrating flashes of light were soon followed by audible sounds of artillery fire, which allowed the airmen to monitor the advance of the Red Army and speculate on their forthcoming liberation.

Several days later, 5 February 1945, the long weeks of endless rumors and speculation were finally dispelled with the announcement that C-lager would be evacuating camp the following morning. Some airmen remember being informed of their pending departure at the "mid-day formation," while others recalled first hearing the order later that evening. John Anderson remembered being told, "We would march for three days, rest one [and] march two more" to get to a new camp. Don Dorfmeier's primary recollection of the evacuation order was, "all hell broke loose," as frantic airmen focused on last minute efforts to configure and pack their makeshift rucksacks with clothing and small amounts of hoarded food. Moreover, each man had to assess the function and value of his personal possessions, and select only those items that were practical to carry on a march of unknown duration.

14

THE HUNGER MARCH

On 6 February 1945, 2,503 ambulatory prisoners of war interned in C-lager were marched out of Stalag Luft IV amid much haste and confusion. Staff Sergeant Don Dorfmeier and the men of his barrack had been wakened early that morning and told, " . . . be ready to move within the hour." Some men recalled being told of their departure the previous evening, and therefore had some advanced notice. Yet, even with advanced notification, the actual order to depart was considerably more sobering. Shortly, those airmen healthy enough to walk without assistance, assembled on the compound's parade field fully dressed in their issued overcoats and carrying makeshift rucksacks or blanket bedrolls. Other disabled men, such as Staff Sergeant Otha B. Huckaby, assigned to barrack number III, and those recovering from dog bites and bayonet wounds inflicted on them last summer, would follow later.

After Don and the other airmen were assembled on the parade field, they marched out of the compound in sequential order of their barrack number. From the compound, the airmen moved first to the Vorlager, where each man was issued one-third loaf of bread and one Red Cross food parcel to sustain him for an anticipated march of short duration. Some men were offered a second parcel, yet few individuals possessed either the strength or capacity to carry an additional ten pounds of weight. The men then proceeded, in isolated clusters, to the one road leading out of the compound where they were greeted by agitated guards shouting commands and exhortations of "*Mach Schell and Rous, Rous!*"

Under an overcast sky, the POWs were pressed four abreast and departed Stalag Luft IV in column formation, which extended some two-kilometers in length. In the lead position of the column was Technical Sergeant John Anderson, along with his roommates assigned to barrack number I. Although ambulatory, the physical and mental health of Anderson and most of the airmen in the column ranged from fair to poor. The majority of these men had lost, at a minimum, ten percent of their body weight while in captivity, which adversely affected their physical and psychological stamina. Moreover, Flight Surgeon Leslie Caplan had speculated that prior to the evacuation 70 percent of the airmen interned in C-lager were wounded or suffered from some form of physical ailment and/or psychological disturbance.[365] Most of these ailing and disabled airmen had been evacuated several days earlier with the departure of some 3,000 POWs transported by rail to other internment camps. However, hundreds of other incapacitated men were now forced to depart Stalag Luft IV on foot.

Throughout that first morning, the airmen moved across a snow-covered countryside, in a northwest direction toward Belgard, and away from the sounds of Russian artillery and the relentless approach of the Red Army. From the German perspective, however, the tactical situation was considerably more alarming. Weeks earlier, Marshal Zhukov's First Belorussian Front had breached German defensive positions on the Vistula River and penetrated some 480 kilometers through western Poland and into Germany to capture the town of Zehden on the Oder River.[366] This rapid and spectacular Soviet advance completely destabilized the Eastern Front, while threatening Berlin and the German forces in Pomerania and East Prussia. Only ad hoc units of the Wehrmacht and the Volksstrum held tentative positions on the west bank of the river. The situation was so desperate that Hitler ordered "more than three hundred antiaircraft batteries" be removed from the cities to augment the new front line until 16–22 divisions were transferred from the West. Other divisions were ordered to assemble east of the Oder, with a specific concentration north of Stargard in preparation for a counter-offensive to halt the Soviet advance into Pomerania. "Over 1,200 tanks had been allocated" for the operation, "but the trains to transport them were lacking."[367] Still, the presence of the German panzer and panzer-grenadier divisions in Pomerania was enough of a force to secure a land bridge along the Baltic coast for thousands of refugees and enemy prisoners of war moving into the interior of the country.

The first few hours of the march were exhilarating for some of the American POWs, and served to create an illusion of freedom for those

[365] O'Donnell, *The Evacuation . . .* , 5
[366] Duffy, *Red Storm on the Reich*, 201
[367] Beevor, *The Fall of Berlin*, 90

airmen who had been held captive for so long. Staff Sergeant Joseph O'Donnell, interned for nine months in B-lager, recalled exalting in the joy of being exposed to novel sensory images, as he embraced the "belief that being on the road was preferable to confinement in the camp." Other airmen actively considered escaping from the column and waiting in the woods for the approaching Russian Army. However, not all the airmen shared O'Donnell's optimism or willingness to contemplate escape. For many men, the evacuation of the camp, with the attendant losses of physical safety and psychological security, provoked great anxiety.

While the psychological orientation of the POWs in the lager varied, all the airmen struggled with the physical demands of the march. Within hours of their departure, the parade dress of the formation had deteriorated dramatically as weaker or less physically fit men had fallen to the rear of their now extended column. These first stragglers were men who developed problems "with blisters, aching feet or joints, and tired muscles."[368] Some of these problems also stemmed from men who did not have adequate shoes for their feet. Corporal Bob Carr, the ball turret gunner on Don's crew, was one whose shoes were too small to fit properly. As men in the column began to falter, Flight Surgeon Leslie Caplan and a few individuals who possessed the compassion to extend themselves to others, fell to the rear of the column to assist those in need. These noble, self-proclaimed medics provided encouragement or offered whatever help they could. In many instances, those offering assistance voluntarily remained with the lame airmen who fell out of formation. Their intent was to protect these individuals from being "bullied by the [German] guards." Yet, these altruistic men were frequently prodded with a bayonet or struck with the shoulder stock of a guard's rifle.

By mid-afternoon, most of the POWs in the column were physically exhausted by the bulky items they carried, and the difficult march over icy, muddy, unimproved roads that numbed their feet. The cumbersome Red Cross parcels, which were mostly carried by hand, created additional strain and muscle fatigue. Earlier, some men had taken advantage of a morning rest break to transfer the contents of their parcels to their rucksacks. Others attempted to transfer individual cans from their bulky parcels into overcoat pockets, shouldered rucksacks, or bedrolls while marching in column. The inherent difficulty in performing this awkward task caused many of them to discard cans of food, soap, and

---

[368] O'Donnell, *The Evacuation . . . ,* 60

toilet paper thought to be expendable. Other personal possessions, along with valuable clothing too burdensome to carry, were also discarded by airmen who feared that if they fell out of formation they would be shot. In short order, the collection of discarded items "littered the area," and transformed the route of their march to resemble that of a defeated army in full retreat.[369]

Staff Sergeant Francis Troy, the lager's Man of Confidence, noticed the number of POWs having difficulty maintaining the brisk pace of the march established earlier in the day. Alarmed, Troy moved decisively to the head of the column to argue, as had others, with the German command authority to slow the pace of the march. Although threatened with the loss of his own life, Troy was adamant in his protest, fearing that the lives of possibly several hundred men depended on his assertiveness.

The Germans seemingly acquiesced to Troy's demand and halted the column in late afternoon, south of Belgard. The men had traveled some 14 kilometers for the day. "Finally," Anderson noted . . . "we arrived at a farm [where the majority of the airmen were quartered in a large, complex barn that enclosed an open] . . . compound, yet not all of the men in the formation got to [sleep in the farm building]." Those men who lagged toward the rear of the column were unable to find any available space inside the barn and were forced to sleep outside in the cold winter night.

Staff Sergeant Don Kirby characterized the night's lodgment as a "formal compound with a double row of barbed wire fences that held other POWs who worked the fields of the surrounding farms." However, the fences did not deter Kirby or Sandy Cerneglia from contemplating an escape while others attempted to find some place to sleep. The two airmen had known each other almost a year and both feared "spending the rest of their life in captivity." Their obsession began when both were interned at Stalag Luft VI at Heydekrug. Cerneglia "was forever cooking up schemes" and always on the lookout for an opportunity to escape. Don Kirby had humored his friend by agreeing to accompany him on some future escape attempt. Now, months later, Cerneglia was expecting Kirby to honor that commitment. Moving with an instinctive sense of urgency, both men quickly climbed the two fences

---

[369] O'Donnell, *The Pangs of the Thorn*, 101

of the compound, but were sighted within moments of their escape. Rifle shots rang out as a search detail was quickly organized to give chase. However, the airmen's desire for freedom was more compelling than the determination of the pursuing guards and they quickly found concealment in the shadows of a nearby forest.

Only a recent warming of local temperature prevented the two escaped airmen and other POWs forced to sleep outside on the first night of the march, from freezing to death. The weather in Eastern Europe during winter 1945 had been severe and merciless. A recent blizzard on the 27th and 28th of January had covered the region with "another half meter of snow," suppressing evening "temperatures down to minus twenty Celsius." However, unseasonably warm temperatures in early February had caused an extensive thaw that melted the snow and broke up the ice on the Oder River, 120 kilometers west.[370]

Early the following morning, after receiving some hot water for coffee, the airmen of the lager were reassembled and resumed their westward trek. In short order, the physical demands of the march began to affect the organizational integrity of the column as men struggled to keep up with others in their assigned barrack and those with whom they shared an emotional connection. By mid-morning, the extended column of POWs had fractured into multiple segments of several hundred men each. Several hours later, John Anderson was one of many who, by mid-afternoon of the second day, thought, "I might not make it" to the evening's bivouac site. Anderson's right foot had started to bother him on the first day and he sought out medic Warren Stevens to wrap it, only to learn that there was no tape available for such purposes. Yet, Anderson managed to persevere and remain with the main body of the lager, which halted for the night near the small village of Stalzenburg. The airmen were then dispersed "in various size groups and [placed] in small barns all over town," about 25 kilometers from the point of their morning departure. The men had only been on the road for two days, yet many of them were already exhausted. Later that night, Staff Sergeant Gerald Ralston noted in his diary " . . . the fellows are really worn out. The march is really torture."

Whenever possible, the Germans attempted to shelter the Americans and British in barns or other structures on various farms

---

[370] Beevor, *The Fall of Berlin*, 27

along the march route. These barns and other enclosures were usually located within two square kilometers of the evening's bivouac site. Most farms also had "storage facilities for potatoes," which were frequently requisitioned by the German military to feed the Allied airmen, if they halted early enough in the evening.[371] On these occasions, volunteers who were still capable of performing additional duties at the end of the day, steamed these potatoes in large vats, while long lines of airmen stood impatiently, hopeful of receiving something to eat.[372] On other occasions, "The Germans would," according to multiple sources, "push you in [a barn], slam the door, and it would be pitch dark as one tried to find a place to bed down."[373]

The barns used to lodge the POWs were "crowded, primitive, and filthy," and most often fouled with standing pools of urine and manure on the floor. Yet these structures provided much-needed respite and shelter from the wet, cold weather. Don and the others were understandably grateful for any opportunity to sleep in a barn which contained enough hay or straw to provide bedding for them. However, some airmen smoked in these flammable structures, causing Don much anxiety over the possibility of a fire.

"Well, you could imagine what would happen," Don said emphatically. "There would be a virtual holocaust. We'd all burn to death. This would really [irritate] me. I used to get so [angry] at these guys," he continued, "and try to make them stop, but when it's pitch black inside [and] you're crawling over bodies, you can't get to people." At other times, equally self-centered men who had found a place to sleep in one of the lofts would urinate on others below rather than make their way out of the barn to use a latrine. Don recalled one such incident, citing "some guy down below got irate. He just got wild and said 'you no good son of a bitch. I don't care who you are, [or] how big you are, I'll beat the living shit out of you.' We were laughing like crazy because we weren't getting hit. But the guy in the loft didn't stop and he didn't say who he was. He just went back to sleep."

By morning, day three, men were being left behind. One of those individuals who could have very easily been left behind that morning, if

[371] O'Donnell, *The Pangs of the Rose*, 102
[372] Deranleau, *Memories of an Aerial Gunner*, 127
[373] Caplan, *Domain of Heroes*, 132

not for the concern of fellow crew members, was 21-year-old Carl Moss. The Michigan native was seriously ill from food poisoning at the end of the second day's march. The previous evening he and former crew member, Edmund Boyce, had eaten a can of liver paste, intentionally punctured by the Germans prior to distribution. Although seen by Flight Surgeon Caplan and given some type of medicine, Moss remained very sick and "lost all recollection of the next five days or so." Only later did Carl learn that his fellow crew members had carried him and his possessions for the past few days until he was well enough to march on his own. [374]

On 8 February 1945, the last of some 6,800 Allied prisoners of war interned at Stalag Luft IV evacuated the compound amid increasing German panic. These POWs, which consisted of 600 American, Englishmen, and other nationalities who had flown for the British RAF, were all that remained in D-lager. One of these airmen was Staff Sergeant Leonard Rose, a radio operator from the 459th Bomb Group, shot down on his 28th mission on 29 August 1944. He had been held in the same compound since his arrival on 6 October 1944. Now Rose and the remaining POWs in his lager were marched out of the compound, accompanied by eight or ten "heavily armed [German] guards," a ratio of one guard for every 60–75 airmen. A mobile kitchen eventually followed this last group of POWs. Yet, the German canteen lagged some three or four days march behind the lead elements of C-lager, which were currently moving across Pomerania as part of the swirling flotsam of war.

These lead elements of Don's lager proceeded to move further west and made chance contacts with German refugees and other Allied prisoners of war, all fleeing from the Red Army advance. The airmen's first contact with a group of approximately 7,500 refugees, in addition to an unknown number of German soldiers, occurred on the third day of the march. Their guards made no attempt to separate or restrain contact between the various groups as stipulated by German POW regulations. The men, according to John Anderson, simply overtook the slower group of German refugees moving along on the right side of the road, "fleeing with everything they had." Many refugees were transporting their possessions on foot, with wheel barrows, carts, and even wagons drawn by old men, rather than horses. The experience was unsettling for the Americans, most of whom were witnessing

---

[374] Caplan, *Domain of Heroes*, 23

such a sight for the first time. However, later similar encounters would generate much aggravation, resentment, and expletives as the POWs were forced to yield the right of way to the refugees, and take a more difficult route.

Days later, the airmen of C-lager would witness another shocking encounter with a long column of Russian POWs, moving toward the German homeland. Contact with these prisoners was particularly disturbing given the Russian's lack of warm clothing, gaunt expressions, and the harsh manner in which they were being treated. The sight forced the airmen to acknowledge the existence of a starker brutality than they had personally experienced, and generated much apprehension about their future treatment. Later that evening, Sergeant Dallas Farris noted in his journal, "[The Russians] looked bad. Some did not have shoes; they had what appeared to be burlap wrapped around their feet walking in the snow. We felt sorry for them." On another occasion, the British airmen in D-lager would have their own encounter with a large group of Russian POWs marching "with rags wrapped around their bare feet."[375] After recognizing the plight of the gaunt Slavs, the airmen of the RAF emptied their pockets to throw the hapless Russians whatever soap or cigarettes they could spare. However, the German guards would not allow their prisoners to receive these token gifts of compassion. According to a British airman, one guard rushed up "to stomp on [the] outreached fingers" of one prisoner reaching to retrieve a pack of cigarettes, " . . . then kicked . . . and began to strike him with his rifle butt." The British responded with "a wild roar of rage" at this sadistic behavior. The incident prompted another airman to exclaim, "My God. I'll forgive the Russians absolutely anything they do to this country when they arrive. Absolutely anything."[376]

By the evening on the third day, the social, organizational, and internal leadership structure of C-lager had practically ceased to exist. Their initial cohesiveness had been based on informal and formal relationships developed following earlier room assignments and the ensuing election of room and barrack's leaders. These early relationships served as the basis for an overarching organizational order that provided three important social functions: an individual identity; a psychological connection to a primary reference group; and

---

[375] Beever, *The Fall of Berlin*, 41
[376] Ibid., 41

a formal chain of command. This latter and familiar function was especially important as it served as a communication network to disseminate information, a distribution system to dispense rations, and an organizational system for directing group tasks.

During the first days of the march, most POWs attempted to maintain close proximity with their roommates and those who had previously demonstrated leadership. Instinctively, the POWs were exhibiting a "herding" response elicited when groups of people are faced with threats of personal injury or harm. However, the demands of the march were such that every day more men became separated from their barracks unit. Invariably, this separation increased individual anxiety, which accentuated a growing sense of isolation and despair within the column. In many instances, men became separated from their friends and roommates for days at a time, if not permanently. This happened to men who Don had known for most of his internment, like Jack Fischer, Chuck Hartney, and Carl Moss. All three men later recalled "never seeing Don again following the evacuation of Stalag Luft IV."

Group cohesiveness was adversely affected by other influences as well. Foremost of these was physical stamina. Many airmen struggled to maintain their place in the column and close proximity to roommates or others with whom they felt an emotional attachment. Group integrity was further compromised toward the end of each day when the more physically fit and robust men would move to the head of the column in the late afternoon, hoping to be assured a place of shelter for the evening. Such efforts usually provided these persons with a first opportunity to claim a more desirable sleeping area, forage within the confines of the structure, or secure a position in the front of the line waiting for rations. Airmen who lagged behind might find themselves arbitrarily placed in a different barn at the end of a day, and assigned to march with a different group of men the following morning.

The collapse of the organizational structure within the column created increasing command and control difficulties for Staff Sergeant Francis Troy, the lager's Man of Confidence. These same conditions created similar problems for Flight Surgeon Leslie Caplan, the only other POW in the column who held a recognized position of authority among the airmen. Prior to the evacuation, both men operated within separate domains of the compound and exercised different types of authority to perform their responsibilities. Troy's leadership authority was sanctioned by the protocols of the Geneva Convention, which stipulated that enlisted POWs would select a representative through popular election. Troy's position of leadership, according to sociologist Max Weber, represented a charismatic authority, based on his ability to inspire others and the willingness of the group to follow. Conversely, Leslie Caplan's authority as a commissioned medical officer represented a traditional and legal (expert) authority sanctioned by law and the Geneva Convention, yet he was prohibited from exercising "command" authority by the same Geneva protocols.* Moreover, Caplan was confined to the Vorlager while interned at Stalag Luft IV, where his contact with, and responsibility for, the men of C-lager was limited to those who presented for sick call and/or were admitted to the camp's lazaret. Yet, Caplan was also a charismatic figure and, according to one of the pilots in his bomb squadron, "very charming, [possessing] a great sense of humor . . . and very popular with us and the remainder of our squadron."[377] More significant, Caplan was a very spiritual man who believed with complete conviction in the binding humanity of all mankind. This orientation would become increasing apparent to the men of the lager during their march; he was much-acclaimed for his compassion.

Following the evacuation of Stalag Luft IV, both Troy and Caplan moved within a chaotic and deteriorating situation. Little organizational structure remained to define their individual responsibilities, much less resolve the ambiguity of their respective roles. This loss of cohesiveness created a chaos that Don later characterized as "pretty much every man for himself," which accounts for why some men stole articles of clothing and food left unattended by more trusting and unsuspecting individuals. Yet, the airmen were trained to function as members of a team, and many men started to align themselves with others, to form small groups to ensure their own survival. The men referred to these informal pairings of two-, three-, or sometimes four-man groups as "combines," which formed on the basis of compatible temperaments, physical stamina,

---

* German sociologist Max Weber argued that individuals will subordinate themselves to leaders who exercise one of three legitimate types of authority: traditional, charismatic, and legal/rational.

[377] Caplan, *Domain of Heroes*, 93

and perceived or demonstrated survival skills. The implicit agreement common to all these groups was that each member would provide whatever physical and psychological support was necessary to sustain the others throughout the demands and hardships of each day.

Some of the airmen in C-lager, who anticipated the potential hardships of a cross-country march, made earlier commitments with specific individuals to support each other in the event of evacuation. In many instances these agreements were based on attachments to former crew members, roommates, or other acquaintances made during their internment. In Don's room, Martin Chavez paired off with M. G. Flores, while Jack Fischer and Harry Feldkamp agreed to stay together on the basis of their amicable history of sharing food with each other. Other men such as Charles Hartney and Frank Dyer would align themselves with others to form three-man combines. Don Dorfmeier and Paul McNally agreed to a similar arrangement prior to the evacuation of their lager. The two Fresno airmen had known each other since their internment at St. Wendel and had become friends during the preceding six months. In time, they developed an appreciation for each other's strengths and tenacious spirit, which inspired mutual confidence. Yet, on the morning of the evacuation, the two men found themselves in different sections of the lager's column due their respective barrack assignment and their designated march order. Initially separated by some 1,200–1,400 other POWs, the two men managed to find each other shortly after their departure. This was most consoling for Don who lacked competency in basic field craft and felt reassured by Paul's survival skills, thought to have been acquired in scouting. Years later, Don recalled, "My buddy Paul [constructed] a pretty good rucksack so we were in good shape to carry [all] that we [possessed], while I carried our blankets."

The mutual cooperation and division of labor exhibited within the combines was most evident when the men bedded down for the evening. In these instances, one man would usually establish a rest or sleeping area for the group, while another foraged for food and/or started a fire for boiling water or cooking their rations. Later, all members of the combine slept together, huddled under the collective weight of their blankets in a futile attempt to keep warm. However, many of them, like Chuck Hartney, recalled this was almost impossible, "especially during the winter phase of the march." Still, the high percentage of airmen who eventually survived the long trek out of Pomerania serves as a testimonial to the care and tenacity exhibited by the men of these combines who encouraged, supported, and at times, literally carried each other from one day to the next, in the face of incredible hardship.

The physical demands of the march, in which hungry, inadequately clothed and physically exhausted men struggled in rain and snow, compromised the immune systems and the health of hundreds of airmen evacuating Stalag Luft IV. The majority of these men were initially infected with diseased fleas and lice after sleeping in barns, on hay used for livestock. This affliction alone caused constant, maddening discomfort. Days later, Leslie Caplan diagnosed his first case of diphtheria, a contagious and life-threatening disease. Presentations of pneumonia, and later tuberculosis followed.[378] However, the one condition that overwhelmed and threatened the health of the entire lager was dysentery, an infection of the lower intestinal track caused by living in "crowded conditions of filth and drinking unsafe, contaminated water." Within days of their departure, this affliction became rampant, although it affected everyone in the column with varying degrees of severity. The primary symptom of dysentery, the loss of bowel control, was exacerbated by the expectation that the airmen restrain themselves until the column halted for a five or ten minute break every few hours. This was, according to Joe O'Donnell, unrealistic. "The intense cold [numbed] our fingers, which made unbuttoning the fly of our trousers difficult [and] it usually took the entire five minutes to urinate." Moreover, few men could "hold the urge" to relieve oneself in spite of "the threat of being shot or [struck] in the back by the butt of a rifle for breaking ranks."[379] Still, such threats were effective. "There were many times on the road," Don said, "that I would be walking with [the discharge of my bowels] running down my leg." Most airmen suffering with dysentery would report similar experiences where they could not help but soil themselves and their clothing.[380] These accidental discharges created social embarrassment, as well as hygienic problems in the absence of having toilet paper, soap; or, more significantly, water to wash themselves and their clothing. Under the best of circumstances, the POWs could only hope to wash their hands in a nearby stream. In the absence of water, the airmen resorted to using snow or dirt to clean themselves and their clothing before resuming their place in the column and continuing the march.

---

[378] Caplan, *Domain of Heroes*, 93
[379] O'Donnell, *The Evacuation . . . ,* 9
[380] Deranleau, *Memories of an Aerial Gunner*, 128–130

The number of sick and seriously ill men in the lager forced Leslie Caplan to start a journal to record the names, diagnosis, and disposition of these afflicted men. These medical annotations were entered into a journal he had carried with him since his first assignment in the US Army Air Force. Caplan's first entry following the evacuation of Stalag Luft IV, dated 8 Feb 1945, noted that "eleven men were left at Stolzberg," unable to proceed further after just two days on the march.[381] Several days later, on 11 February 1945, he documented his first case of diphtheria. Aside from providing an assessment of literally hundreds of afflicted airmen, Caplan's medical journal, void of personal sentiment and speculation, represents one of the more accurate records produced by any participant on the march.

The harsh physical demands and the psychological trauma of the first week of the march caused many men to withdraw into an emotional, dissociative state. This narrowing of one's external focus was so pronounced that years later few airmen could remember little more than intense, fleeting impressions of any phase of the march, much less their first days on the road. One such vivid impression, recalled by Chuck Hartney shortly after departing Stalag Luft IV, was that of an older woman who attempted to offer soup to the cold and hungry airmen of his lager. This maternal gesture was exceedingly poignant for Hartney, who was fascinated by the woman's compassion and tenacity. Fixated by her persistence, the airman watched this determined woman "walk along the length of their column, in shoes made of straw," attempting to offer sustenance and comfort to the Allied airmen. "The memory," Hartney said, "would haunt me for the rest of my life."

Staff Sergeant Don Dorfmeier experienced a similar gesture of kindness extended to him by one of the older German guards early in the march. "[Many] of the German guards," Don recalled, "were considerably older than their prisoners and also experiencing great difficulty on the road. Around mid-day an older . . . guard collapsed in a snow bank. He just couldn't make it. So I reached down and pulled him up and grabbed his weapon, which I believe was an automatic rifle that weighed about 20 pounds. So I made the deal with the old fellow, stating 'I'll pack this weapon for you [if] you share your [rations] with me.' So the rest of the day [and for some time later] . . . I carried this guy's weapon until such time as the obergefreiter, the senior ranking

---

[381] Caplan, *Domain of Heroes,* 23

member of their escort detail, who would march up and down the line to keep men moving, would come into view, then I would [momentarily] pass the weapon back to the guard.* Come lunchtime, or any time we had a break, he'd give me a slice of bread and cheese. Over time we got to be great pals. He had lost his sons in the war . . . He had literally [lost everything] . . . he was just an old man like my grandfather would have been."**

A week after evacuating Stalag Luft IV, the exhausted airmen of C-lager had marched approximately 140–160 kilometers over snow-covered roads, consumed the last of their Red Cross food parcels, and now, according to an anonymous airman, were living exclusively on "butts and coffee" to jolt their bodies to function. The following day, this same individual noted he was "seeing a lot of courage these days . . . [as] men with drawn faces and bad stomachs [cracked] jokes while they [marched] through mud up to their knees." Years later, Leonard Deranleau characterized the first week of the march in a less cavalier manner, as "fighting complete exhaustion from lack of sleep, food, and water," frequently marching "late into the evening, always with the thought of being shot if [one] fell [out of formation]."[382]

The constant, repetitiousness movement, in addition to the prolonged exposure to freezing weather had created a monotony that dulled their immediate focus, as well as the later recollections of most airmen who had not kept a journal.*** Yet, regardless of efforts to record events, every airmen of C-lager remembered the extreme hardships they endured on Valentine's Day, 14 February 1945. The day started with the usual early morning head count, followed by a meager breakfast ration of

* The primary weapon used by the German Wehrmacht during WWII was the bolt-action Mauser Karabiner 98K, which weighed 8.2 pounds.
** Staff Sergeant George Guderley corroborated this phenomenon on the march out of Pomerania. Arthur Durand also cited similar occurrences . . . during the evacuation of Stalag Luft III, where airmen of the South Compound, "carried rifles for some of the exhausted guards."[383]
*** The relationship between psychological trauma and pathologies of memory are now recognized as a characteristic feature of dissociative amnesia and Post Traumatic Stress Disorder.[384]

[382] Deranleau, *Memories of an Aerial Gunner*, 125
[383] Durand, *Stalag Luft III*, 331
[384] Durand, *Stalag Luft III*, 331

several small potatoes prior to moving again in the "gray, dismal . . . freezing rain and the relentless[ly] cold" morning.[385] Throughout the day, the airmen marched in a constant precipitation of rain and snow flurries, while moving over slippery, icy roads. Around mid-afternoon, most airmen drew on their own internal sense of time and physical exertion to surmise they had marched as far, if not further, than on any previous occasion. Yet, there appeared to be no slowing of the pace of the march or any indication of halting the column to find lodging for the night.

Angrily, Don and other airmen in his immediate vicinity expressed their resentment by forging ahead at a faster pace in an effort to humiliate the older German guards who could not keep up. "We just kept moving," Don recalled, "and it got later and later in the day, and we were pissed off. So, a defiant spirit rose up," he continued, and we said, "'Alright, if you guys want to march, we'll march' and [a bunch of airmen] in our group started [to move] out at a fast vigorous pace. And then we began to sing "Lili Marlene," which was a German marching song from their heydays of 1941.* [This really upset them] . . . they tried to make us stop, yet they couldn't."

Darkness soon settled over the Pomeranian landscape as the airmen continued to march until late in the evening. Finally, after covering some 35 kilometers, the column halted and moved into the large open clearing of a pine forest. The men were then forced to sleep outside, and without shelter, although Leslie Caplan would later state "there were many barns in the [immediate] vicinity." Moreover, the POWs had to camp in complete darkness and were denied the opportunity to start a fire for either warmth or to cook rations. Don recalled, "We finally arrived [at our final destination], a large open field, around 2000 hours. [The ground was wet] as it had rained during the day, yet recently cut boughs [were strewn on the ground]. On Paul's [suggestion], we gathered several boughs to serve as insulation from the wet ground and set up our sleeping area on an elevated spot so the water would [drain away] from our position." The field where the airmen slept was not only wet from a week-long precipitation of rain and snow, but also fouled, according to Caplan, by the "feces of dysenteric prisoners who had stayed there

---

* "Lili Marlene" was the universal anthem of all soldiers fighting in the European Theater during the Second World War. The song was first broadcast on German Armed Forces Radio 18 August 1941.

[385] O'Donnell, *The Evacuation . . .* , 9

previously." In sworn testimony following the war, Caplan further stated, " . . . many stragglers and sick men who could barely keep up" arrived at the bivouac site late and [were] unable to find a decent place to sleep. Regardless, all were forced to bed down for the night, lacking rations, and expected to sleep in impossible conditions.

The following morning those men who were fortunate to have slept at all, awoke cold and numb to discover several inches of snow that had fallen on their encampment. Dispirited and hungry, they were quickly assembled and forced to move on, "without food or water at the same pace [and just as far] as the previous day, on just plain guts," according to one airman. Later that same morning, the Germans ferried the POWs across the channel of the Oder River estuary that separated the Stettiner Haff from the Baltic Sea. The exhausted airmen disembarked near the port village of Swinemünde, on Usedom Island, 38 kilometers southeast of Peenemünde, were Don and his crew were shot down six months earlier.

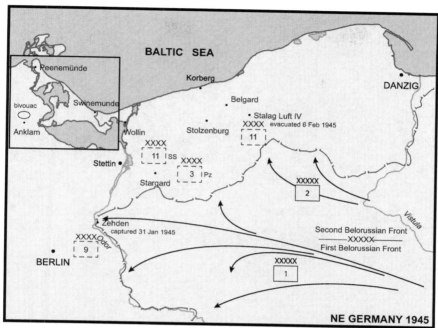

Evacuation of Stalag Luft IV

Author's collection

The Soviet Winter Offensive of 1945 started on 12 January as armies subordinate to the First Belorussian Front advanced 480 kilometers from the Vistula to the Oder River in just over two weeks. Days later, Stalag Luft IV evacuated the first of 6,800 ambulatory American and British POWs– moving northwest toward Belgard–while an ad hoc collection of German units were transferred from the west to stabilize the Eastern Front. Ten of these divisions were assigned to the newly organized 11th SS Panzer Army assembling east of the Oder River.

15

STARVATION & DESPAIR

Disembarking near Swinemünde, Don Dorfmeier and the other POWs in his column marched across Usedom Island toward the German mainland. Cold and miserable, the airmen remained defiant and the men in Staff Sergeant George Guderley's group voiced their resentment through song. Their first selection, according to the Illinois radio operator, "included an unfavorable reference to German character," which understandably, irritated their guards. "Noting this reaction," Guderley continued, "the airmen decided to push the anger further by singing the service song of the Air Corps." Yet, with the first few words of the opening line, "Off we go into the wild blue . . . ," the senior NCO of their escort detail halted the column. Infuriated, the German sergeant announced tersely, "With any more singing [they] would be shot." Other guards chambered rounds in their rifles to emphasize this intent. The airmen responded to this show of force by moving on in insolent silence and, according to Staff Sergeant Gerald Ralston, spent the next few days without " . . . food or water, [sleeping] in the open again on the 16th and living [solely] on [cigarette] butts."

Several days later, the International Red Cross estimated that 6,165 Allied POWs from Stalag Luft IV crossed over the Usedom Peninsula into central Germany, suggesting some 750 airmen had, for various reasons, fallen out of the march.[386] Most of these men were stragglers, too sick or disabled to press on, and were left at various points along the road. Some of these men may have been transported to military hospitals, or have died from physical exhaustion, illness, or possibly, execution. Others may have fallen into Soviet captivity, an equally uncertain fate as not all Allied POWs liberated by the Red Army were returned at the end of the war.

However, not all the missing POWs had perished. At least two of those initially unaccounted for airmen had escaped. Staff Sergeants Don Kirby and Sandy Cerneglia had successfully taken flight in the

---

[386] O'Donnell, *A History of Stalag Luft IV,* 127

late afternoon of the first day's march when their column moved into a secure compound for evening bivouac. While most other men were looking for a place to sleep, Don and Sandy quickly climbed over the compound's two barbed wire fences and eluded a patrol assembled to give chase. Wet and chilled after crossing a stream, Kirby and Cerneglia moved on through the cold night and the next few days without food or sense of direction. Incredulously, the airmen managed to travel openly for two days without arousing suspicion by simply telling those who inquired that, "They were sick airmen sent off to report to the nearest hospital for treatment." Eventually, a more perceptive German NCO challenged their ruse and they were promptly apprehended. The following day a vehicle returned the two escapees to Stalag Luft IV, now crowded with captured Mongolian soldiers of the Red Army. Days later, Kirby and Cerneglia again departed Luft IV as the only two Allied airmen moving among a horde of Soviet prisoners who were, according to Staff Sergeant Kirby, "horribly mistreated."

Days later, the last elements of the Stalag Luft IV column crossed to the German mainland, and merged with the massive refugee population evacuating the eastern provinces of the Third Reich. German authorities initially estimated the number of evacuees moving toward the perceived safety of the country's interior homeland at approximately 4,000,000.[387] However, this assessment was later revised upward to 7,000,000, and by 19 February 1945, it was estimated that 8,350,000 fugitives were moving into the German interior. Week after week, crowded passenger trains from East Prussia, Pomerania, and Silesia emptied bewildered and unfortunate refugees seeking shelter in cities such as Berlin, Brealue, and Dresden. In Berlin alone, an estimated "40,000 [to] 50,000 transients were arriving in the city every day, although much of the German capital had been reduced to ruin by Christmas 1944."[388]*

Further south, the majority of the refugees evacuating the province

---

* The German capital, Berlin, has been characterized by author Cornelius Ryan, as "a second Carthage," after 363 Allied raids "laid waste more than ten square miles of built-up districts–ten times the area destroyed in London by the German Luftwaffe."[389]

[387] Beevor, *The Fall of Berlin,* 48
[388] Ibid., 48
[389] Ryan, *The Last Battle,* 15–16

of Silesia were fleeing toward the medieval city of Dresden in the Elbe River valley, 160 kilometers south of Berlin. Ranked as the seventh most-populated urban center in the country, Dresden had not been a target of the strategic bombing campaign until later in the war, and the city was perceived by many refugees as a safe haven.[390] This perception attracted thousands of fugitives, swelling the city's population from 600,000 inhabitants to over one million. Similar to Berlin, refugee trains continued to arrive with displaced persons "too hopeless and tired to move further into the interior of the country."[391] Many evacuees also became stranded after full rail priority was restored to the Wehrmacht. The earlier diversion of all available rolling stock to evacuate refugees from the east had created a transportation crisis throughout Germany, disrupting shipments of food, coal, and other supplies necessary to sustain the flagging war effort.[392]

This vast concentration of refugees in Dresden soon attracted the attention of Allied military and political leaders seeking a target to serve as a ruthless expedient to break the morale of the German people. The destruction of Dresden would also provide an opportunity for England and the United States to demonstrate their airpower, and intimidate the Soviet Union. Both nations were increasingly alarmed by the Red Army's relentless advance into central Europe, and looking beyond their present alliance with the Soviets in anticipation of a postwar conflict in Europe.

The proposed destruction of Dresden called for a massive air assault, surpassing the devastation inflicted on Hamburg in 1943.[393] To achieve this degree of annihilation, British Bomber Command, acting in consort with the US Army Eighth Air Force, planned a series of four consecutive raids that would be conducted on 13–15 February 1945. The initial RAF raid was a dual strike by a force of 800 British Lancaster bombers, executed with faultless precision against an undefended target.* Half of the first mission's 2,658-ton bomb load,

---

* Weeks earlier, all of the city's antiaircraft batteries were redeployed "to bolster the antitank screen on the Oder Front."[394]

[390] McKee, *Dresden 1945*, 31
[391] Ibid., 31
[392] Beevor, *The Fall of Berlin*, 51
[393] McKee, *Dresden 1945*, 63
[394] Keegan, *The Second World War*, 515

consisting of light-weight incendiaries filled with highly combustible chemicals, produced a firestorm of unspeakable carnage and destruction. A second raid followed just hours later, and two additional missions were conducted by the US Air Force during the next 48 hours. Over 11 square miles of the city were destroyed and, according to local officials, some 22,000 persons were killed, considerably fewer than the number of those who perished during the Hamburg raids.[395]

German reaction to the bombing of Dresden was one of understandable outrage following graphic newspaper descriptions of the Allied raids as "a coldly calculated plan of murder and destruction."[396] The government also unleashed a tirade of vengeful rhetoric in response to the attack. Joseph Goebbels, the Reich Minister of Propaganda, in addition to others, urged immediate retribution; that enemy prisoners of war, specifically Allied airmen, be executed in reprisal or moved into the very cities targeted by the American and British air forces. Days later, while attending a senior leadership conference, Adolph Hitler further threatened to denounce the Geneva Convention and vowed "to make the enemy realize that we are determined to fight for our existence with all the means at our disposal."[397] However, the threat to renounce humane treatment to enemy POWs, as stipulated in the Geneva Accord, was motivated as much by Hitler's desire to stop the high desertion rate of his own armies in the West, as it was to administer revenge.

Hitler and his ministers continued to argue the fate of the Allied POWs six days after the Dresden raid when the lead elements of Don's lager went into bivouacs near Anklam, 150 kilometers north of Berlin. Many of the small barns and other makeshift facilities in the area served as improvised hospitals during the airmen's first sustained period of rest since their evacuation from Stalag Luft IV two weeks earlier. The decision to halt the march was influenced, in part, by the recent stabilization of the Eastern Front along the Oder River, and the initiation of a major German counterattack in Pomerania. Although the German offensive miscarried–"rain and mud confined the tanks to the roads"–it did force the Russians to halt their drive on Berlin.[398] For the moment, the focus of the Red Army turned northward to eliminate the

---

[395] Keegan, *The Second World War,* 515

[396] McKee, *Dresden 1945,* 268

[397] Shirer, *The Rise & Fall of the Third Reich,* 1000

[398] Ziemke, *Stalingrad to Berlin,* 447

remaining German forces in Pomerania and East Prussia.

This temporary cessation of the march allowed German authorities an opportunity to account for all their POWs, and provide the airmen a modest ration of soup and bread. Later, Red Cross parcels were distributed on the basis of one package for every three or four men. The halt also provided a much-needed opportunity for the men to conserve their strength and care for their feet. Sergeant Jack Fischer was one of many individuals who benefited from this and other brief respites sanctioned during the next few days. Later, Fischer acknowledged his good fortune to have spent several days "sheltered in an enclosed pig sty, out of the weather; otherwise I would have lost my feet."[399]

German field kitchen   German Federal Achieves

Days earlier, Staff Sergeant Francis Troy and Flight Surgeon Leslie Caplan succeeded in winning some concessions for more humane treatment for the weak and failing airmen of their lager. Both men had become alarmed by the increasing number of incapacitated and faltering airmen, and initiated multiple protests on behalf of the men in their charge. The first concessions granted by the Germans allowed the POWs to proceed at their own pace."[400] Caplan was also granted the authority to organize and direct a hospital staff of volunteers to move as an advanced party to prepare sites for the evening's bivouac. The primary responsibility of these volunteers was to clear designated sections in the barns and gather straw bedding for the ailing and incapacitated. Other men dug latrine pits, if shovels were available,

---

[399] Jack Fischer, video, Andersonville Historic Society Site, 1994
[400] O'Donnell, The Evacuation . . . , 60

and/or gathered wood for fires to either boil water or prepare whatever potatoes were available. Later on, the Germans provided several large-wheeled farm wagons with horses to transport men too sick or lame to walk.

Caplan's first reference to these wagons was noted in his medical journal 17 February 1945.[401] The previous day he had encountered a small party of emaciated American POWs from Stalag IIB at Hammerstain. These men were all sick and had left their column to find a hospital. However, they were denied admission and forced to resume their march "with little or no rations." The next morning, "these men were left behind, but late in the day were placed on wagons and caught up with us after dark." Caplan then requested Hauptman Weinert, the senior German lager officer, to provide "rations, rest, and hospitalization," citing "these men were exhausted and might die soon." Weinert refused this request, according to Caplan, replying "there was no hospital available and these men were not his responsibility." Later, he agreed "to leave these men in a barn for rest," and, as Caplan noted, face an uncertain fate when their fellow airmen moved on the following day.[402]

The dedicated transportation cited in Caplan's journal afforded only limited assistance to the Hammerstein POWs. Yet, these aptly characterized "sick wagons" provided relief and lifesaving opportunities for hundreds of other weak and feeble airmen. Many of these men waited in long lines that formed early each morning in hope of being assigned a place on one of the wagons–and not march another day. However, securing placement on the wagons was a mixed blessing. The sick men were exposed to cold weather, and some men even developed equally or more serious conditions of frostbite resulting from the extended periods of physical inactivity.

The men who rode the sick wagons during the march were mostly too weak or lame to walk. Moreover, they were frequently carried into the barns at the end of the day by volunteers and placed in the hospital area to rest. Still others stood for hours in the cold rain and waited for what limited rations were available to those in most need of nourishment. Sergeant Stratton Beesley was in the first group who

[401] Caplan, *Domain of Heroes,* 28
[402] Ibid., 29

benefited from Caplan's efforts to establish a field hospital system. Beesley was diagnosed with diphtheria on 19 Feb 1945, and according to Caplan's journal notation, " . . . left at Seltz to be picked up by D-lager."[403] Stratton's primary recollection of this incident was one of "riding on the sick wagon for several days and resting at night in one of the hospital barns."

Later on, when horses were no longer available, other airmen volunteered to form 12-man teams to pull each wagon for as long as they were capable. One volunteer who assisted with this effort was Technical Sergeant Bob Cash. The Oklahoma native had originally departed Stalag Luft IV with his roommate, Ed Dobran, with whom he had shared the initial hardships of the march. Weeks later, Dobran fell ill and was subsequently placed on the sick wagons by Leslie Caplan, who according to Cash, "was concerned with the swelling in [Ed's] throat." More specifically, Caplan was monitoring the "[inflamed] membrane [of] both tonsils."[404] Cash, who had already experienced traumatic loss and serious injury when shot down on 20 June 1944, would not abandon his friend. Rather, the twenty-one-year old radio operator elected to stay with Dobran and assist with hauling the wagon that carried his friend until Ed's health improved and he was again ambulatory.

The momentary halt of the march around Anklam allowed Leslie Caplan to attend to many other airmen held in barns around the surrounding area. Although Caplan and his volunteer medics lacked adequate medications, they nevertheless possessed "a small supply of bandages, tape, aspirin . . . and salves."[405] These items, obtained from medical parcels sent by the International Red Cross, allowed them to treat "infected blisters . . . ugly abscesses . . . frostbite and in some cases, gangrene."[406] While Caplan attended to those afflicted with foot-related problems and the seriously ill, a number of other men cited complaints of aching joints, weight loss, and severe dysentery. These latter reports, while alarming, only served to confirm Caplan's earlier fears that many of the men were now suffering from moderate to severe malnutrition.

---

[403] Caplan, *Domain of Heroes,* 31

[404] Ibid., 60

[405] O'Donnell, *The Evacuation . . .,* 61

[406] Ibid., 61

Caplan's concern for the health of POWs in his care first surfaced prior to the evacuation of Stalag Luft IV where many airmen assigned to C-lager were already exhibiting early signs of malnutrition. This medical condition, which is generally diagnosed by physical examination to assess body weight and composition, in addition to a neurological assessment to detect disorientation, usually develops in stages, and in response to a restrictive or poor diet, infection, and/or excessive loss of nutrients due to heavy perspiration or diarrhea. The basic metabolic response to malnutrition is conservation of energy, wherein stored fats and muscle tissue are used to sustain life. Individuals whose diet lacks proteins, fats, and other nutrients essential to meet energy requirements usually manifest noticeable symptoms of weakness, tiredness, and other pathology, in addition to psychological and social problems. The loss of protein in one's diet also affects the function of the gastrointestinal tract, which limits the body's ability to absorb nutrients, further restricting the function of vital organs, the maintenance of skeletal muscles, and the healing of wounds. Ultimately, extreme malnutrition will lead to deficiency and toxicity in most body systems and result in death from starvation within eight to twelve weeks.*

Caplan attributed the dramatic deterioration in the medical condition of these airmen during the past two weeks to the harsh, physical demands of the forced winter march while inadequately clothed and nourished. He would later calculate that these men received an average of only 770 calories per day throughout the duration of the march, from a limited distribution of a few potatoes, an occasional slice of bread, and through individual efforts to forge for turnips or other root vegetables. These meager rations were occasionally augmented by an additional 600 calories when the men were lucky enough to receive rations from International Red Cross.

This most meager allotment of food was wholly inadequate to maintain one's body weight under normal, much less the extraordinary

---

* Ancel Keys conducted the definitive study of malnutrition and semi-starvation at the University of Minnesota in 1944–45. The initial study, referred to as the "The Minnesota Experiment," consisted of 32 male subjects (increased to 36 in subsequent trials) who were restricted to half of their former food intake for six months. During this period, these subjects lost an average of 25 percent of their original body weight, while all participants exhibited "symptoms of depression, irritability, and general

circumstances of this march. Dietary standards recognized by the US Army during the war recommended that individuals exposed to extreme physical hardships or harsh environmental conditions, as experienced by the transitory airmen, consume an average of 3,800 calories per day to maintain normal body weight. This 3,000 calorie deficiency caused most airmen to loose, at a minimum, one-half to one pound of body weight per day, although larger men such as Don Dorfmeier would have experienced an even greater loss of normal body weight during the first phase of the march.* This conservative estimate of weight loss, averaging between 10–14 pounds per man during the first weeks of the march, is significant when considering most airmen had already lost approximately 10 percent of their normal body weight prior to their evacuation.

The distribution of Red Cross parcels near Anklam enabled the Allied POWs to now trade in earnest with the local civilian population, although such activity was strictly prohibited. In spite of this prohibition, many airmen would either bribe their guards, or risk the consequences and trade soap, chocolate, and cigarettes from their Red Cross rations, along with "watches and rings, anything they [had] . . . for 'brot' or other food stuffs." A 21 February 1945 diary entry of one airman marching with Chuck Hartney noted, "The guys did a land office business [today]. Cards, shaving sticks, gum, coffee . . . for bread, butter [and] liverwurst."

Given the airmen's collective history, it was understandable that they initially feared German civilians. These fears were further aggravated when their guards, on some occasions, preceded the passage of the airmen's column through a village or town by announcing them as "terror fliegers," thus provoking a hostile response. Yet, in less urban settings, the airmen soon learned that not all contact with the civil population would be hostile or negative. Staff Sergeant, and later

---

emotional instability," in addition to "social withdrawal, a narrowing of [personal] interests and difficulty concentrating." Keys' study demonstrated a 20 percent loss of bodyweight was associated with "very serious [social disorder and conflict]."[407]
* A reduction in the body's basal metabolic rate will reduce the amount of calories needed to perform normal physiological processes, which accounts for two-thirds of all energy requirements.

[407] Keys, *The Biology of Human Starvation,* 917

author, Joseph O'Donnell cites an incident reported by John Carr of the 390th Bomb Group, who recalled "[marching] into a little village that had a large water fountain in the middle of the square. We were lined up along the street waiting to get some water [as] the villagers were calling us 'luft gangsters' and even worse names." A woman approached the column, while berating them, only to reveal four loaves of bread concealed in her apron, which she freely distributed to the surprised airmen.[408] Other members of the German civil population were often quite willing, provided the opportunity, to trade with the Allied POWs, exchanging bread and other foodstuffs for American sundries like soap and toilet paper. Sympathetic foreign laborers also provided individual airmen with a turnip or carrot if given an opportunity.

Two other accounts are worth noting, if only to illustrate the fuller spectrum of the airmen's contact with the civilian population. The first incident involved airman Clair L. Miller of the 351st Bomb Group, who managed to convince a German woman to trade two loaves of bread for a "large bar of chocolate Ex-Lax from a Red Cross parcel." Apparently, the woman and her children had "not seen chocolate for years" and were quite amenable to making a trade, and immediately consumed the "whole bar right then." Only later, Miller continued, "would the guards come around looking for the guy who had [traded] the Ex-Lax to [the] German family."[409] The second incident was cited by Leslie Caplan, who noted in a postwar article, "Death March Medic," "some frauleins would give anything–and that means anything–for a chocolate bar," insinuating some of the healthier and more robust airmen in the lager traded for sexual favors.[410]

Following a brief respite, the large assembly of POWs quartered in the vicinity of Anklam was split into three separate columns and marched to different internment camps located within the interior of the German Reich. Two groups, approximately 1,500 men each, headed north toward Stalag Luft I at Berth, on the Baltic coast, while the second faction moved south toward Stalag VIIA at Moosberg. The third and largest group, approximately 3,000 POWs, which included the airmen assigned to C-lager, continued to move westward across northern Germany toward Fallingbostel and Stalag XIB.

---

[408] O'Donnell, *Luftgangsters Marching across Germany,* 37
[409] O'Donnell, *Luftgangsters Marching across Germany,* 24
[410] O'Donnell, *The Evacuation,* 62

The resumption of the halting, southwest trek toward Fallingbostel and the specific direction of movement for this third group, varied among the marching elements of the column. Few airmen, with the possible exception of those who kept personal diaries, could accurately chronicle the specific route or events of their movement, which seemed to be circuitous and nonsensical. Richard W. Burt of the 460th Bomb Group, recalled moving [west] "through Jarmen, Demmin, Malchow, [and] Ludwiglust," a route that was forested and offered some shelter on nights when they were not billeted in large barns. Burt noted that "we would also pass camouflaged airfields, and aircraft that had been pushed back into the trees"[411] for protection against Allied attacks. Once across the Elbe River Burt's group saw more air activity, including being strafed several times by British fighter-bombers.

Don recalled passing tank blocks, constructed of dozens of felled trees cleared from nearby forests. These barricades were erected by driving four vertical poles into the ground, which then formed a slot to hold dozens of trees that had been stripped of their branches and laid horizontally on the road. Most likely, the clearing occupied by the airmen on the night of 14 February, prior to crossing to the Island of Usedom, had been cleared of trees to construct the same type of barricades on the east bank of the Oder. Now, on the other side of the river, the airmen encountered these tank blocks every few kilometers along the roadways and other avenues of approach leading into the Reich. Yet, more impressive than the barricades, was the size and formidable appearance of the German tanks moving toward the Eastern Front in an effort to stop the Russian surge. "These vehicles," Don recalled, " . . . were mammoth, weighing 50–75 tons."*

Airman Gerald Ralston's group rested again on 22 February 1945 after "marching 15 kilometers on very poor roads through the village of Tarnow" and receiving "plenty of spuds . . . soup for one meal [and]

* Following the aborted Ardennes' operation, significant numbers of German forces were transferred to the Eastern Front in an attempt to halt the Russian offensive that began in January 1945. Some 16–18 divisions, with most of their new equipment, to include 1,674 new armored vehicles, were diverted in February 1945 alone. An additional 10 panzer and panzer-grenadier divisions were assembled in Pomerania for a counterattack, which was launched on 16 February 1945.

[411] O'Donnell, *The Pangs of the Thorn,* 133

one third of IRC parcel." The following day, the group resumed their march and moved some 6–8 kilometers before doubling back half that distance. At this point, it started to rain, prompting a mad dash to the nearest barn. There Gerald noted, "A lot of men have bad cases of [diarrhea] and plenty [are] sick . . . passing blood through their bowels, [while others] are coughing and spitting up blood. Some men strayed over the hill to a nearby village to trade for food and were caught . . . beaten with rifle butts, canes, and clubs, also shot at, but no one was seriously hurt."

With the resumption of the march, the number of stragglers increased daily due to the collective influence and debilitating effects of malnutrition, diarrhea, and illnesses. Many POWs were also experiencing a variety of problems with their feet. The primary difficulty was incorrect shoe size. Most airmen had either abandoned their shoes or were blown out of their aircraft without them. Consequently, many airmen in captivity were forced to wear shoes provided by the IRC or YMCA, regardless of fit. This problem alone accounted for much misery and suffering; the airmen walked long distances every day in poorly fitting shoes with socks that were frequently wet and fraying. Such conditions caused painful blisters, which contributed to further difficulty in marching, and many men were only able to continue when supported by other members of their combine. Don cited only one reference of assisting another airman during the march, stating, "I helped carry another [guy] for [the better part of one day] before he waved me on saying, 'It's okay Dorf—you go on. I'll be all right.'" In these instances, failing airmen fell back to join those lagging behind, or possibly to be placed on one of the sick wagons.

Throughout the march, most airmen were forced to move for days at a time with the ever-present pangs of hunger and constant fatigue accompanying the monotonous repetition. In written correspondence, Bob Carr indicated that the airmen in his cohort only "received bread rations six times during the first 30 days of the march, and only allotted one-tenth of a loaf per man." Jack Fischer didn't seem to fare much better in his group, noting he went as long as "four days at one point on the march without having anything to eat."

The focus on food, and the attempt to alleviate one's hunger, became an all-consuming activity that challenged the resourcefulness and character of every airman, as well as the relationships they forged over many months of captivity. Moreover, general alertness and comprehension declined as a direct consequence of starvation. Yet, preoccupation with thoughts of food, although seldom discussed, became obsessive. For Technical Sergeant Jack Browder, such preoccupation had become a daily and ritualistic activity. Once on the road, Browder would completely dissociate from his environment and withdraw into an inner fantasy world where he would repetitively construct, with lavish attention to the smallest detail, his "ideal breakfast of pecan waffles."

The airmen also stole food whenever possible, even though they were " . . . threatened with death if they were caught stealing food from the farmers." Still, the airmen would take advantage of whatever opportunities were at hand. One airman recalled "we ate anything we could beg or steal. We ate raw sugar beets . . . cabbages, potatoes, and grain in any form. These items were seldom available, but when they were we would take what we could."[412] In such circumstances, a "country boy" like Jack Fischer possessed a decided advantage over men like Don Dorfmeier, who was raised in a more urban environment. Elaborating further, Fischer stated, " . . . if you knew what to look for in a barn you could, on occasion, find a hen's nest or get by a guard to milk a cow."

These same skills were also helpful to Technical Sergeant Tony Capone, 95th Bomb Group, who recalled that "the Germans would push you in [a barn], slam the door and it would be pitch dark" as one tried to find a place to bed down. On one occasion his group marched so late into the evening that it interfered with the distribution of the usual day's rations. Rather, a pile of uncooked potatoes was simply dumped on the ground, in the middle of the poorly lit barn, already fouled by the animals that lived there. A chaotic rush ensued to grab what one could and in the process most of the potatoes were ground into the filth of the dirt floor. Those individuals closest to the potatoes managed to secure some food while others simply recognized that it was pointless to join in the fray. Later, while most were asleep, Capone noticed several cows in stalls near the back end of the barn. Quietly, he crawled toward one of the animals, intent on using his experience of milking goats in his youth for his younger sister who was allergic to cow's milk. Once in

---

[412] Caplan, *A Domain of Heroes*, 209

position, Capone was able to milk the cow, quenching both his thirst and securing some nourishment for his evening meal.

Less resourceful men were forced to conserve whatever rations they received from the Germans or shared among themselves. In these circumstances, the hoarding of food, or an inequitable division of rations with other members of one's combine, would unleash a torrent of bad feelings and ill will. One occurrence fractured the close relationship between Frank Dyer and Chuck Hartney, who parted company on the march over some dispute related to how they rationed their food. This rupture occurred in spite of their earlier joint effort to escape from the compound at St. Wendel and sharing the same room for the past six months prior to the evacuation of Stalag Luft IV. Fortunately, the two men were able to reconcile their resentment and reestablish their relationship after the war.

As the Allied POWs continued to march into the interior of a collapsing Third Reich, humanitarian organizations were monitoring with great concern the evacuation of German-held POWs from Eastern Europe. Field delegates representing the International Red Cross and the YMCA were shocked by the hardships of the evacuations and took personal risks to persuade German officials to adhere to the accords of the Geneva Convention's protection of prisoners of war. The same delegates further noted the plight of these POWs in field reports sent to the Red Cross in Bern, Switzerland, which then enabled the American Legation in Geneva to apprise the United States government of the status of their interned airmen.

On 28 February 1945, the State Department in Washington, D.C. received a telegram from the IRC in Bern, Switzerland identifying the configuration, axis of march, and general physical condition of three groups of allied and American POWs marching into central Germany. "The largest and southern most group . . . [which] included 25,000 Americans, [had moved] through the Sudetenland of Czechoslovakia, where they assembled at Teplitz Schonau and [then later] moved to Stuttgart, Nüremberg, and Munich. This group . . . suffered particularly because it [had] been repeatedly strafed by Allied planes, [caught] in bad weather and . . . crossed the Czech mountains with little food."[413]

---

[413] O'Donnell, *A History of Stalag Luft IV,* 22

A central group of "some 60,000 prisoners [had moved] west in the direction of Leipzig, Berlin, and Dresden . . . although 300 severely wounded American officers interned at Stalag Luft III were abandoned in the camp hospital." The condition of the other POWs on the road was thought to have been less severe as a result of "relatively good [weather] conditions." Moreover, a supply of approximately 100 tons of food parcels was established at Luckenwalde for later distribution.[414]

A northern group of approximately 100,000 POWs, which included the airmen evacuated from Stalag Luft IV, was identified as having moved "along the northern coast to the west [toward] the region of Hamburg, Bremen, and Lübeck . After making a severe forced march across Pomerania, this group was allowed to rest for several days in the vicinity of Anklam, New Brandenburg, Deumin and Swinemünde." The Bern telegram further cited the establishment of a storehouse in Northern Germany at NeuBrandenburg where 60 tons of food parcels were shipped for later distribution to the POWs as they continued their westward march. However, an agent for the Red Cross reported that local units of the German Volksstrum were generally confiscating the IRC food parcels from warehouses . . . and distributing these rations to the local populace prior to issuing them to the Allied POWs. "The prisoners, German officers and guards" were, according to the American Litigation, "eating the same rations which [required] selling everything they have in order to obtain food but with little success. Eighty percent of [these airmen] were also cited as suffering from dysentery."[415]

The Bern wire clearly identified the northern group of POWs as experiencing the greatest hardship of the three columns moving into the German homeland. On 1 March 1945, some three weeks after the evacuation of Stalag Luft IV, with the physical strength and emotional stamina of most airmen eroding, strong winds, followed by several days of snowstorms, engulfed the POWs moving toward Fallingbostel. "March," according to John Anderson, "roared in like a lion." The following day, Anderson and his group marched another 28 kilometers in "fierce winds and constant snow."

The next morning, Anderson, who was suffering with chronic diarrhea and aching feet, was finding it "difficult to keep going" and

[414] Ibid., 22
[415] O'Donnell, *A History of Stalag Luft IV*, 22

reported to morning sick call along with 30 other men who were similarly exhausted. There, Caplan, characterized as "doing his best to keep everyone going," determined that Anderson's condition warranted placement on the sick wagon. However, John's assignment required that Caplan remove a man suffering from rheumatoid arthritis. His decision, according to Anderson, is one "I have regretted the rest of my life," fearing he had caused the other man considerable pain in having to walk. In retrospect, John's acquiescence to Caplan's intervention was also the worse possible course of action for the ailing airman. During transit, Anderson's feet froze from lack of movement and circulation; at the end of the day "[he] could hardly walk."

Over the next couple of days, Anderson's condition continued to deteriorate, requiring assignment to the hospital group supervised by Caplan and his cadre of volunteer medics. By his own admission, John was "getting weaker [every day] . . . and had to be helped on and off the wagon." He could no longer stand on his feet, much less walk. On 10 March 1945, Anderson was identified as one of 25 airmen pending transfer to a stationary hospital near Beckendorf. Yet, John preferred to ride the sick wagon and expose himself to the cold harsh March winds for another day, rather than being abandoned in a barn as an unknown person. After a day's rest at another location, which included substantial nourishment of eggs, potatoes, and salmon from an IRC parcel, Anderson felt strong enough to walk again without his pack. However, he could not finish the last three kilometers of the day's march. By the end of the week, John's diarrhea had subsided, yet his "frostbitten feet were beginning to turn black." More alarmingly, Anderson's "feet were so bad," that Caplan was "considering amputation" yet such a procedure was not possible . . . he possessed only a razor blade for surgical operations. Eventually, the incapacitated Anderson, along with 75 other airmen under the care of medic, Warren Stevens, was transferred from Caplan's mobile field hospital to a barn hospital at Nebbenstadt.

In spite of Anderson's poor prognosis, he would not regret his decision to remain with Caplan, whom he credits with saving his life. The lager's flight surgeon not only worked tirelessly to secure extra food for the men in his hospital, but also provided spiritual care, conveyed through his compassion, which inspired hope. This attentiveness alone was therapeutic, conveying a powerful message that each individual life had meaning and value. It is, therefore, no exaggeration to credit this exceptionally spiritual man as singularly responsible for saving the lives of hundreds of airmen–men who would have died without his medical intervention or, more significantly, his inspiration to persevere.

One of many individuals inspired by Caplan's compassion was George Guderley. The Illinois radio operator had volunteered to attend to the sick, although he himself was ill and under Caplan's care. Guderley's motivation was influenced, in part, by his emotional connection and concern for Staff Sergeant Wayland Buchholz, the younger brother of a close high school friend, also part of Caplan's sick party. Guderley had discovered Wayland's presence at Stalag Luft IV while making the rounds in the lager to ask if anyone was from Chicago. Now, anxious that Buchholz and others in the mobile hospital might not survive without proper nourishment, the assertive airman took advantage of an opportunity, although at great personal risk, to steal a can of cream left unattended by a local farmer.

The stolen cream was presented to Caplan with instructions to distribute the milk as he saw fit, as long as Wayland had the first opportunity to drink the rich, life-sustaining emulsion. Caplan readily agreed, elated to provide for his men. One of these individuals was John Anderson, who noted in his diary, "received a spoonful of milk from a bottle, as did others in the sick group." However, Guderley's selfless act of generosity almost cost him his life. After the cream had been consumed and the can hidden, irate guards found Guderley and accused him of stealing property of the Third Reich, a crime for which he could be shot.* Yet, Guderley, who had successfully evaded capture for eight days prior to being apprehended, refused to panic or be intimidated. While standing at a very respectful position of attention, the young staff sergeant feigned ignorance of all accusations and denied complicity in any theft until the guards left in frustration, bested by the performance of this spirited and audacious airman.

---

* Rationing in Germany and subsequent legislation prohibiting hoarding started with the invasion of Poland in 1939. Almost immediately, cream, chocolates, and coffee disappeared prior to more severe cuts in other rations by late 1941. In addition to looting, other capital offensives warranting a death sentence included espionage, sabotage and subversion.

Allied airmen March 1945   Pegasus Archive

Staff Sergeant Karl Haeuser was another airman on the road to
Fallingbostel who was significantly affected by the demands of the
march. Earlier in the month, he had become so hungry he traded his
prized " . . . [gold Gruen Curvex] watch, [a gift] his parents had given
him when he graduated from high school," for food. Shortly after, he
started to suffer from dysentery. Then, an event happened several days
later, "in mid-March" that shocked both Haeuser and the other men of
his group. "A guy dropped out of line one day," Karl recalled, "who I
hardly knew, and therefore did not feel compelled to stop to lend any
assistance." Moments later, after Karl and the other members of his
unit moved on, "we heard a shot [and] . . . looked at each other [in
surprise]." Their disbelief was all the more complete "when the guard
came walking back by himself, and we were shocked." The incident
served to remind Haeuser and the other airmen that the Germans really
where "their enemy," who, regardless of age or similarity between
cultures, would kill you with indifference. This awareness became all
the more pronounced when, this scenario was "repeated another twenty
or more times . . . in that last month" of the march. "Sometimes," Karl
continued, "the POW could recoup and catch up, sometimes not."[416]

Karl Haeuser's account of airmen being shot on the march has been
corroborated by other participants. Clarence Bower, 96th Bomb Group,

---

[416] Phillips, "The Long March." *Destination Discovery* 9.11 (Feb 1994) : 37

reported similar incidents of shootings during the later phase of the march. More specifically, Bower stated, "We had a lot of [men] who fell behind for one reason or another, then a guard would disappear . . . we [then] heard a shot and a few minutes later you would see the guard . . . back up with the group so you knew the prisoner was laying in the timber somewhere." Yet, Bower, who was featured in the documentary film, *Behind the Wire*, also stated that he witnessed POWs being shot one morning as the airmen in his group were forming for another day's march. "We spent one night at a big barn," Bower explained, "and in the morning not all of the prisoners fell out for the mandatory formation and head count. Some men remained in the barn, hiding. The German's sent their dogs in to flush out the other men, yet some men still would not come. "So," Bower alleged, they " . . . set the barn on fire then shot the remaining airmen as they fled out of the burning structure."[417]

---

[417] *Behind the Wire*, Al Zimmerman, video, Eighth AF Historic Site, 1994

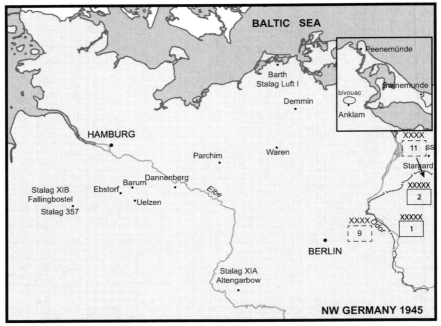

The March to Fallingbostel   Author's collection

By late February 1945, approximately 6,000 POWs from Stalag Luft IV had crossed to the German mainland and occupied temporary bivouac sites north of Anklam. Days later, these wanting airmen were separated into three elements and marched to different camps. Two contingents of 1,500 men each were sent north to Stalag Luft I and south to Stalag VIIA at Moosburg. The larger column of over 3,000 airmen, including the majority of men assigned to C-lager, proceeded to move west–through Demmin, Parchim, and Ebstorf–toward Stalag XIB at Fallingbostel.

16

FALLINGBOSTEL

By mid-March 1945, the American and British airmen who evacuated Stalag Luft IV, some 40 days earlier, had marched approximately 375–400 kilometers across northern Germany. This arduous trek, according to Flight Surgeon Leslie Caplan, was marked by a "trail of slime" as the extended column moved toward their final destination, Fallingbostel. Twenty-eight-year-old airman, Tom Farrow, characterized the disposition and mood of the men in his group, at that time, as having sunk to "our lowest ebb."[418] Farrow noted, "In spite of the guards' urging we could only move at a slow walk. There was little conversation [as our combine] struggle[d] to keep up with the rest of the group. We were eating only rotten potatoes and dehydrated sugar beets, which were used mainly for cattle feed." Similar descriptions of desperation were also noted by Staff Sergeant Gerald Ralston in his 16 March 1945 diary entry, " . . . food is very scarce. The men are digging in garbage for spuds or onions . . . just anything at all to eat."

The pervasive monotony of the march, characterized by starvation and despair, continued unabated for days on end. Yet, over the next two weeks the POWs experienced some improvement in the weather, and enjoyed respites of longer duration before moving to new locations. These favorable developments allowed the airmen to attend more frequently to their personal hygiene and care for sores and blistered feet. They could also disrobe more often to remove lice from their bodies and seams of their clothing. One airman marching with Frank Dyer's group noted these developments in his 22 March 1945 entry: "[It] was a beautiful day for walking anywhere but where we have to walk. [The] sun shone all day. Went 22 kilos . . . through Danneberg today on our way here. What beautiful loaves of bread in that town. Had [plenty] of spuds and a cup of coffee for chow. Couple of Polish women did most of the cooking."

The following day, Dyer's group "Laid (sic) over" and basked in

---

[418] O'Donnell, *Luftgangsters Marching Across Germany*, 32

the morning sun that was "out bright and early . . . after consuming Jerry brew (German coffee) and soup for breakfast." Later, the same diarist continued, he had "washed his feet and only pair of socks," which improved his mood, noting, "Feel better. Got a fifth of a loaf of bread . . . but no Red [Cross parcel]." Early the next morning Dyer's group was off again. "Supposed to march another 18 kilos. [Yet] T. J.'s boys passed us on the road and got our spot for the night." This forced the group to press on for an additional six kilometers to find another barn and establish their evening bivouac in Barum. The next day, Palm Sunday, the good weather continued to hold for "another fine day." Monday morning, the airmen pushed on another 16 kilometers, only to later discover "we got the shaft [on the bread ration] yesterday. Better get Red [Cross parcels later] or we'll 'have had it.'" Yet, the distribution of paltry rations at the end of the next day forced Dyer to trade "a ring for one seven pound loaf of bread, some sorghum, and sugar." The following morning the group rested for a second day. Later that afternoon, C-lager's Man of Confidence, Francis Troy, visited the airmen to circulate a roster, and to inform them that they would "move out on train from here . . . probably won't get our parcels until we leave."

Two days later, 28 March 1945, most of the estimated 3,000 Allied airmen concentrated in the vicinity of Barum and other small villages 65–70 kilometers southeast of Hamburg, were aroused earlier than usual from their fitful sleep. Dyer's group, in particular, was hurriedly assembled and force-marched nine kilometers to the rail station at Ebstorf. En route, anxious guards continually prodded the airmen to move faster with exhortations and promises of rations. Yet, to no one's surprise and everyone's disappointment, the "promised Red [Cross] parcels at the station failed to materialize." Rather, only a meager bread ration was issued later that day.

Following the distribution of a small, partial loaf of bread to each man, Don and a majority of the men at Ebstorf were ordered into the boxcars already positioned at the town's rail station. Once loaded, the airmen found themselves crowded "60 men or more to a car," then left stranded in the rail yard for the next 20 hours, without water, ventilation, or buckets for their sanitary needs."[419] Airman Dick Eagles observed the initial anxiety of the men in his car, noting, "While sitting here . . . waiting to move, I have studied some of the fellows. Things are getting really desperate [as] the [men] are already trading [their] bread for [cigarettes]. With the little food we get [I am surprised] these guys think they can't go one day without smoking. I've seen rings, watches and yes, wedding [bands] trade[d] for bread. I'm glad I have no jewelry with me or maybe I would be tempted also, even though I am starving."[420] Staff Sergeant Joseph O'Donnell recalled other equally pragmatic concerns, noting he was "confined with 64 other POWs, all of [whom] had chronic dysentery and the only [manner] to relieve ourselves was [through] a small opening in the boxcar floor."[421]

Those men not loaded on the train at Ebstorf were marched another 6–10 kilometers farther south to Uelzen and ordered on to waiting boxcars with other airmen who had arrived earlier that morning. One of these men was Gerald Ralston, who cited similar conditions in his car as those noted at Ebstorf. Ralston recalled, "We have no water or ventilation and [much] dysentery! We took turns digging a [six inch] hole in the floor to relieve ourselves. The only tools we had were our table knives to cut through [thick] oak." Other groups of airmen continued to arrive at Uelzen later that same day. One airmen recalled, "We started to walk south in the late afternoon. After dark we could see a glow in the sky to the west and could hear occasional rumbles of [artillery]. Many German troops were on the road. We walked 12 [kilometers] to Uelzen where we were locked in boxcars." Later, their train "pulled out during the night" and proceeded to travel south for a two-day transit to Stalag XIA at Altengrabow.[422]

The prolonged confinement of the other airmen left in the boxcars at Ebstorf reactivated memories of earlier traumas associated with their transits from Heydekrug and St. Wendel. This was most pronounced for Staff Sergeant Don Dorfmeier and the men evacuated from St. Wendel who spent five days in the infamous "40/8" rail cars traveling 850 kilometers across Germany to Stalag Luft IV the previous September. Yet, unlike their earlier transit, the airmen crowded in the stationary boxcars at Ebstorf were no longer the healthy, confident men who openly sang to express their camaraderie, defiant spirit, and unwavering faith in their survival. The stress and hardships of the past

[420] Ibid., 118

[421] O'Donnell, *Luftgangsters Marching Across Germany,* Overview

[422] O'Donnell, *The Pang of the Thorn,* 103

six months, including the most recent deprivations of the march, had diminished their physical health, psychological resiliency, and social cooperation. The airmen now stranded in the rail yard were physically sick, emotionally drained, and extremely fearful in their present circumstances. Airmen Ralph Mattera later recalled this incident of confinement as "the ultimate dehumanizing experience [of the entire march]."

The psychological anguish experienced by the airmen crowded in these box cars was further aggravated by the "considerable aerial activity in the area at the time." Most men knew they were vulnerable to being strafed and killed by Allied aircraft when herded into unmarked cars. Joseph O'Donnell and others even believed the Germans intentionally repositioned the wagons in the rail yard to attract and encourage such attacks from the air.[423] John Anderson recalled his fear of being attacked during this prolonged confinement as "traumatic." Anderson, who had been placed in a slightly less-crowded boxcar specifically designated for the sick and lame, was also shocked by the hysterical and unrestrained behavior of his fellow airmen.* "The [POWs] in my car became more like animals than men," John would later recall, and then concluded, "This was the worst experience of my life."

This harsh, callous treatment of these men was later characterized as "unnecessary suffering," according to Flight Surgeon Leslie Caplan. In a sworn deposition following the war, Caplan confirmed that they "were provided little to no water while locked in the boxcars, although potable water was readily available in the rail yard."[424] Equally offensive, none of the airmen were let out of their confinement to relieve themselves, which caused "conditions in the boxcars [to become] unbearable . . . from the stench of POWs racked with dysentery, who had to urinate and defecate on the boxcar floor."[425]

* Multiple documented accounts cite numerous instances of semi-starved POWs exhibiting "abnormally strong [emotional] reactions" to situational stresses. These finding were later replicated in Keys study on malnutrition, linking starvation with exhibited symptoms of depression, irritability, "nervousness" (anxiety) and general emotional instability.[426]

[423] O'Donnell, *Luftgangsters Marching Across Germany*, Overview.
[424] O'Donnell, *The Evacuation . . .* , 22
[425] O'Donnell, *Luftgangsters Marching Across Germany,* 27
[426] Keys, *The Biology of Starvation*, 907

The aggravated tension among the confined airmen abated somewhat around midnight on 30 March 1945. Departing Ebstorf, an estimated 35 rail wagons carrying Staff Sergeant Don Dorfmeier and approximately 2,000 other POWs, started slowly moving southwest 50 kilometers to Fallingbostel. This group represented one-third of the 6,800–7,000 airmen who had originally marched out of Stalag Luft IV in early February 1945. All entrained hoped they would soon arrive at their final destination to await liberation from the approaching Allied armies, now advancing through the Rhineland. One airman, who chronicled their halting journey, noted, "[We] traveled off and on during the night, sweating out two air raids, one in the morning and one in the yard." Tom Farrow described the 12-hour rail transit from Ebstorf to Fallingbostel, recalling, "On Thursday evening we began moving slowly through the night, stopping Good Friday morning. The doors were opened and everyone struggled out, gulping fresh air. I never knew completely about [the] casualties of the trip. Everyone in our car made it, but at least two in the next car died."[427]

Once off-loaded, the stiff and disoriented airmen, who had been confined for 33 hours, were organized into a loose formation and marched the short distance from the rail station at Fallingbostel to their new camp. The compound, designated as Stalag XIB, originally housed workers who constructed troop barracks when the site was first established as part of a larger training center to support the expansion of the German Wehrmacht in 1935. Four years later, these quarters were designated as a "working camp" for Polish POWs who labored in the surrounding community. Shortly thereafter, the facility expanded with the arrival of Dutch, French, and Russian POWs following German triumphs in Western Europe and Belorussia in 1941–1942. Two years later, the stammlager had become an "international camp," which occupied a "vast area of ground, holding some 96,000 POWs of various nationalities."[428]

As the airmen approached the new compound, they recognized familiar smells of burning wood and coal emanating from the camp, which stimulated memories of warmth and comfort. With much anticipation, this exhausted group of airmen, who had endured great hardship during the past seven weeks, expected to receive shelter and

---

[427] Ibid., 32
[428] O'Donnell, *Luftgangsters Marching Across Germany*, 77

rations in the new camp. Sadly, such expectations created one of the greatest ironies of the march. The new arrivals, eager to get into this permanent camp, confronted thousands of other prisoners, already interned in the crowded compound, who were just as anxious to escape their squalid confinement. Still, Staff Sergeant Don Dorfmeier and the majority of the men in his column were initially thankful to have arrived at their terminal destination.

Airmen not interned at Fallingbostel were marched a short distance to Stalag 357, a nearby compound at Orbke. This camp had been relocated from Poland in summer 1944 following the German evacuation of Eastern Europe.[429] The camp was opened two months later to alleviate the overcrowding at XIB. It primarily held Allied aircrew and soldiers of the US Army. Many of these prisoners had recently been taken captive during the German Ardennes Offensive, although "a large contingent of [Poles] captured during the Warsaw Uprisings . . . arrive[d] shortly afterward."

Initially this camp was "well-run." However, tension between the airmen and soldiers created much dissension. Both groups held differing views about their respective roles as enemy POWs. The airmen of the US Army Air Force and British RAF were members of highly disciplined services, with great espirit de corps, and predisposed to causing the Germans as much trouble as possible. Conversely, the soldiers of the Army Ground Forces were more passive, possibly due to their abusive treatment following capture, and " . . . wanted as little trouble as possible." This conflict was resolved through a popular vote in January 1945. RAF Sergeant James Deans was elected as the compound's Man of Confidence, which established his authority and a unified policy of active resistance in the camp.

Sergeant Deans, a 30-year-old RAF navigator shot down on 10 September 1940, had been held in four different camps during his five years of captivity. A natural leader, Deans was a legendary figure responsible for organizing "a highly secret group of POWs while interned at Stalags I, III, and VI, prior to arriving at Stalag 357. Collectively, these specially trained POWs relayed vital information to British Intelligence, M-19, through a system of coded messages

---

[429] Ibid., 77

inserted into prisoners' written correspondence."[430] Dean's leadership was exceptionally valuable at 357. By February 1945, both XIB and 357 "were in a deplorable state, lacking food and medical supplies." Excessive overcrowding during the last year of the war had overwhelmed the infrastructure of the German armed forces, which could no longer care adequately for their many prisoners. This became increasingly apparent as more camps were being evacuated from Eastern Europe and thousands of "new POWs were arriving [almost daily], many after long forced marches."[431]

Once the airmen of C-lager were interned inside the two compounds, they soon realized their hope for permanent shelter and regular rations were unfounded, as neither was available. Rather, most, such as the men in Don's group at Stalag XIB, were assigned to large open tents, with only a light scattering of straw as ground cover to "shelter" a hundred men each. Still, one philosophical individual was thankful he "at least [could] stretch out more than in that [boxcar]." Airman Clair L. Miller recalled his good fortune to have been assigned to a barrack where he could sleep.[432] Only later that evening would the new arrivals receive "a little soup and Jerry coffee for an evening meal," which offered no more nourishment than the rations they received on the road.[433] For other men, survival was less dependent upon food than rest and medical treatment, regardless of how rudimentary the level of care. John Anderson, who could hardly walk without assistance, was especially appreciative that he and a number of other sick and lame prisoners in his group were admitted to the camp's hospital, only a brief march from the rail station. Yet, the camp's lazaret was overcrowded with an estimated 600 patients, many of whom were dying from starvation at the rate of ten a day.[434]

The initial excitement and optimism of the recently arrived airmen contrasted sharply with the recoil with which they were greeted by other nationalities in the camp. Understandably, the stench alone of several thousand unwashed and dysenteric airmen in uniforms repeatedly fouled during the past seven weeks on the road, would have been

---

[430] O'Donnell, *Luftgangsters Marching Across Germany*, 77
[431] O'Donnell, *The Pangs of the Rose*, 77
[432] O'Donnell, *Luftgangsters Marching Across Germany*, 19
[433] Ibid., 19
[434] Caplan, *Domain of Heroes*, 52

repulsive and offensive under any circumstances. Nevertheless, the sneering disdain exhibited by several French POWs in the compound, dining on Red Cross rations supplied by the Unites States, was readily noticeable and infuriating to Ralph Mattera and others.[435]

The airmen were equally appalled by the deplorable conditions in the camps. Most were shocked by the staggering number of prisoners, in particular the "tens of thousands of men from all nationalities and [cultures]" who were interned at Stalag XIB. Moreover, both camps were administered by the more austere German Army, as opposed to the fraternal Luftwaffe. These conditions alone created a different camp culture from what the airmen experienced at Stalag Luft IV. Noticeably absent was a sense of order, camaraderie, and a willingness to share with others. These conditions, along with inadequate quarters and limited rations, were extremely disheartening, causing one airman to comment, "What a hole we've come to. No grub in sight . . . I'm so disgusted."

Staff Sergeant Don Dorfmeier was similarly shocked by the camp conditions at Fallingbostel, although he did not state this directly when recounting his march experiences. Rather, the tone and quality of his voice changed noticeably when describing the appalling state of the camp. His recollection seemed to have elicited an intense emotional insight; an epiphany regarding the magnitude of the worldwide effort and enormous personal suffering required to defeat Adolph Hitler and a militarized German nation.

Out of necessity, the dispirited and apprehensive airmen were forced to adopt a more pragmatic, self-serving orientation to survive in such an environment, "living side by side with Russians, Poles, Serbs, Greeks, Czechs, and Italian prisoners, all representing different values and attitudes, amid crowded and filthy conditions." Years later, Joseph O'Donnell recalled his reaction to the shocking conditions in the camp. "Survival at Stalag XIB became increasingly difficult. The Red Cross parcels were [simply not available], which meant that we were totally dependent on the inconsistent rations [provided by the Germans]."[436] Food was available for those prisoners who were considered permanently assigned to the new camp, but not for the transient airmen.

---

[435] O'Donnell, *Luftgangsters Marching Across Germany,* 27
[436] O'Donnell, *The Evacuation . . . ,* 22

"The only means of survival was every man for himself," O'Donnell continued, acknowledging that his hunger forced him to submit " . . . to the shameful act of scavenging for scraps of food thrown away by other men." More specifically, Joe admitted to "Following Russian POWs around the camp, picking up [and eating] . . . discarded kohlrabi skins."

To retrieve his sense of self-respect, O'Donnell sold his watch for food. The hungry airman recalled, "The Russian POWs were [sent] on daily work details outside the camp, and were in a position to barter with the local citizens." Their access to food enabled O'Donnell, with the assistance of a member of his combine who acted as an interpreter, to exchange his watch for seven loaves of black bread. He immediately ate one of the loaves to satisfy his intense hunger. The other six loaves provided a means with which to potentially barter for other commodities at a later date. However, fate would intervene shortly, and Joe would not be able to fully capitalize on his earlier trade.[437]

Easter Sunday dawned on 1 April 1945 and most of the POWs awoke having dreamed of their families and baskets of food filled with "ham, kielbasa, and eggs." Many of these men believed the war would end soon and that they would be home shortly to satiate their fantasies. Yet, the only food distributed to most airmen that day consisted of a mere "quarter of a Red Cross parcel," in addition to "three spuds, rutabaga soup, [and] Jerry brew. [It] wasn't much," according to one diarist, "but we ate like kings. Seems as if it doesn't take much to satisfy a man here." Other men, after almost eight weeks of limited rations, were starting to pass out during roll-call formations, lacking the stamina to stand for any prolonged period in the warm sun of an early spring. On these occasions, the weak and unsteady airmen were usually taken to the hospital where, at best, they would receive a few vitamin pills and be allowed to rest for a while.

Although the airmen received only limited rations following their arrival at Fallingbostel, they were deloused and allowed a brief shower several days later. For many men, the shower would be their first opportunity to bathe in months. Yet, they were highly suspicious and fearful of the German's true intent when they were marched out of their compound to a small wooden building located in an open clearing. The airmen's apprehension was based on earlier rumors, circulating at

---

[437] O'Donnell, *The Evacuation . . .* , 23

Stalag Luft IV, that the Germans were exterminating various ethnic groups, and that they might experience a similar fate. Arriving at the . . . clearing, the airmen were "commanded to strip down, balls-naked, and told our clothes would be deloused [while] we were able to take a hot shower with soap."[438] Yet, the suspicious and resistant airmen only allowed 12 men to initially enter the showers as a precaution to prevent the entire group from being murdered.

The airmen's fear at the shower point was traumatic enough for some men, such as Jack Fischer, to have reacted similarly to their early experiences at Stalag Luft IV. Don Dorfmeier's recollection of the incident was typical of his self-depreciating humor, choosing to characterize his reaction and the reaction of others as "humorous . . . all laughing at each other because of how skinny we all were." Others focused on the "black and blue" coloration on the bodies of some men "from the bites of lice and fleas." The experience at the shower facility was noted by other men as an event of only secondary significance compared to the limited rations they received later that evening. One diarist noted, after bathing and returning to his camp "around 1000 at night," he received "four small spuds and cold grass soup for dinner" and glad for it because "it was the only thing I ate all day."

As the Allied airmen were adjusting to the routine and demands of their new camps, American and British armies were continuing their advance into central Germany. Two weeks earlier, American forces seized the intact Ludendorf Bridge at Remagen. This fortuitous event presented an opportunity for Allied forces to cross the Rhine "nearly two months earlier than anyone had anticipated." However, General Eisenhower and his staff needed additional time before they were able to assemble the necessary logistical support and landing craft to exploit this tactical advantage. Once across this last defensive barrier, the American First and Ninth armies maneuvered to surround the Ruhr and some 350,000 German soldiers defending the nation's heavy industry in the region. The encirclement was finally completed with the capture of Lippstadt on 4 April 1945. Allied forces were now just 162 kilometers southwest of Fallingbostel. North of Lippstadt, the British Second and Canadian First armies moved toward the northern open water ports of Bremerhaven and Hamburg. Further south, General George Patton's Third Army was dashing through the southern regions of the country

---

[438] O'Donnell, *The Evacuation . . .* , 60

at the rate of "more than [48 kilometers] a day."[439] Rumors of the rapid Allied advances in the West and Soviet preparations for a final assault on Berlin now started to circulate in Stalag XIB and 357 on a daily basis. One rumor related to these recent developments was captured by an airman in early April 1945, noting, "[the] Russians–Yanks are 100 kilos away, should be here in five or six days."

The German authorities responded to the continuing advance of the British Second Army toward Fallingbostel by initiating an evacuation of both compounds. Hurriedly, columns of a thousand men or more moved out of these camps, and back toward the Elbe River. Only the sick and lame were to be left behind. For the newly arrived American and British POWs from Stalag Luft IV, the speculation and threat of a resumption of the march was beyond comprehension. Tempers flared when on 5 April 1945 "a roster was circulated . . . [to identify] men unfit to march," raising the prospect of yet another evacuation. Such contemplation caused one diarist to note, "If we hit the road again, I doubt that I will last long. Why in the hell don't these [Germans] quit. The bastards are beaten, [they] don't have a damn thing left and [yet] they're still hanging on. I would admire this in anyone else, but I hope [we] kill every goddamn one of them."*

Germany's continued willingness to fight at this late stage in the war was attributable to several explanations. In November 1944, Adolph Hitler delivered a major speech in which he threatened that "capitulation means annihilation." In this address, the German Fuhrer warned that "if the Bolshevists won, the fate of the German people was destruction, rape, and slavery."[440] This theme was further exploited by Joseph Goebbels' repeated reference to the "atrocities at Nemmersdorf, where soldiers of the Red Army had captured an East Prussian village the previous autumn and raped and murdered its inhabitants."[441] Goebbels was also very effective in exploiting the leaked details of the

---

* The American soldier, according to author, John Laffin, "hated the Germans with bitterness more savage than that held for the Japanese,"[442] resulting in multiple atrocities against unarmed German soldiers during the closing months of the war.

[439] Korda, *Ike, An American Hero*, 563–4
[440] Beevor, *The Fall of Berlin*, p. xxxiii–xxxiv
[441] Ibid., 4
[442] Laffin, *Americans in Battle*, 157

Morgenthau Plan, sponsored by the United States, "to strip the country of all its industrial capacity and reduce the economy of the country to one of a 'pastoral state.'" According to Franklin Roosevelt, the plan was intended "to castrate the German people" and Goebbels effectively used this threat to strengthen the resolve of the country to continue the war against the United States and England.

While the German population was manipulated by fear and threats, German soldiers were also threatened with "execution for anyone who deserted or retreated without orders."[443] Threats alone, however, were insufficient to stop the panic and collapse that enveloped East Prussia shortly after the start of the Soviet Winter Offensive in January 1945. Panic in Danzig and elsewhere, caused units of the SS to seize "stragglers at random and [hang] them from trees as deserters."[444] Weeks later, on 9 March 1945, Hitler signed an order establishing the authority of special, highly mobile courts to try and execute soldiers who became separated from their units, although this order only formalized a policy that had already been implemented months earlier. Ultimately, this practice would become more pronounced over the entire Eastern Front, according to Soviet sources, who claimed that "25,000 soldiers and officers [of the Wehrmacht] were summarily executed for cowardice in 1945."[445] Still, threats and executions alone could only account for part of the country's willingness to continue the war. A more accurate explanation for the continued resistance that captures the essence of the national character, at this late stage of the war, might be best summarized by one German officer who stated, "We simply fought on because no one told us otherwise."[446]

Some airmen interned at Fallingbostel gave in to despair as they contemplated another evacuation, others like Staff Sergeant George Guderley, obstinately refused to even consider the possibility of going back on the road. Guderley also had the good fortune of being informed of the pending departure during a chance encounter with an older German guard who had befriended him at Stalag Luft IV. The paternal guard further suggested Guderley might find momentary refuge in another section of the compound reserved for "the untermenschen of

---

[443] Ibid., 11–12
[444] Ibid., 120
[445] Ibid., 247
[446] Beevor, *The Fall of Berlin,* 259

all nationalities who were sick and dying at the rate of 40 per day." Guderley responded to this forewarning by enlisting the cooperation of twenty other like-minded airmen who also preferred to remain in the camp. These individuals formed a mock detail, with the aid of "40 rusty pails" to further their deception. Guderley then proceeded to march his squad of airmen out of the compound, in column formation, while counting cadence in the best military tradition. Although initially challenged by a gate sentry, Guderley invoked the authority of a much-feared German Oberfeldwebel to explain their assignment, which sufficiently intimidated the attending sentry to present arms and allow the mock detail to pass out of the compound without incident.

The following day, the airmen's worst fears were realized when Staff Sergeant Francis Troy and Flight Surgeon Leslie Caplan were forced, with only a few hours notice, to assemble their contingent of airmen from Stalag Luft IV, and evacuate the two camps. The notification was so abrupt that Caplan scarcely had enough time to identify those individuals too ill or lame to walk, which could have created a significant, life-threatening problem for those who were truly sick. Hundreds of airmen, including John Anderson, and more recently, Chuck Hartney, whose leg had swelled unexpectedly two days earlier, were hopeful of liberation. German authorities intended to challenge the validity of those claiming to be truly sick, warning that "every tenth man found to be malingering would be shot." However, no doctor ever showed up to examine these men, and the Germans never followed through with their threat.

As the airmen in the compound were reacting to these emerging developments, Staff Sergeant Dorfmeier recalled several alarming rumors that were circulating throughout the camp in the days prior to evacuation. The most disturbing rumor speculated, "Hitler would fight to the last man and that all prisoners of war would be shot before [Germany] would surrender." The validity of this and other rumors were later acknowledged to have merit based on investigations and testimony obtained after the war. Authorities in the United States were certainly aware of the precarious circumstances of the American POWs in Germany, and were of the opinion that many would perish or be executed during the closing months of hostilities. In February 1945, Mr. Binder, a delegate representing the Protecting Powers, had warned "[Americans] who had loved ones held in German captivity to expect the worst." Several months later, the president of the International Committee of the Red Cross, Mr. Carl Burckhardt, released a written statement as a supplement to the IRC's June 1945 *Prisoners of War Bulletin.* In this statement, Burckhardt cited a late March 1945 order by Adolph Hitler "to execute all American and British airmen held captive in Germany." Hitler's motivation for this order was further cited as "revenge for the bombing of German cities."[447] Yet, the airmen assembling to march out of Stalag XIB and 357 didn't need any official acknowledgment to validate their fears about the future. Their exposure to the disarray within the camp and beyond was sufficient to alert them to the unprecedented dangers they would face once again out on the road.

The group of airmen hurriedly assembled by Troy and Caplan consisted of approximately 1,500 of the 2,000 Allied POWs that had arrived the previous week. Stunned and disheartened by the prospects of another evacuation, the dispirited airmen stood in the rain for hours as a result of confusion and multiple delays associated with their departure. One delay was attributed to the chaotic distribution of inadequate food rations that consisted of a half loaf of bread and a quarter of one Red Cross parcel per man. These rations, supplemented with a small portion of coffee and a dozen or so cigarettes, were to sustain the airmen for the next seven days.*

The disheartened and forlorn gathering of airmen eventually departed Fallingbostel late afternoon 6 April 1945. A noticeable pall of apprehension gripped the column as the POWs marched out of the camp into the swirling chaos of the war now raging throughout Germany. The majority of these airmen were participating in their third evacuation from an interment camp during the past year. However, this exodus was noticeably different from the two previous evacuations. Earlier, comparatively healthy airmen sensed that as long as they adhered to

---

*The order for evacuation could not have come at a more inopportune time for Joseph O'Donnell. Just two days earlier he had traded his watch for seven loaves of bread. The six remaining loaves weighed approximately 15 pounds that he could not manage, given his lack of strength and limited capacity for carrying personal possessions. Joe's misfortune, however, benefited those who remained behind when he made a reluctant decision to "donate" half of his recent acquisition to other men left in the hospital.

[447] O'Donnell, *A History of Stalag Luft IV,* 129

the demands of the German authorities, regardless of how harsh or arbitrary, they could survive. Now, the physically and emotionally exhausted airmen feared for their safety. Most were afraid they would not be physically capable of enduring the demands of another march and would be unable to keep up with the group. They all feared the unknown as the pending defeat of Nazi Germany created unparalleled disorder, and an uncertainty that allowed wild speculation and rumors to assume an unprecedented degree of authority.

17

ESCAPE

After much confusion and hours of standing in the rain, the long column of wet and demoralized airmen departed Fallingbostel mid-afternoon on 6 April 1945. A formal protest, noting the physical impairment and exhaustion of these POWs, was registered with the German authorities the day before their evacuation–yet, to no avail. Staff Sergeant Don Dorfmeier and the other airmen of C-lager were marched out of the two compounds as foretold by various camp rumors. Flight Surgeon Leslie Caplan's journal entry on the departure date reads, "On few [hours] notice left Fallingbostel. Scarcely had time to [identify] some sick to stay. Twelve men left behind in chapel area (400 men) and others were selected in tent area to stay behind. Only 1,500 men marched out (all three lagers) and others scheduled to leave tomorrow."[448]

In spite of their late departure, the airmen moved directly east for 15 kilometers before halting well after dark in the vicinity of Wardbohnen. An anonymous airman, marching out of Fallingbostel with the main column, noted, "I'm sure beginning to hate the sixth of the month," referring to their previous evacuation from Stalag Luft IV on the same day, two months earlier. "The weather was bad [and] rained a hell of a lot for awhile. Started south [then] heading north. Came into town in the dark, but got a lucky break being in the rear of the formation. Put about 75 of us up in a little barn."

The following morning, a second group of airmen evacuated Stalag 357 as cited in Caplan's journal. One of the POWs in this group, Staff Sergeant James W. McCloskey, recorded their movement for the day as only 12 kilometers, suggesting they also experienced similar confusion and delays prior to departure. Yet, McCloskey's column made even less progress the next day, halting for the evening shortly after passing through the town of Wietzendorf, some 20 kilometers northeast of Fallingbostel. The advance of both columns of airmen then lagged for

---

[448] Caplan, *Domain of Heroes,* 54

the next several days as they were marched across country roads congested with German troops and civilian refugees fleeing the all-encompassing conflict. Correspondent Alan Moorehead characterized this chaos as a "scene almost beyond human comprehension . . . Everyone was on the move, and there was a frantic . . . quality about their activities. Life was sordid, aimless, leading nowhere."[449]*

The initial sluggish pace of the two columns of POWs, slowed by congestion on the roads, was mostly attributable to the poor physical condition of the airmen. The brief respite at Fallingbostel, while welcomed, was inadequate for the men to recover from the physical and psychological exhaustion of the past two months. The vast majority of these prisoners were starving, and the resumption of the march reactivated their many ailments. Shortly after their departure, Caplan identified thirty new cases of dysentery and other illnesses. The demands of the march were equally difficult for some of the older German guards. Tom Farrow noted, "Our column headed northeast and we soon noticed our guards had been replaced by a much older group, probably members of the home guard, [the Volksstrum], men . . . in their fifties and sixties. [Soon] the guards were limping with some falling down. One [even] had a heart seizure and died."[450]

The physical demands of the march were further exacerbated by the harassment of German guards who insisted the airmen keep moving and not fall out of formation, regardless of their physical condition. This was especially difficult for the hundreds of men suffering from dysentery who were incapacitated for days throughout the entire march. Staff Sergeant Leonard Deranleau recalled experiencing two such attacks of diarrhea shortly after departing Fallingbostel.[451] In the first instance, Deranleau abruptly broke ranks and left the column formation to relieve himself on the far side of the road, ignoring the demands of a young German soldier to "Keep moving!" Outraged by the airman's unwillingness to comply with his order, the belligerent adolescent went

---

* Royal Air Force Sergeant and Man of Confidence, James Deans, would lead a larger, separate group of Allied POWs out of Stalag 357 around the same time and move on a similar route as the airmen who departed Fallingbostel.

[449] Hastings, *Armageddon*, 477
[450] O'Donnell, *Luftgansters Marching Across Germany*, 33
[451] Deranleau, *Memories of an Aerial Gunner*, 144–45

so far as to draw his service pistol to enforce his authority. In spite of this threat, a weak and disoriented Deranleau refused to return to the formation, which incensed the agitated youth to the point of almost shooting the exhausted, humiliated airman. Fortunately, Leonard's life was saved by the intervention of an older guard and two other POWs, who broke ranks to assist Deranleau to his feet and carry him back to the column.[452]

Days later, Deranleau experienced another incident where he recalled, "Terrible abdominal cramps . . . immobilized me to the point I couldn't walk." Although assisted by two other POWs, the stricken airman again fell to the side of the road. He remained there until the lager's Man of Confidence, Francis Troy, and two volunteer medics arrived to intervene. In an attempt to be helpful, the two medics recommended the hapless airman be placed on the column's sick wagon. Yet, this suggestion only increased the anxiety of the already ailing airman who feared being separated from the main body. Sensing Leonard's apprehension, Troy attempted, unsuccessfully, to reassure his former crew member. Then, according to Deranleau, Troy realized that further efforts were futile so he "stooped down in front of me and pulled me up on his back . . . and [proceeded to] carry me three or four hundred [meters] until my cramps subsided."[453]

As Leonard Deranleau's intestinal seizures abated, he and the other dispirited men in his column continued to move in a northeast direction; the German authorities doggedly moved their prisoners away from the Allied armies advancing from the West. In utter disbelief, exasperated airmen noted that their route "doubled back and covered a good bit of the same territory we had just come over a month before." More ominously, the airmen were marching into the maelstrom swirling throughout central Europe. Author James S. Lucas, who served as a young soldier with the British Army in spring 1945, would later characterize the last month of this epic struggle as "an Armageddon," where hundreds of thousands of more soldiers and civilians would die during the last 30 days of conflict.*

---

* A quarter million German soldiers, alone, died in April 1945.[454]

[452] Deranleau, *Memories of an Aerial Gunner,* 144–45
[453] Ibid., 145–146
[454] Ziemke, *Stalingrad to Berlin* 682

The fury raging through Germany during the closing days of the war was intensified by unrelenting Allied efforts to interdict and destroy all ground traffic moving on roads and rail networks in the country. The last elements of the once-powerful German Luftwaffe had been destroyed months earlier in their effort to support the unsuccessful counteroffensive in the Ardennes. From January 1945 on, Allied air forces seized domination of the skies over central Europe and were able to attack at will across the entire country. This dominance was achieved in spite of the long-delayed production of the German ME 262, the world's first jet aircraft, which was superior to any Allied fighter.* However, the Germans could not produce enough of these planes, nor did they have adequate fuel or trained pilots to make anything but a token effort to oppose the ongoing destruction of every city and industrial region in their country. Sadly, the relentless air pursuit and attack of ground targets would prove tragic for a number of Allied POWs still moving across central Europe in April and May 1945.

Accounts of Allied air activity were noted in the diaries of most airmen within days of departing Fallingbostel. This was especially true once the airmen became snarled on the same roads used by the Wehrmacht, and exposed to multiple strafings. An early April 1945 diary entry by an airman several kilometers north of Don's column wrote, "[We] had to hit the ground fast . . . about half an hour after [moving] into a small village. [A] P-51 [fighter was] strafing in the area . . . ." Days later, James W. McCloskey noted in his diary "British Typhoon [fighters] over us all day, shooting up everything in sight."[455]

In spite of the airmen's physical limitations and the road congestion, the constrained movement in Staff Sergeant Don Dorfmeier's column changed abruptly on 10 April 1945. One diarist reports, "[We're] up at 0430 and hit the road early. Did 24 [kilometers] with few breaks. Had a cigarette for breakfast [and] no other [food] all day." The next morning, the airmen were again pressed just as harshly, according to the same individual who cited, "marched another 20 K[ilometers] on a

* German industrial production "turned out 3,000 fighter aircraft in September 1944." The first jets starting coming off the production lines the following month.[456]

455 O'Donnell, *Luftgangsters Marching Across Germany,* 86
456 Ibid., 411

cigarette and a few spuds. Went to bed hungry and on a stomach partially empty." Two days later, the Germans announced the death of the president of the United States, Franklin Roosevelt, reporting that he "died of a brain hemorrhage." This news caused much sadness among the POWs. Roosevelt was very popular and Don, as well as many other young airmen, perceived him as a father figure whose leadership over the past twelve years had brought the country through the Depression, and now the war. Caplan later noted, "The news of Roosevelt's death depressed [everyone]. Many nearly on the verge of tears."[457] However, one philosophical airman speculated that perhaps Roosevelt's death "was a sign that the war would end soon and [that] the Lord figured his work towards its end was done."*

On 12 April 1945, the actual day of Roosevelt's death, Staff Sergeant Don Dorfmeier observed his 21st birthday. Instead of celebration, he spent most of the day reflecting on his past seven and a half months as a prisoner of war and speculating about his future. Such contemplation had occupied much of his time since departing Fallingbostel. For days, Don, along with many of the POWs in his column, had experienced mounting anxiety about their fate as they continued moving east, away from advancing Allied forces. For some men, this anxiety was becoming unbearable as the looming anticipation of crossing back over the Elbe River became symbolic of death itself. In response to these mounting fears, small groups of men started to think of escape while they still had the opportunity.

Days earlier, on 7 April 1945, James W. McCloskey noted that four airmen in his group escaped on the very evening of their departure from Stalag 357, yet he provided no other information regarding their

* President Roosevelt's death was perceived by German Minister of Propaganda, Joseph Goebbels, as an intervention by the "Angel of History" who would reverse the fortunes of war for Adolph Hitler and the Third Reich. A similar incident, known as the "Miracle of the House of Brandenburg," occurred almost two hundred years earlier, when the unexpected death of the Czarina of . . . Russia fractured the coalition of forces aligned against Frederick the Great and prevented a Prussian defeat during the Seven Years War of 1756–63.[458]

[457] Caplan, *Domain of Heroes,* 54
[458] Shirer, *Rise and Fall of the Third Reich,* 1108–1110.

status.[459] Presumably, these individuals thought their best chance to escape was during the initial confusion of the evacuation, or while they still possessed the physical and psychological stamina for such a daring venture. Others, however, waited until the monotony associated with the earlier part of the march resumed and proved to be unbearable. Yet, with the repetitiveness and boredom that returned within days of their departure, came increased physical difficulties, hunger, and more recently, the unintentional strafing of their columns by Allied aircraft.

Although many POWs on the march contemplated escape, the actual number of individuals who attempted such an audacious undertaking was exceedingly small. A postwar study, published in 1997, concluded that less than two percent of American prisoners of war even initiated an escape, much less succeeded in such an attempt. In spite of official US Army policy stipulating that escape was "a prisoner's duty," many considerations account for why this did not happen on a larger scale. The simplest of explanations is that most prisoners became lethargic and settled into a routine when confined. A second and perhaps more compelling reason for not attempting an escape was the execution of airmen captured after the mass breakout of 76 POWs from Stalag Luft III in March 1944. All but three of these men had been apprehended, and 50 of them were subsequently executed by the Gestapo. This tragedy was followed by a later announcement that the German government had implemented a new, use-of-deadly-force policy to prevent any future attempts.[460] This consideration also served as the rationale for Allied intelligence services who instructed the POWs not to attempt any escapes during the last year of the war since an Allied victory was all but assured in 1945.

Escape from a marching column seemingly presented more opportunities than being confined in a compound. Yet, for these airmen, the endeavor was considerably more risky considering their depleted physical and psychological state. Moreover, prisoners who attempted to escape during the later phases of the march and were caught, or voluntarily returned to the column, were openly beaten–an ominous warning to the other airmen. As a result, serious contemplation of escape from captivity, much less an actual attempt, required a significant degree of bravery or an overwhelming sense of desperation.

---

[459] O'Donnell, *Luftgangsters Marching Across Germany,* 86.
[460] Doyle, *A Prisoners Duty,* 137

At first light, 15 April 1945, Don and the other men in his column woke to perform the same routines of the past 68 days. However, on this morning, according to Leslie Caplan, the airmen had "good hot water and [8 ounces] of potato soup [cooked with] one pig . . . for 1,100 men." Once fed and assembled, the column marched an estimated 10 kilometers to the village of Brenenbute. The day's weather was "hot," Caplan further noted and "that the men exercised poor water discipline" during the march, resulting in "much diarrhea and many stragglers." The column's sick wagon, however, could only accommodate some of these men and by the end of the day, Caplan identified another 62 airmen who could no longer march and needed to be hospitalized.[461] One of those identified was Bob Cash, whom Don had known since their first internment at St. Wendel. Yet, neither Don nor Paul McNally appeared affected by the day's road march; both men were preoccupied with Paul's intent to escape later that evening.

For several days, the two acquaintances had discussed Paul's contemplation of joining three other men planning an escape in the "near future." All three individuals had been POWs longer than either of the Fresno airmen, and according to Don, were "just about ready to go around the bend." Or perhaps the three plotting airmen, in addition to feeling desperate, also felt emboldened by the enveloping chaos of the moment. In any event, Don recalled, "the leader of their party had a small compass from an escape kit, a plan of how to proceed, and the conviction of not wanting to cross back [over] the Elbe [River], nor die."

Later that afternoon, Don had agreed to present the escape plan that he and Paul had discussed to a committee in accordance with established military protocol. Such procedures, directed by the US Army Military Intelligence Service, required individual "barracks' subcommittees [report to the senior individual in each lager] to determine whether an escape proposal merited support."[462] The two conspirators also enlisted a guard to act as an accomplice prior to "all 1,500 airmen" being confined for the night in a single barn.*

---

* Caplan's journal reference to "1,500 airmen" does not account for attrition resulting from straggling, hospitalization, or escapes since departing Fallingbostel.

[461] Caplan, *Domain of Heroes*, 66
[462] Doyle, *A Prisoner's Duty*, 125

Around midnight, Don and the four members of the escape party assembled at the barn's entrance. He knocked on the door and told their German accomplice outside, "I have five men who are sick." Earlier, this same guard had been bribed, Don recalled, "with cigarettes [to help] us get out of the barn, although this was simply a ruse to gain access to Caplan and discuss the merits of an escape." The guard then led the small group out of the barn, he continued, "Over to the pigsty where . . . it was warm and we [placed] the men who were ill." Once inside the designated hospital, Don presented the escape plan, which was then sanctioned by Caplan. Don also listened very attentively to the ensuing discussion as the flight surgeon briefed the group on how "they should get out and [what] to do once on the outside [of the compound]." Part of his suggestions included "using peppers and onions to mask the trail of their escape." At the last minute, Don continued, "I asked, with my heart in my mouth, if I could be included [in the escape]" and Caplan consented.* He then gave the small party a "prepared list of some 900 men [compiled in anticipation of evacuating Fallingbostel], some iodine crystals to purify water, and his blessing. And that was about it." The group then slipped through a door in the hospital that "had been left ajar, [and they moved] into the pigsty, crept out, and laid alongside the hogs in the mud."

Once outside, the airmen noticed a lone German sentry with a dog, posted on the other side of the fence that separated the pigsty from the rest of the farm. "The sentry and his dog walked past the group of escapees three times" Don said, "without the dog detecting the presence of the airmen." Later, he recalled thinking, "their scent was [probably] masked by the odor of the pigs," although he also recognized that the airmen didn't smell that much better than the animals after living in the same clothing for the past ten weeks. "The sentry continued to walk his post," Don continued, "while he and the others counted the lapse in time between the guard's departure and return to his original position. This procedure allowed the men to determine when the guard would be farthest from the group on his next rotation and present the best

---

* Don's presentation and request for permission to escape is noteworthy for two reasons. First, it suggests some continued resemblance of discipline and leadership within the column, despite the chaos of the past two months of the march. Secondly, it illustrated the high regard the airmen had for Leslie Caplan, although as a medical officer he held no formal command authority within the group.

opportunity for them to slip over the fence, one at a time." Once over the fence, each man "ran out about 50 meters before throwing himself to the ground." The airman then "crawled torturously for about a half mile to the neighboring woods." After all the men had assembled at the wood line, their anxiety reached a feverish pitch. Each man was acutely aware of having made an irrevocable decision that, if caught, might result in their execution. The experience was both terrifying and exhilarating. Such tension would have been similar to the moment of escape from their crippled, burning aircraft months earlier.

With intense focus, their hearts racing, and fueled by a continual surge of adrenaline, everyone in the group was primed to respond to the slightest threat. That moment presented itself almost immediately, Don recalled, when a "German soldier put them to flight." The group then "began to run" in response to a real or imagined sense of being pursued, " . . . dropping onions and peppers, while all of us [thought] we could hear the sounds of the dogs behind us. Later, around 0300 or 0400 [hours] in the morning, the airmen stopped running to rest. All I recall [after that] . . . ," Don continued, "was [being] wakened by the shaking of my shoulder and the hand of another man of the escape party [covering] my mouth so I would not cry out." The men had stopped running sometime earlier, and spent rest of the night sleeping "about 25 meters from a major road and [awoke to discover] the whole damn German Army was going by on bicycles, heading toward the Western Front."*

This abrupt discovery initiated what Don would later characterize as "the start of seven days of literally hell!" During this trying week, the escaped airmen hid in the forests during the day, lived off food stolen from farms in the evening, and traveled only at night to avoid detection. Their travels, however, were aided significantly by following fire breaks in the forest "that led in an east/west direction." While they were moving the next evening they "met two English soldiers, also evading, yet continued to travel their separate ways. The following day, the airmen "were told by two other fugitives that the Englishmen they

---

* By April 1945, the strategic bombing of the German rail system and fuel refining plants had paralyzed the nation's transportation system. The motor vehicle industry was also hard hit. By January 1945, the German Army was forced to mount many of their panzer grenadiers on bicycles.[463]

[463] Ziemke, *Stalingrad to Berlin*, 411–12

had encountered earlier had been killed."

The tension and interplay within the small party of evaders was as perilous as the dark night in which they moved. The five men did not know each other before the evening of their escape. This lack of familiarity and trust, even under normal circumstances, would have a negative impact on group cohesiveness and the willingness of its members to subordinate themselves to a leader. Yet these airmen found themselves in anything but normal circumstances. Furthermore, their deplorable physical condition would have had already created deficits in their psychological functioning and ability to cooperate as a group. According to Ancel Keys' study on starvation, this cooperation would have been affected by symptoms of depression, irritability, and general emotional instability, which undoubtedly caused much angst and disagreement as the men negotiated numerous obstacles and were forced to make critical decisions to evade capture.

Don provided few details about how they acquired food for their survival. However, the group might have been aided by some German families who routinely left food in the small outbuildings that surrounded their farms for "those traveling at night." Through a chance encounter with a woman who lived on such a farm during the war, the author learned "many mothers routinely put out food, especially during the last months of the war, in the hope that other mothers across Europe might do the same for the men in her family who were serving in the German Army."

On the group's third night they "were caught in the middle of an intense [artillery] barrage with incoming rounds falling [to our rear] as retaliating fire from Allied artillery shells started landing in front of [our position]. Frantic," Don said, "we dug ourselves [shallow depressions] with our knives, some two to three feet deep." There the airmen were "forced to remain in hiding," and "pulled dirt and debris over us [to protect us from shrapnel], and 'sweat out' that battle for two days." According to a later newspaper account, "The activity swelled and reached a climax the following day when Allied fighter planes began to strafe the woods to clear them of enemy fire." In the meanwhile, the frightened airmen "laid in their [protective hollows] and listened to the screaming shells [flying overhead] and hitting around us." In addition to exploding shrapnel, the men were also exposed to flying splinters from the trees. "Air and artillery bombardments in such conditions," according to author Antony Beevor, "produced a panic [even] among experienced soldiers."[464]

The group's fourth day of evasion was "comparatively quiet and the airmen, fatigued by the strain of the previous two nights, slept most of the [day]. A continuous rain fell for the next 48 hours as their food supply dwindled, along with their hopes." Still, they continued to move in a westward direction in expectation of finding deliverance. Eventually, the group "ventured away from the forest and [moved toward] a creek" in search of food and water. Once in the vicinity of a small stream, Paul McNally continued to move into an open clearing, against the better judgment of the rest of the group, and was immediately spotted by "two German civilians." Panicked, the airmen recalled they quickly "returned back to our hiding place [and] thought we'd had it." At this point " . . . despair began to overtake them."

"On the morning of the seventh day after their escape, the five airmen spotted a small artillery observation plane and could only hope they were close to their own forces." The despondent evaders were also wet, hungry, and exhausted, which had undermined their resolve. "We were," Don recalled later, "beat [and] decided to give up. So we sent two of our companions, one who spoke Polish and the other German, out to find anyone but the SS, to say we were forced laborers who had strayed away from camp and to take us back."*

The two designated airmen of Don's group departed with instruction "to [find] food regardless of the consequences or whom they might meet, while the rest of the group waited" in anxious anticipation. In the interim, the pervading anxiety and sense of despair among the other escapees stifled any meaningful conversation or consideration of other options. Hours later, the two airmen tasked with finding provisions returned, "loaded down with all sorts of rations, candy bars, and cigarettes." They had, Don recalled, "run into elements of the 11th

---

* Special units of the German SS roamed throughout the country, attempting to instill resolve in the population by executing soldiers found separated from their units, housewives caught stealing bread, or anyone else undermining the authority of the Third Reich.[465]

[464] Beevor, *The Fall of Berlin*, 332
[465] Beevor, *The Fall of Berlin*, 120

Armored Division of the British Second Army", which "picked them up in a [reconnaissance vehicle] and now returning [for the other three airmen in hiding.]"

British reconnaissance vehicle   Imperial War Museum

At first sighting of the approaching British vehicle, Don and the two airmen who remained in hiding were flooded with emotions. Long repressed feelings associated with their ordeal as POWs engulfed them. Earlier incidents of terror, the harsh realities of their long march, and the uncertainties of their recent escape surfaced, then diminished, during those first fleeting moments of realizing they had been found.* More focused thoughts of home would emerge later, but in this instant, all that mattered was their release from ever-present, unrelenting anxiety and fear. Once reunited, all five airmen were consumed by the emotion of the moment. Even the most steadfast of the group could not maintain his composure. Overwhelmed by their good fortune, the five airmen "managed to cry, laugh, and pray all at the same time."

---

* Current models of chronic stress cite, "unconscious thoughts as well as conscious memories of the trauma" are a constant presence that "intrudes on the mind in the form of daydreams, flashbacks, nightmares, and intrusive thoughts."[466]

[466] Williams, *Post-Traumatic Stress Disorder*, 78

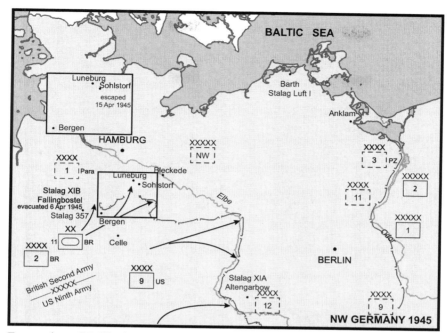

Evacuation of Fallingbostel and escape   Author's collection

One week after arriving at Fallingbostel, the advance of the British Second Army prompted the evacuation of Stalags XIB and 357 on 6 April 1945. Many of these POWs feared they were being sent north to their death. Nine days later–after moving east to Bergen, then northeast to Luneberg, Don and four other POWs in his cohort escaped their evening's lodgment on a small farm near the village of Sohlstorf. Moving only at night, these exhausted airmen were recovered a week later by reconnaissance elements of the British 11th Armored Division on 21 April 1945.

18

REPATRIATION

Following the few brief moments of euphoric celebration, the five thankful airmen were quickly evacuated to the rear of the British lines and debriefed. "The British treated us [very] well," Staff Sergeant Don Dorfmeier recalled, "and [fed] us a big meal, which we immediately . . . threw up because we weren't used to eating." Later, "they took us to town . . . and handed me a .45 [pistol] . . . which I hadn't had in my hand since qualifying . . . and told me to guard a poor German youngster who was scared to death. So, there I [sat], an emaciated 155 lb, 20-year-old . . . POW with a [weapon] in my hand, and he didn't know what I was going to do. [Well], all I did was tell him not to worry [as] I put the safety on the damn thing so I don't do anything crazy and just sat there."

The tone of Don's comments suggests he was lapsing into a state of complete exhaustion with little interest or conscious thought of anything other than sleep. Physically and emotionally depleted, hours, if not days, would pass before he or anyone in their group could fully appreciate their change in status from one of "captive" to "recovered" prisoners of war. That any of them actually succeeded in their escape was a considerable accomplishment. A later study concluded "only 213 officer and enlisted US Army Air Force POWs successfully escaped from captivity in the European Theater of Operations during the Second World War. [However, these figures only reflect the] "official numbers of officers and enlisted men whose return were not facilitated by uninterrupted escape lines and could be [documented] by British Intelligence."[467] Furthermore, these statistics, in all likelihood, do not include the escapes of dozens of men during the closing months of the war. Events in Europe were simply moving with such rapidity that few, if any, formal reports or records were made of these last days.*

---

* Another 2,692 US airmen of all ranks successfully evaded capture after being shot down.[468]

467 Doyle, *A Prisoner's Duty,* 286
468 Ibid., 286

While Don and the other four airmen were evading capture in the forests of northwestern Germany, dramatic changes were occurring throughout Europe. On 11 April 1945, the US Ninth Army reached the Elbe River, which had been previously determined as the line of demarcation between the Soviet and Western occupation zones in Germany. That same day, American forces liberated the Mittlebau-Dora factory at Nordhausen, a vast slave labor camp established to mass produce V-2 rockets, "designed to reverse the tide of war, and bring large scale destruction to London."[469]* The following week on 16 April 1945, just four days after the death of President Roosevelt, the British Second Army liberated Fallingbostel and the tens of thousands of Allied POWs left behind in Stalag XIB and Stalag 357. An unknown number of these freed prisoners included the sick and non-ambulatory airmen referred to in Caplan's earlier journal entry, in addition to Staff Sergeant George Guderley and the other conspirators of his mock detail. This brazen collection of individuals had returned to their former compound the day after the departure of Caplan's column. The airmen had intimidated the newly posted, older guards to allow their reentry into camp; there they waited the arrival of advancing Allied forces 10 days later. Regrettably, the liberation of the town and camps had been resisted, causing the "[deaths] of 35–40 Russian POWs" when British aircraft strafed one of the compounds. Yet, when the Reconnaissance Troop of the 8th Hussars arrived at Stalag XIB, they found an honor guard of British paratroopers "drawn up, as if on parade." The camp had been taken over by the POWs several days earlier, "once the majority of the [camp] guards had fled."[470]

The excitement and sense of relief in the liberated camps was, according to George Guderley, "indescribable." British authorities moved quickly to identify and evacuate airmen who could be moved from the lagers to an airstrip and loaded onto C-47 transport aircraft. They were then flown to a Recovered Allied Military Personnel (RAMP) camp near Brussels, Belgium. Weeks earlier, in March 1945, the mission of Allied military hospitals in Europe was changed from

---

* The first V-2 rockets started falling on London, then Antwerp, on 8 September 1944. Attacks on these cities and other targets averaged 370 per month until the end of the war.[471]

[469] Gilbert, *The Day the War Ended*, 9
[470] O'Donnell, *Luftgangsters Marching Across Germany*, 78
[471] Middlebrook, *The Peenemünde Raid*, 370

supporting military combat operations to providing care for recovered Allied military personnel. American and British forces advancing into Germany were liberating POW camps in the western regions of the country, and the condition of many prisoners in these camps required immediate medical attention.

Technical Sergeant John Anderson, one of the non-ambulatory POWs left at Fallingbostel, recalled that "he and the other airmen started to sing as they evacuated the camp." Perhaps Anderson, who loved music, was the inspiration for this emotional expression. It is also possible that some of these men were with Anderson during the evacuation of St. Wendel seven months earlier, when they sang to express their defiance on the first day's movement in crowded boxcars across Germany. Their singing may also have been a manifestation of the spirit of the US Army Air Corps, ingrained much earlier during long months of stateside training. However, Anderson and the men evacuating the recently liberated camp were singing on this day to express their deep sense of pride in being an American serviceman. They knew that if it were not for the United States, there would be no liberation of Europe and no release from captivity.

The freed airmen from Fallingbostel were deloused and issued fresh British uniforms soon after they arrived in Belgium. George Guderley later recalled he was, "Paid the equivalent of $100 in Belgian francs and told he could stay there as long as he wished." Ten days later, having enjoyed the open and warm hospitality of the city, Guderley was ready to move on to Namur, Belgium where he received "a temporary service record, Staff Sergeant chevrons, and a typhus immunization" en route to another RAMP camp, Lucky Strike, near Le Havre, France.* John Anderson arrived at the Le Havre embarkation camp around the same time, yet continued to be afflicted with gastrointestinal problems. This condition might have influenced his

---

* In September 1944, following the Allied capture of the French port of Le Havre, numerous "cigarette camps" were established as staging areas for new soldiers arriving in theater. Six months later, several of these camps were designated specifically for American POWs being evacuated from Germany. The most notable facility, Camp Lucky Strike, was established at San Riquie en Caux. The camp had a hospital to care for those who were seriously ill and malnourished, in addition to two bars open every night from 1900–2200 hours.

perception of the camp's food, characterized as "just terrible." Two weeks later both men sailed home to the United State for an extended 60-day furlough.

On the same day Fallingbostel was liberated, Caplan's column of airmen crossed the Elbe River and moved another 14 kilometers toward their evening's lodgment at Thomasburg.[472] The march to the river and the site of the previous evening's bivouac at Sohlstorf, where Don and the other four escaped, had been stressful. The preceding week, the weather was hot, and many men who could not keep pace with the group, became stragglers. The column was also exposed, according to airmen Richard W. Burt, of the 460th Bomb Group, to incidents of strafing by Allied aircraft. One such strafing occurred shortly after departing Fallingbostel and "not far from the front lines [where] German units were moving around us in all directions. One day we were laying over in a group of barns . . . where antiaircraft gun emplacements were being dug to [protect] an engineer unit . . . frantically trying to put a pontoon bridge across a river. All of a sudden . . . four British Typhoon fighter-bombers came in low, firing their guns and dropping bombs . . . while receiving return fire from the gun pits . . . all within 25 yards of us. When the shooting [finally] stopped . . . we ventured outside [to see] the remains of the pontoon bridge slowly floating downstream. That was as close as I ever want to be to that kind of action."[473]

Another column of American and British POWs who were moving in the same vicinity, were also strafed several days later. This incident involved an element of the several thousand airmen and soldiers who departed Stalag 357 a week earlier and were converging on the town of Greese, north of the Elbe River. These airmen had already started to bivouac in the area where their Man of Confidence, Sergeant James Deans, was supervising the transportation and distribution of long-anticipated Red Cross rations. Men who had already received their parcels were beginning to consume their corned beef and biscuits when the British planes found them. At first, the nine RAF Typhoon fighters circled overhead without raising suspicion. Then, they descended from the sky, and someone who recognized what was happening cried, "My God! They're coming for us!" Moments later, "sixty POWs were dead. Scores of others were injured, " . . . some of whom would later die of

[472] Caplan, *Domain of Heroes*, 66
[473] O'Donnell, *The Pangs of the Thorn*, 134

their wounds in German hospitals.[474]

On the morning of 16 April 1945, Soviet forces one hundred and eighty kilometers to the southwest of Greese, breached the Oder River and overran German defensive positions on the west bank. Days later, the Red Army "stood ready to assault the city."[475] However, the ensuing battle for the capital would be unorganized and sporadic, reflecting the diminished significance of Berlin for all but its symbolic value. The capital had been destroyed months earlier, reduced to a "second Carthage,"[476] according to author Cornelius Ryan, by the cumulative effects of some 363 Allied air raids conducted during the past three and one half years of war. The city was intentionally abandoned by the German Army and only an ad hoc collection of under strength units offered any resistance.*

Russian artillery started to shell Berlin at the time Don and the other recovered men in his party were moving through the US Army's elaborate and complex evacuation and hospitalization systems. A newspaper article recounting the escape noted, "The group was taken back to the British rear lines, where they received first aid and later transferred to an American medical unit. Shortly after, they were sent to France and then taken to England where they convalesced in an American rehabilitation hospital." The evacuation system cited in this article was established in late 1944 and devised primarily to triage and evacuate combat casualties from the European continent. The first priority of triage was to identify those soldiers requiring less than thirty days of hospitalization from patients requiring longer-term care and evacuation to the United States. Soldiers who were retained in theater were evacuated to Britain by air, whenever possible, and those needing long-term or specialized care were then sent on to the 91st General Hospital at Oxford, England, 65 kilometers northwest of London. In mid-March 1945, the number of American combat casualties started to

* Ironically, the German chancellery and Hitler's underground bunker in Berlin were defended by French and Spanish volunteers of the 33rd SS Grenadier, "Charlemagne" Division, who were inspired to enlist in the Waffen-SS "to save Europe from Communism."[477]

[474] Ryan, *The Last Battle,* 410–11
[475] Keegan, *Second World War,* 521
[476] Ryan, *The Last Battle,* 16
[477] Beevor, *The Fall of Berlin,* 322

decline and the system became burdened primarily by the recovery of Allied military personnel and German POWs.

After arriving in London, Don recalled that "he and the other four men in his group were given the royal treatment by English women in uniformed service, who carried our gear" en route to the hospital. Once admitted, all five of the emaciated airmen were placed in the malnutrition ward of the US Army 91st General Hospital in Oxford.* Don's medical records indicate that he received his first evaluation on 23 April 1945, where his body weight at the time was recorded as 155 pounds. A later comparison between this initial screening and Don's last physical examination prior to deploying overseas, documented a minimum weight loss of 45 pounds–nearly 25 percent of his normal body weight. Other airmen who participated in the extended Hunger March out of Stalag Luft IV experienced similar losses during their ordeal.

Although the five recovered airmen were now safe in England, weeks would elapse before the US Army sent notification to their families to inform them their sons were alive and well. Still, the Western Union telegrams were ambiguous, if not misleading. Noticeably absent was any reference indicating how these men acquired their freedom. The telegram sent to Paul McNally's family on 25 May 1945, simply stated, "The Secretary of War desires me to inform you that your son, S/SGT McNally, Paul E., returned to military control on 15 April 1945," which was inaccurate. Rather, that was the day the five airmen had escaped. The terse message further indicated their son was "hospitalized [in] European area not due to enemy action. Further information and new address follows direct from hospital."

At the time Staff Sergeant Don Dorfmeier started receiving treatment at the 91st General Hospital, the airmen of the 398th Bomb Group at Nuthampstead were standing down as the operational tempo of the war was diminishing. The past year, the bomb group had flown

----

* The 91st General Hospital was a 1,800 bed treatment facility that deployed to England in March 1945. The following month, Don's group was among the first of 64 repatriated POWs to arrive at this hospital on 23 April 1945. Upon admission they were deloused, and then bathed prior to being immunized, placed on special diets, and quarantined for 16 days. Over the next four days, another 770 patients arrived in Oxford for similar treatment.

194 missions to support the strategic bombing campaign against Germany.* During these operations, the 398th lost 58 aircraft and over 500 aircrew were killed or wounded, including the Group Commander, Colonel Frank Hunter Jr., who was shot down and perished when his aircraft crashed 23 January 1945. Another 287 airmen were declared Missing in Action and interned as POWs. With the hostilities in Europe drawing to a close, nobody in the unit wanted to be the last man killed in a war that seemed all but won.**

Most of Don's original crew, with whom he had deployed to England a year earlier, had long since departed Nuthampstead. One of the last members of this crew to return home was Lieutenant Wallace Blackwell, who flew his final 35th mission on 28 December 1944.[478] However, former crew member John Bell was still at Nuthampstead, working at the air field the last week of April 1945, when he was notified that he had received a call in the Operation's Office. This news startled Bell–few servicemen received personal calls while overseas– and his first reaction was concern for the safety of his brother, currently serving with the US Army in Italy. Fearing his brother had been killed or wounded, John dashed across the flight line, while his anxiety mounted, and grabbed the phone. Yet, John's most pressing concern was not addressed. Instead, he heard the slow, deliberate cadence of a soft baritone voice asserting, "We'll never surrender . . . never, never surrender!" Exasperated, Bell demanded to know who was on the line. Only then did Don identify himself, telling his friend he had just returned to England after escaping, and was now a patient at a hospital

---

* Combat tours for aircrews were extended from 25 to 35 missions in early February 1944.
** The 398th Bomb Group would participate in the last mission conducted by the Eighth Air Force during the Second World War. On 25 April 1945, the Group supported a 120 plane raid to the Skoda Armament Factory, an industrial target near Pilsen, Czechoslovakia. The factory was bombed primarily to keep it from being captured by the rapidly approaching Red Army. Regrettably, two planes from the 398th Bomb Group were shot down over the target by heavy flak. Only three men were able to get out of the first plane, one of whom "was later found shot to death." The other plane crashed and "according to some witnesses, four of [the airmen] were executed by the Germans.[479]

[478] Wallace Blackwell, "Timeless Voices," www.398th.org
[479] Streitfeld, *Hell from Heaven*, 187–188

in Oxford, 18 kilometers from Nuthampstead. An excited, yet brief conversation followed. Don then asked Bell to come immediately to visit him at the hospital, suggesting his friend ask for an overnight pass. Bell quickly agreed and found his operations sergeant who authorized his request for a three-day leave of absence. However, in Oxford, Bell's first effort to gain entrance into the hospital was denied by a military policeman, who informed the airman he was not authorized to visit any patients. John responded brazenly by asserting that "I have come to see my brother."

Once admitted to the hospital and directed to the correct ward, Bell recalled he was "shocked to see Don, who looked God awful having lost so much weight." Yet Don, always a study of contrasts, according to Bell, "possessed a bright and burning spirit," that persuaded John to spend the next three days on the ward. "This was arranged," he recalled, "after Don ordered the ward nurse to prepare another bed so I would not have to find lodging in town at my own expense." For the next three days, Bell listened to the exploits of the five airmen, sharing the details of their experiences at Stalag Luft IV, the hardships of the march, and their recent escape.

In later conversations with the author, John Bell stated, "Don would not let me leave or take lodging in town." Rather, "your father ordered the head ward master to have another bed made up so I could stay in the hospital, and the staff complied." He continued, "The stories of the escapees were compelling," yet his strongest impression of those three days was "the degree of deference extended to Don by the other group members," giving John the impression that Don had either organized or led the escape. I corrected this misperception stating, "My father had only requested permission to join the escape party at the last minute," motivated, in part, by Paul's involvement. Moreover, I speculated that leadership and decision-making within the group was probably very fluid and likely fluctuated throughout the week as result of one's physical stamina and emotional composure.

While Don and Paul recuperated in England, Soviets forces continued to penetrate into Eastern Europe. "Among those in flight from east to west were tens of thousands of Russians seeking to escape the advance of the Red Army."[480] Some were anti-Bolsheviks who had

---

[480] Gilbert, *The Day the War Ended,* 64

lived in Germany since fleeing Russia after the revolution of 1917. Others were White Russians, Slovenians, and ethnic minorities of the Soviet Union who openly greeted the Germans as liberators following the initial invasion of their country.[481] Thousands of these minorities –the majority of whom were Cossacks–volunteered as early as 1941 to serve in various legions fighting in frontline units against the Red Army. Hundreds of thousands of Russian POWs also volunteered to serve in the German Army, performing various rear echelon duties as army auxiliaries,[482] or as *Osttruppen* (anti-partisan forces).

The fate of these Russian volunteers and former auxiliaries was sealed at the Yalta Conference in February 1945, when a paranoid and vengeful Stalin forced England and the United States to accept a forced repatriation of all citizens to their country of origin. Stalin and most Soviet authorities had nothing but "harsh contempt . . . for any Russian POW who enlisted in the German Army" or who had been forced to work as a laborer for the Wehrmacht.[483] Equally reviled were those who had openly fought against the Red Army. These individuals were either "shot without much ado" when first apprehended or executed on their return to Russia.[484] Reports of such atrocities started to surface in early 1945 after thousands of former Russian POWs, serving in the Wehrmacht, were captured by Allied forces in Normandy and returned to Murmansk in December 1944. Several months later, as Soviet forces moved into central Europe, hundreds of liberated Russian POWs were executed by the Red Army, the most notable incident occurring in the streets of Graz, Austria. [485]

The repatriation of former Russian POWs included the return of those who had already been sent to the United States, as well as those held in the American and British Zones of Occupations within Germany. Enforcement of this accord was "painful in the extreme, causing considerable uneas[iness] among many of the Allied soldiers who had to carry out the physical task of forcing men into trains and trucks at bayonet point."[486] Many Russians, after learning of their fate,

---

[481] Lucus, *The War on the Eastern Front 1941–1945,* 29

[482] Ziemke, *Stalingrad To Berlin,* 20

[483] Doyle, *A Prisoner's Duty,* 142.

[484] Gilbert, *The Day the War Ended,* 368

[485] Doyle, *A Prisoners Duty,* 143

[486] Gilbert, *The Day the War Ended,* 368

"committed suicide, or tried to escape and were shot." In at least one instance, a delegation of Russians asked British soldiers if they could be shot on the spot rather than be returned to Soviet authorities.[487]*

To ensure Western compliance with the forced repatriation of the Yalta agreement, Stalin forcefully detained over 50,000 Allied POWs liberated during the Red Army's thrust into central Europe. Some 28,662 of these prisoners of war were American airmen and soldiers of the US Army.[488] One of those detained, Staff Sergeant Leonard E. Rose of the 459th Bomb Group, was "liberated" by Russian soldiers on 24 April 1945 near Annaberg, Germany, 85 kilometers south of Berlin. The following day, Rose and a number of other American POWs attempted to cross the Elbe River at Torgau, yet were denied access to the recently positioned pontoon bridge by Russian soldiers who, instead, sent the airmen to Riesa. "Two days later," according to Rose, "a US Army major riding with a convoy arrived to transport [him] and approximately 3,500 American POWs detained by the Soviets to American hospitals, but again the Russians would not release their Allied prisoners." After the convoy departed, the compound gates were closed and guards were posted to prevent the Americans from leaving. Twenty days later, Rose and an unknown number of others decided they had better escape. The airmen concluded that the Soviets had no intention of ever releasing them, but planned to take them to Russia. Making their escape that evening, Rose and others got over the wall of their compound and walked west all night. At first light the following morning, 15 May 1945, one week after the war in Europe had ended; Leonard and four other men in his group were able to convince American soldiers of the 69th Infantry Division that they were indeed American POWs attempting to get home.

* General Eisenhower was so angered by this disagreeable process he ordered the discontinuance of forced repatriation of Russian nationals." However, the State Department overruled the senior Allied Commander's instructions.[489] By December 1946, "5.5 million people had been returned to the USSR, of which over 1,500,000 former POWs were sent to the Gulag or to labor battalions in Siberia."[490]

[487] Ibid., 368
[488] Doyle, *A Prisoner's Duty,* 143
[489] Gilbert, *The Day the War Ended,* 370
[490] Beevor, *The Fall of Berlin,* 423

A post-war study group concluded, incredulously, that all but 280 POWs held by the Red Army during the end of the war, and soon after, were eventually repatriated.[491] Yet, Leonard Rose disputed these figures, citing his own anecdotal experience that a number of airmen he met in captivity were never returned to Allied control.* Moreover, persistent rumors regarding the abandonment of American POWs motivated "the Defense Intelligence Agency to continue to conduct active searches in Russia for traces of American POWs from WWII."[492]

Ninety kilometers southwest of Berlin, Staff Sergeant Gerald Ralston and hundreds of airmen, separated several weeks earlier from the larger group of POWs sent to Fallingbostel, were also on the road again after evacuating Stalag XIA on 12 April 1945. With less than half a Red Cross parcel per man, the airmen were moving south toward Annabery, along with retreating German soldiers and civilian refugees fleeing the Red Army's thirst for revenge, indiscriminate use of force, and communist ideology. Their column moved 14–20 kilometers a day, then slept in fields or surrounding forests at night. Over the next 10 days, Ralston's group experienced significant air activity as Allied aircraft "straf[ed] and bomb[ed]" targets in close proximity to their positions. Still, their spirits soared the day "two [US Air Force] P-51 [fighters] flew down [along] either side of us and waggled their wings!" Days later, quartered in an old factory, Gerald recalled that he and others were forced to seek refuge in a nearby cemetery as Allied air strikes "landed close by [and] the concussion was more than we could handle. We became nauseated, deaf and bleary eyed [and while] . . . [our] condition cleared up the next day . . . it left us pretty shaken with ringing in our ears." The next morning this same group "marched in the rain all day" and spent that night in the woods, "on the ground with wet blankets and clothing." Two days later, on Monday, 23 April 1945, Ralston and his men moved along with panicked German soldiers, "some going to the front . . . others retreating . . . scared to death of the Russians and [wanting] to get to the American side [in] the west."

---

* A 1985 VA study identified 78,773 American soldiers still listed "Missing in Action" from WWII. In all likelihood, these figures include many other POWs detained by the Soviet government.[493]

[491] Doyle, *A Prisoner's Duty*, 143
[492] Ibid., 143
[493] Beevor, *The Fall of Berlin*, 423

Four days later, the morale and discipline of the Wehrmacht on the Eastern Front, buoyed for months by fear of the Red Army, collapsed. The morning of 27 April 1945, Soviet tanks broke through the defense positions attempting to hold a line at Prenzlau, 60 kilometers north of Berlin. Later that evening, "an hour and a half before midnight," the commander of the Third Panzer Army reported that "half of his divisions and the flak artillery had quit fighting" . . . [that] a hundred thousand men were fleeing west. "The war was over," he continued, "the soldiers had spoken."[494]

The collapse of the northern most German Army on the Eastern Front allowed Soviet forces to threaten the German Experimental Works at Peenemünde and to liberate Stalag Luft I at Barth. However, the Russians could claim little credit for freeing the approximately 9,000 American and British POWs in the Baltic compound. The German security guards of the camp had voluntarily departed the evening of 30 April 1945, and the Russian forces who arrived shortly thereafter agreed to provide food, but little else. Days later, Colonel Byerly, the Senor Allied Officer of the camp, flew to England to report on the status of Allied airmen in the compound, prompting the decision to evacuate these prisoners by airlift. On 8 May 1945, "two hundred British Lancaster bombers brought back more than 13,000 former British prisoners of war, [to include those interned at Barth], to Britain. Yet, the homecoming for the POWs was often hard, their exposure to freedom difficult," and few found a hero's welcome.[495]

The Soviet occupation of Peenemünde on 5 May 1945 was anticlimactic for the Russians. All production activities and foreign labors were relocated following the RAF bombing in 1943, and three subsequent Eighth Air Force missions in July and August 1944 further damaged various structures. Moreover, German scientists who had continued to work at the peninsula facility departed in early 1945, or just days prior to the Soviet arrival, to avoid capture.* Still, this did not

---

* Walter Dornberger, von Braun, and others had moved south to Oberammergau during the last days of the war, where they later surrendered to American forces. Shortly thereafter, von Braun and 492 other German scientists were sent to the United States and eventually worked on the American Apollo 11 space project.

[494] Ziemke, *Stalingrad to Berlin,* 487
[495] Gilbert, *The Day the War Ended,* 155–156

prevent the Soviets from dismantling what remained of the facility and sending it back to Russia.[496]

Further south, panicked German guards, fearing the advancing Red Army, pushed long columns of tired airmen [all day], "through two villages with white flags flying from every house. The men, according to Gerald Ralston marched " . . . until three o'clock the next morning, covering some 30 k[ilometers]," before reaching their destination, Prima. There, the Allied POWs bivouacked for three days, then moved another 15 kilometers to Bittersfeld. To their surprise, American soldiers of the 104th Infantry Division greeted them on their arrival. Ralston captured some of the emotion of this moment–"We marched through our lines across a bombed-out bridge . . . with tears of joy [in our eyes]." One of the many airmen who completed this 13-day trek out of Stalag XIA was Bob Carr, the ball turret gunner from Don's crew out of Nuthampstead, who walked across this bridge with "feet bloody from shoes that didn't fit."

While the Russians were detaining American POWs at Riesa, and Ralston's group rested further south at Prima, the column of airmen that departed Fallingbostel on 6 April 1945, remained in their bivouacs and shelters, 28 kilometers north of the Elba River. One airman took advantage of this extended rest period to calculate the distance his group had marched since evacuating Stalag Luft IV in early February; "We walked 778 kilometers or 485 miles as of 27 April 1945, the 81st day of the march."[497] The realization was staggering. Three days later, this same diarist, and the other men in his column, moved another 18 kilometers, arriving late at night in the vicinity of Borze, then dispersed in three separate lodgments, some 10 kilometers apart.[498] Earlier that day, Clair L. Miller, who was as interned with Don Dorfmeier at St. Wendel, "cut [his] thumb on a rusty can." The cut was deep enough for Clair to "see the bone" yet, the wound "did not exactly bleed." Rather, " . . . a sudsy orange substance ooze[d] out of the [gash]." Alarmed, the airman reported to Leslie Caplan, who, examining him, said "Unless I was liberated within a couple of days I would die. My red blood cells were almost depleted."[499]

---

[496] Middlebrook, *The Peenemünde Raid,* 227
[497] O'Donnell, *Luftgangsters Marching Across Germany,* 25 ?
[498] Caplan, *Domain of Heroes,* 81
[499] O'Donnell, *Luftgangsters Marching Across Germany,* 25

Fortunately for Clair Miller and countless other POWs in his immediate vicinity, liberation would soon follow. Resting again on 1 May 1945, the weather turned cold enough to snow on them–they hoped it would be for the last time. Later that evening, secure in their lodgments, the men saw "artillery flashes [and heard] guns going off pretty steadily" during the night. Some were told "The Allies are 14 kilometers from [their position] and if they don't come to get us, we're going to them."[500] Staff Sergeant Leonard Deranleau recalled the excitement of that evening, "You [could] almost sense the war was coming to an end. Even the [Germans] seemed to be anxious for it to be over as they became [friendlier]." Later on, Leonard was approached by one of these guards, who in broken English said, "'Mussolini kaput, Hitler kaput, Roosevelt kaput! All is comrade,'" as if to say if it hadn't been for these [world] leaders there wouldn't have been a war!"[501]

The next morning, the German officer in command of the column, sent for Leslie Caplan and told the flight surgeon, "We were cut off by the British," and requested that he find the English forces to coordinate their surrender. Caplan responded to this directive immediately and located Francis Troy. Together these two airmen, accompanied by an interpreter and a German NCO who carried a white flag, moved some two or three kilometers toward the British lines. Eventually, they found a scouting element of the First Royal Dragoons, and in an open clearing, the two senior representatives negotiated the surrender of their escort detail and arranged for the safe recovery of the airmen in their care, ending their long ordeal.[502] This final arbitration concluded their 86-day "forced Hunger March" across northern Germany that began with the evacuation of Stalag Luft IV on 6 February 1945 and ended, 2 May 1945. Of the 6,800 Allied POWs who marched out of Pomerania twelve weeks earlier, this small contingent of less than 1,500 airmen, lodged north of the Elbe River, had drawn the short straw of fate. This group alone, which included a significant number of men originally assigned to C-lager, had marched for the longest duration and the farthest distance of any group of Allied POWs held captive in the European Theater of Operations during the World War II. They had, according to Al Zimmerman, the writer and producer of the documentary, *Behind*

---

[500] Deranleau, *Memories of an Aerial Gunner,* 147
[501] Ibid., 147
[502] Caplan, *Domain of Heroes,* 84

the Wire, endured "the cruelest march of all."[503]

Several hours later, a British reconnaissance vehicle, followed by a few tanks, arrived to formerly liberate the American POWs who had been waiting in their bivouacs, hoping for freedom. Now their moment of deliverance had finally arrived and, with it, all hell broke loose. German guards offered no resistance to this anticipated change in the fortunes of war. Without ceremony or an overt display of emotions, they voluntarily stacked their weapons and formed ranks to acknowledge the abrupt, yet long-expected change of roles between the guards and their prisoners. Jack Fischer recalled this moment, noting, "After mingling with their British liberators, we were told to remain where we were and wait until morning . . . before proceeding to cross no-man's land toward British lines for processing." These instructions were fine with Fischer, who characterized his physical condition that morning as "nothing more than skin and bone . . . covered with lice, half sick, and [speculating] that he could not have survived another week of the march." Then tears welled in his eyes and Jack acknowledged the next morning's passage toward British lines "was the hardest seven or eight kilometers I ever had to walk."[504]

Airman James W. McCloskey and his group quartered at Hackendorf, left their bivouac site at 0800 hours on 3 May 1945, and moved toward the British position. Later, passing through Lauenburg, James noted in his journal, "the town showed significant damage resulting from intense fighting." Yet, outside the town, "the road was jammed . . . and blocked with [German] equipment: tanks, trucks, half-tracks, reconnaissance vehicles, and motorcycles. There were also . . . artillery pieces, small arms, and ammo. Such wreckage can hardly be imagined. British soldiers were stopping German POWs and taking watches, knives, and almost everything from them. The road was jammed with thousands of POWs, German soldiers, British guards, and refugees. It was a huge mess . . . ."[505] Leslie Caplan also passed through the same town, and recalled that movement through Lauenburg was further hindered, in part, by elements of three German divisions in the area who had recently surrendered and were moving to their own

---

[503] *Behind the Wire*, Al Zimmerman, video Eighth AF Historic Site, 1994
[504] Jack Fischer, video, Andersonville National Historic Site, 1994
[505] O'Donnell, *Luftgangsters Marching Across Germany*, 89

internment camps.[506]

On 7 May 1945, with Hitler dead and and his country in ruins, the German Wehrmacht surrendered unconditionally to the Western Allies in Reims, France. A similar ceremony was conducted the following day in Berlin, to appease the Russians, thus ending the Second World War in Europe.* The war, which lasted from 1939–1945, killed an estimated 55 million people. Germany lost over 5.5 million persons, while inflicting more dreadful losses on other countries, such as Poland, which lost eighteen percent of its prewar population. However, no country or ethnic group suffered more grievously than the Soviet Union, which endured horrific losses in excess of 26 million dead. Best estimates suggest the Red Army alone suffered losses approximating 8.5 million soldiers. Another eighteen million Russians perished during the German occupation. Countless numbers of other persons were wounded or displaced throughout Europe, many of whom were part of the eight and a half million foreign labors "departing the rubble-strewn cities of Germany,"[507] all searching for a new life.

German POWs moving to internment camps . . .   US Army

Within this swirling mass of humanity, tens of thousands of Allied

* Hundreds of thousands of other German soldiers in East Prussia and northern Latvia would continue to fight for another week. Thousands more, who served in the Waffen-SS, would conduct a guerrilla war in Estonia until 1954.

[506] Caplan, Domain of Heroes, 95
[507] Gilbert, The Day the War Ended, 374

airmen were starting to move to designated airfields throughout Germany, traveling through numerous villages and the carnage of a nation in ruins. From these collections points they would be airlifted to medical clearing stations in Belgium and France. To expedite this, a vast airlift of US Army Air Force B-17 heavy bombers and C-47 transports flew from air bases in England to various assembly points in Germany, extracting thousands of anxious POWs. Sadly, some of these early airlift flights ended in disaster. Airman Bob Engstrom witnessed one such incident at his airfield when a pilot aborted his take-off and "veered to [the] left and crashed into a line of waiting C-47s, which burst into flames. Maybe four guys jumped out but the rest never did."[508] However, most airmen such as Richard W. Burt simply recalled, "waiting several days at an abandoned Luftwaffe airfield" after being informed on 8 May 1945 that the war was over. The next day several C-47s landed and Richard Burt was loaded with other sick airmen bound for a hospital in France. Years later Richard recalled, "We all gave a cheer as we took off and said farewell to a nightmare that would continue to haunt us for many years to come!"[509]

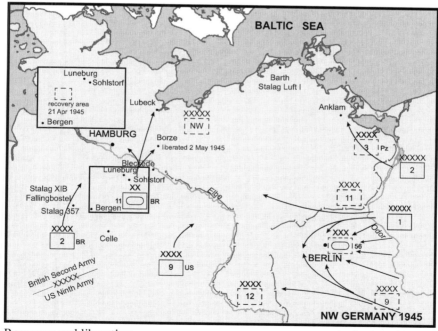

Recovery and liberation

Author's collection

[508] Carlson, *We Were Each Other's Prisoners,* 16
[509] O'Donnell, *The Pangs of the Thorn,* 135

The airlift of recently liberated Allied airmen . . .   USAAF

. . .boarding C-47 transports   USAAF

As the wheels of Richard Burt's C-47 were lifting off, Leslie Caplan was moving by train to Namur, Belgium. Caplan had arrived in Brussels the previous day and, in all likelihood, his reputation had preceded him. Weeks earlier, following the liberation of Stalag XIB, ten airmen who participated in the long march out of Stalag Luft IV, yet had not evacuated Fallingbostel, petitioned the US Army to recognize the "indomitable spirit" and heroic efforts of this extraordinary flight surgeon of C-lager. The airmen's appeal went on to cite, as would many others in years to come, that this "modest, unassuming man . . . walked twice the distance of the [other] men to [provide encouragement] and often traded [sundries] from his own Red Cross parcels for eggs, so that the sick men [in his care] might get the nourishment they [required]."[510]

The recognition and laudable exploits cited in the airmen's petition

[510] Caplan, *Domain of Heroes,* XII–XIII

might have embarrassed this unpretentious man who was reluctant to recount his own accomplishments. This fact is readily apparent when reading Caplan's first letter home following liberation. In correspondence to his family, dated 8 May 1945, the dutiful son first reported he was in "excellent health," in spite of having "witnessed and experienced great dangers and hardships." Leslie continued to offer a brief account of the adversity and deprivations of the march without specific reference to his role. He then closed with the comment, "I survived this ordeal well. I did not get dysentery or any other disease, but I never worked so hard or felt so discouraged in my life."[511] Contrary to his own assessment, Caplan was, in fact, malnourished and sick from tuberculosis, a significantly debilitating infection that usually attacks the lungs. Moreover, Caplan's physical condition, in spite of his optimism, required immediate medical intervention; and from Namur he was transferred to a hospital train in route to Camp Lucky Strike. From this location, the 36-year-old self-described medic of the Hunger March continued to pass through three more field and general hospitals prior to departing Cherbourg, France on the US Army hospital ship, *Acadia*, on 18 June 1945.[512]

Once stateside, Leslie Caplan would be hospitalized for 10 months at Fitzsimons Army Hospital, Denver, Colorado where he was later discharged.* Prior to retirement from active duty on 8 July 1946, Doctor Caplan was promoted to the rank of major and awarded the Legion of Merit for his heroic role in attending to and saving the lives of untold numbers of POWs during the long march out of Stalag Luft IV. Appropriately, the citation reads, in part, "For exceptionally meritorious conduct in the performance of outstanding services as medical officer for 2,600 American prisoners of war . . . ."[513]

---

* Other POWs were not so fortunate. A 1954 follow-up study of WWII POWs noted "the frequency of tuberculosis deaths was not unexpected; more pertinent is the question of whether the extraordinary incidence of tuberculosis is symptomatic of . . . large proportion of the ex-prisoners, such as those following prolonged malnutrition described by Keys et al." The study also notes concerns for "the future survival potential of those still alive and their long run morbidity and disability expectations."[514]

---

[511] Ibid., 80

[512] Ibid., 71

[513] Caplan, *Domain of Heroes*, XIV

[514] Cohen, *A Follow-Up Study of WWII Prisoners of War*, 64

While he recovered at Fitzsimons General Hospital, Caplan petitioned the Adjutant General of the Army to recognize the "tact, courage, and good judgment" of Staff Sergeant, Francis Troy. In a recommendation dated 8 July 1945, Caplan cited Troy for his "endless efforts to secure better food, shelter, or transportation for his men. In spite of threats, rebuffs, and humiliation," he continually argued "for better conditions [for] the seriously sick," which ultimately "saved many lives and frostbitten limbs." Troy was later awarded the Bronze Star for his "exceptionally meritorious service."[515]

Caplan and some of the more seriously ill airmen were promptly evacuated to receive medical treatment, but thousands of other liberated prisoners of war remained stranded throughout Germany. To help expedite their passage, aircrews from the 398th Bomb Group at Nuthampstead, England were ordered to support the massive, two-week airlift operation. Pilot and First Lieutenant John Mikulus of the 603rd Bomb Squadron, recalled flying one such rescue mission to Stalag IIIB–with a crew of only four men, without ammunition or ordnance, in order to extract as many POWs as possible. Writing about the experience years later, Mikulus recalled, "Upon landing in a large open field and taxiing toward the camp buildings . . . [we] deplaned [and] look[ed] at what must have been a miserable life for so many POWs." Then, "one of the assembled groups . . . started running toward us [and] we were mobbed, hugged, kissed and lifted up as if we were angels from heaven. I heard crying and hysterical laughter . . . [and] many [men] kissed [our] B-17 while they climbed aboard." After loading the 36 liberated airmen, Mikulus negotiated the short field and barely managed to "clear a fence by about ten feet" as he struggled to gain 8,000 feet of altitude en route to an airfield north of Paris. However, he would not know until years later that once airborne, the spirited POWs had hurriedly lined up to use the urinal in the main fuselage of the aircraft, all hoping for one last chance to piss on Germany before going home![516]

When the POWs from Stalag IIIB and other liberated airmen and soldiers arrived at the field hospitals in Belgium and France, they were provided showers and new uniforms. Once clean and fed, they were medically triaged prior to being evacuated to the RAMP camps, which,

---

[515] Recommendation provided by Jesse Franklin in letter dated 8 October 2001
[516] Mikulus, "Stalag Luft . . . ," *Flak News* 17.1 (Jan 2002) : 9

were purposely established near embarkation ports on the English Channel to expedite their return home. However, approximately 20 percent of all airmen who participated in the evacuation of Stalag Luft IV, as well as POWs liberated from other internment camps throughout Germany, required immediate hospitalization for malnutrition. Others, such as Frank Dyer, who suffered from scabies, would be hospitalized once returned to the United States.

Staff Sergeant Joseph O'Donnell, one airman who had marched out of Fallingbostel with Caplan, required hospitalization and was evacuated to the 91st General Hospital in England. O'Donnell recalled, "We arrived in [Oxford] . . . about 9:00 p.m. One hanger was set up to receive us . . . where we were then seated at an informal table and given tea and cookies." Each individual was [then] . . . attended to with concern that "gave us that warm feeling that, again, we were human." Once admitted to the hospital, the airmen showered again and were told "the mess hall was open and would remain open 24 hour a day, seven days a week and that we could eat all we wanted, whenever we wanted." Understandably, everyone in O'Donnell's group "overate and was sick." The men then returned to their ward where, for the first time in months, if not years, "we crawled between clean, sweet smelling sheets, and pulled the blankets over our heads . . . without scratching, freezing . . . starving . . . or dying [and] said a prayer of thanks [before falling] off to sleep."[517]

The airmen who did not require hospitalization were transferred to the new RAMP camps to receive physical examinations. Yet, these evaluations were cursory and superficial procedures, according to Jack Fischer, and "not intended to identify illnesses or psychological problems." Rather, Fischer continued, the Air Force's primary concern was to simply conduct an administrative protocol "to remove the airmen from flight status."[518] Once terminated, Fischer argued, "The Army was freed of its obligation to pay the airmen their incentive allowance for performing hazardous duty, which was equal to fifty percent of their base pay." Understandably, most airmen resented this policy and the fact that they were denied an adequate physical to remedy legitimate medical problems. Some men attempted to take this in stride and adhere to the sentiment of a popular top *Hit Parade* single of the day,

---

[517] O'Donnell, *The Evacuation* . . . , 33
[518] Jack Fischer, video, Andersonville National Historic Site 1994

"Accentuate the Positive." For others, this treatment would engender a lingering resentment and angst. For such men, their joy of having survived would fade in time and unresolved feelings of resentment would coalesce with other disturbances tending to manifest itself in alcoholism and/or other psychological disorders.

General Dwight D. Eisenhower, the Supreme Commander of all Allied Forces in Europe, and the future 34th president of the United States, addressed a group of 40,000 liberated American POWs at St Valery, France, 23 May 1945. Staff Sergeant Leonard Deranleau recalled, "Eisenhower was very impressive . . . stressing the importance of the Army Air Corps [and] thanking us for our efforts in winning this war."[519] He also said he was personally going to do everything to get them home as soon as possible. The general went on to state, "Speaking for everyone in America I want to express our gratitude to you all in helping to defeat Germany. You men carried the ball for us and we will not forget it."[520] The Eisenhower's comments were well received and were a direct acknowledgement that the Army Air Corps had been attacking German-occupied Europe two years before the US Army landed in France, 6 June 1944.

In spite of Eisenhower's apparent sincerity, the liberated airmen who were returning from Europe were afforded little recognition or special consideration of their status by the American public. Aside from what was extended to them by their individual families, the general public had stigmatized these servicemen for having surrendered.[521] Weeks earlier, senior American officers refused to endorse the creation of a specific medal designed for service members who had been held as enemy prisoners of war.[522] Sadly, these senior officers, along with the American public, were uninformed or indifferent to the harsh realities faced by the nation's POWs. Moreover, the country and agencies like the Veterans Administration, were simply unprepared to recognize or acknowledge the difficulties these men suffered, or the profound and lasting impact of their experience. Yet, none of the tens of thousands of liberated airmen or soldiers populating the RAMP camps of Europe in May and June of 1945 could have imagined they would be forgotten.

---

[519] Deranleau, *Memories of an Aerial Gunner,* 161
[520] Ibid., 161
[521] Carlson, *We Were Each Other's Prisoners,* viii, xvi
[522] Ibid., xvi.

The recovered servicemen were too jubilant, too hopeful, to think that America would not care about them or the severity of their ordeal.

Honorable Service Lapel Pin

This lapel pin was awarded to all US military service members honorably discharged during WWII. The decoration allowed service members to legally wear their uniforms for thirty days following separation from active service.

19

HOME: FRESNO STATE

Staff Sergeants Don Dorfmeier and Paul McNally woke early on 11 June 1945 and quickly dressed for an occasion that would be experienced by countless US servicemen. The two airmen had been discharged from the 91st General Hospital weeks earlier, and at sea for the past seven days. Now, they and hundreds of other returning veterans would line the portside of their troopship to catch a morning glimpse of the 151-foot Statue of Liberty as they sailed into New York harbor. For many of these servicemen the towering grey-green icon symbolized all that was right with America. Don and Paul certainly felt as much, as did countless other veterans returning home for an extended furlough authorized to all repatriated prisoners of war.

US Army soldier returning from Europe   US Army

Besides this one remembrance, Don didn't make any other specific references to his return voyage from Europe. However, he and the other veterans on his ship undoubtedly reflected on their earlier passage when their individual encounter with war stilled loomed undefined. Returning home with "experiences that would haunt them them for many years to come," Don and the other veterans hoped to embrace a new beginning. For the moment, the anxiety generated by their personal experiences of war was channeled into the excitement of what they would do with the rest of their lives, now that they had survived.

The ship docked in New York and the two Fresno veterans proceeded to Camp Shanks where several days later they received orders to report to the Army Air Force Redistribution Station at Camp Beale, Santa Monica, California. Departing New York, Don and Paul were given first class passage on a "nice train." An hour or two later, the two men were transferred to [second class accommodations] "typical [of a] troop train and [continued] across the States in that fashion." Several days later, former C-lager roommate, Jack Fischer experienced a similar affront after his return to the States. Arriving in New York on 13 June 1945, Fischer recalled that "he and other repatriated POWs bound for San Antonio, Texas, were given second class seating on a train while German POWs were riding in [first class] Pullmans with [bed] sheets."* Still resentful years later, Fischer asserted, "only the presence of armed guards prevented us from physically ejecting the Germans from the more desirable seating."[523]

This was not the only offense Fischer and the former POWs in his party would experience on their return from overseas. After they arrived in San Antonio, the repatriated airmen were assigned to barracks that were dirty, and were instructed by a junior captain to have their quarters cleaned by the following morning. Jack and the others balked at this directive. A senior NCO, acting as spokesman for the group, responded to the young officer stating, "We were told aboard ship we would have no duties [upon returning to the States] and that assigned orderlies would attend to basic house-keeping." The Captain promptly disappeared, returning several hours later, invoking the authority of a senior officer, who "threatened to court-marshal all those who failed to comply with his orders." However, the airmen, according to Fischer, would not be intimidated, and the group spokesman told the Captain, "The Colonel could go fuck himself. They weren't cleaning the barracks. Furthermore, they would go to the local radio stations and newspapers in town to expose the shabby treatment of recently returned POWs." The two officers ultimately backed down and the following morning

---

* A total of 380,000 German POWs were interned at 155 camps in the United States during WWII.[524]

[523] Jack Fischer, video Andersonville National Historic Site, 1994
[524] Carlson, *We Were Each Other's Prisoners,* xix–xx.

orderlies appeared to clean the airmen's quarters.

Neither Don nor Paul seemed to have encountered any of the difficulties cited by Fischer once they arrived in California. From Santa Monica, the two airmen, acting in accordance with Special Order 169, furnished "their own transportation on or about 18 June 1945, with reimbursement at 3 cents per mile and $1.00 per meal . . ." and proceeded "to points specified for 60 days of rehabilitation, recuperation, and recovery." Arriving home on the same day, the two men were overwhelmed with emotion on reuniting with their families. Their relatives were similarly affected. All had yearned for this day, and it was understandable that the airmen's parents would greet their   sons with reverence. Their sons, however, did not think of themselves as special, nor did the general public, who thought "there is nothing heroic or ennobling about becoming a prisoner of war."[525]

Still, the ordeal of the two escaped airmen was compelling and it was most likely that they would be approached by a Fresno reporter who asked for an interview. Regrettably, the published article about the escape of the two POWs was inaccurate and segments of the story were presented out of context. Yet, there was no denying that the account, printed with accompanying photographs of the two young men, captured the essence of a dramatic exploit. Perhaps the airmen, still traumatized by their past experiences or emotionally overwhelmed by their return home, could not have provided a more coherent account of their hardship. Or conceivably, the newspaper reporter was too excited by the accounts of the two former prisoners of war to have asked more exacting or clarifying questions. The harrowing account of their escape also stood in sharp contrast to the photographs of the two airmen who, while projecting confidence and resiliency, still possessed the look of innocent youth. Without question, the photos, provided by the War Department or the veterans' families, were taken in their early days of service training, prior to enduring the rigors of war. A later photograph of Don, taken in mid-July 1945, captures more accurately the expression one would associate with the experiences cited in the article.

The returning Fresno veterans, along with all repatriated POWs, had only recently been authorized to grant interviews with the press as

---

[525] Carlson, *Were We Each Others Prisoners,* vii

a result of a change in War Department policy. A new Pentagon memorandum, dated 29 March 1945, regarding "Publicity in Connection with Escaped, Liberated or Repatriated POWs," cited an amendment to an earlier directive stating, "personnel who have evaded, escaped, or been released from liberated areas may relate stories of their experience after clearance with the [appropriate] agency." However, the memorandum continued to state "no references may be made to the following: 1) Existence of unannounced organizations established to assist evaders or escapees . . . . 2) Names, pictures or other identification of [individuals providing assistance] . . . . 3) Treacherous acts of Allied POWs . . . . 4) Sabotage activities of Allied Prisoners of War . . . . 5) Briefings. and equipment for escape and evasion . . . and other intelligence activities within the camps . . . ."[526] All repatriated POWs were introduced to this change in policy while processing through the RAMP camps in Europe or various military bases prior to returning home for extended furloughs. The airmen were also required to sign a nondisclosure statement with the Army Air Force to safeguard sensitive information acquired through official briefings and their individual experiences as prisoners of war. This requirement was part of a concerted effort to protect the tradecraft identified in the Army's MIS-X Manual on Evasion, Escape, and Survival in the event of another conflict.* Most airmen perceived this policy as reasonable, especially those veterans choosing to remain on active duty, like Chuck Hartney, who later served as an Escape and Evasion instructor. However, continued adherence to a vow of silence decades later only served as a convenient rationale for men to refuse to talk about very painful experiences.

The Army's requirement for returning POWs to sign the nondisclosure statements does not imply that these servicemen were debriefed or provided any kind of transitory care. They were not. Rather, author Lewis Carlson notes, "Most were [given an extended furlough home, then] quickly mustered out of the service and left to their own devices to deal with painful memories, inexplicable and debilitating anxieties, and even acute antisocial behavior."[527] Still, most

---

*The Army MIS-X manual was used to train service personnel and assisted POWs captured during the Korean and Vietnam wars, and not officially declassified until 31 August 1994.

[526] WD, Memorandum; Publicity . . . 29 Mar 1945
[527] Carlson, *We Were Each Other's Prisoners,* 200

airmen enjoyed their first few days at home and attempted to relax and appreciate their immediate families, along with other curious, well-intentioned relatives and friends.

However, Don Dorfmeier and many POWs, soon manifested a discernible, underlying tension and irritability, noticeable to their family as, "out of character" with the son or brother they knew prior to their overseas deployment.* Don's brother, Alton, and mother, Marie, said as much years later. "Don acted as if he were ashamed of something" and the family was surprised, if not shocked, to learn "he now drank [alcohol]" and, in their opinion, "to excess."**

In spite of the warm welcome from their families, neither Don nor many of the other repatriated prisoners of war returning home in 1945 were proud men. Most of them thought of their experience as shameful and degrading.*** Moreover, the general public unfairly stigmatized the country's POWs as "fainthearted" and "sitting out the war while others did the fighting." This attitude was prevalent enough in the general population to appear in correspondence sent to POWs who were held in captivity. Author Lewis Carlson cites one thoughtless and insensitive spouse, writing to her husband in 1944, "I still love you even if you are a coward and a prisoner."[528]

This offensive assessment of American prisoners of war as cowards might have been attributable to the anxiety aroused in the general public following the surrender of 78,000 American and Filipino soldiers and the loss of the Philippine Islands in April 1942. The loss of the Islands and its garrison, following the damage to the US Pacific Fleet

---

* Traumatic experiences are linked to subjective feelings of tension, anxiety, outrage, and/or anger frequently manifested as irritability.[529]
** Later studies would find that many of these POWs would still "experience nightmares, persistent flashbacks, and extreme reactions" to their ordeal 35–50 years after their release from captivity.[530]
*** Former POW and Field Service Officer for the American Ex-POW Association, Fred Campbell, cited shame as the pervading characteristic of the hundreds of WWII POWs he helped to obtain medical treatment and compensation for their war-related service.

[528] Carlson, *We Were Each Other's Prisoners,* vii
[529] Williams, *Post Traumatic Stress Disorder,* 78
[530] Carlson, *We Were Each Other's Prisoners,* 61

at Pearl Harbor, generated fears of a possible Japanese invasion of the West Coast during the early phase of the war.* A similar sense of shock and disbelief was no doubt elicited several years later when 23,000 US soldiers were captured in the Ardennes during the German winter offensive of 1944.[531] Later remarks, attributed to Eleanor Roosevelt, referring to American POWs as "animals that need to be rehabilitated,"[532] further disparaged the integrity of the country's prisoners of war and served to reinforce a negative perception of these men as lacking in moral qualities.

Many repatriated POWs found they could only stay at home for a few days before gravitating to the local bars and clubs in their respective neighborhoods. The continual assault of intrusive thoughts and emotional arousal caused general irritability during the day and sleep disturbances at night. Sadly, this distress prevented these men from making the psychological transition from the reality they had recently experienced to the more ordered world of their youth. Parents, spouses, and others, all with good intentions, further exacerbated the veteran's sense of isolation with manifest expressions of disbelief to horrific stories they heard from the returning servicemen. Moreover, these families did not know how to respond to disturbing accounts of the veteran's ordeal. Such reactions conveyed the all-too-clear impression that family and former friends couldn't cope with the distressing information or images generated by the veterans' stories.

Equally problematic for most returning veterans was the difficulty integrating their wartime experiences with long-held beliefs and attitudes about themselves and the world. Countless numbers of these servicemen were disturbed by the disparity between their idealized sense of self and their actual behavior during times of stress, which left them feeling confused by their experiences. Many lost their earlier belief in God and sense of a moral order in the world. Others suffered from a perceived or real sense of survivor's guilt, characterized by a pervading belief that they were not worthy to survive while others, of

---

* This fear of invasion on the West Coast was part of the rationale that lead to the internment of 130,000 Japanese-Americans, most of whom lived in California, in the spring and summer of 1942.[533]

[531] Carlson, *We Were Each Other's Prisoners,* xviii
[532] O'Donnell, *Pangs of the Thorn,* 149.
[533] Ross, *America 1941; A Nation at the Crossroads,* 193

equal or more redeeming qualities, had died. This was especially true for those airmen who managed to escape from burning or exploding aircraft when fellow crew members could not get out. A variant of this theme may have also affected Don, who might have felt conflicted about his escape and abandonment of men for whom he still felt some personal responsibility.

The experience of war had torn, if not ripped the fabric of most veterans' lives, leaving many feeling isolated and disconnected. "Many [POWs]," according to Lewis H. Carlson, "turned to alcohol to drown out painful memories."[534] Establishments that served alcohol and provided less intense, if not superficial, social interaction became increasingly attractive. One of the clubs visited by Don and Paul in Fresno was the High Life on Maroa Avenue, where, according to Paul's son, Gary, "[they] couldn't buy a drink." At the High Life and elsewhere in the United States, servicemen came together to drink with other men with whom they shared the universal fantasy of home–in addition to experiences of disappointment, if not disillusionment. For these veterans, alcohol served to dull the intrusive memories of the war and to ease the awkward moments with family and other acquaintances. Alcohol also calmed the anxieties of every veteran's pending return to active duty, and possible reassignment to the Pacific Theater of Operations. Although the war in Europe was over, the Japanese were still actively fighting for survival and, in spite of suffering staggering losses during the past two years, showed no indication or willingness to surrender.* Fierce battles for the islands of Iwo Jima and Okinawa resulted in exorbitant American losses. US casualties for the battle of Okinawa alone numbered 50,000 servicemen. Another 36,000 Marines, soldiers, and sailors were medically evacuated for psychiatric care.[535]

---

* The Japanese invaded Manchuria in 1931. Ten years later, Japan launched a preemptive strike against Pearl Harbor as a prelude to assaulting Malaysia, the Dutch East Indies, and the Philippine Islands. The subsequent capture of the Philippine protectorate forced the surrender of the US garrison, resulting in the death of 25,000 Filipino and American soldiers from wounds, disease, or brutal treatment during the notorious Bataan Death March in April 1942[536]

---

[534] Carlson, *We Were Each Other's Prisoners*, 232
[535] Hastings, *Retribution*, 402
[536] Keegan, *The Second World War*, 266

The detonation of a second atomic bomb over Nagasaki, 9 August 1945, ultimately forced Japan to surrender and ended the Second World War just as Don and Paul returned to Camp Beale in Santa Monica for "processing and reassignment." Days later, in early September, Don was hospitalized at the Army Air Force Regional and Convalescent Hospital in Santa Ana, California. His diagnosis at the time of admission was "chronic amoebic dysentery and persistent diarrhea [contracted in] early February [1945]." The diagnosis was remarkable given his current weight, noted at the time of admission as 205 lbs.[537] Equally surprising, he remained hospitalized for 18 days do to only marginal improvement in his condition prior to discharge. However, someone at the hospital was perceptive enough to speculate his "symptoms may be secondary to mild anxiety."[538]

Following discharge, Don was transferred to Greensboro, North Carolina, while Paul remained in California, processed for separation and discharge from active duty service on 5 October 1945. In all likelihood, he was back in Fresno before Don even signed into his new unit on the East Coast. The purpose for Don's official reassignment is unclear, other than to "play football for the Air Force's 1060th Distribution Command." Six weeks later he reported for his final physical exam prior to separation. The examination form was a single page, two-sided document asking a total of 48 general questions pertaining to his heath. The annotations on Don's record are unremarkable except for two comments noted in Block # 48, where he reports sustaining a back injury while "Bailing out [of his aircraft] on August 4, 1944 . . . [and continues to experience] occasional pain." The second notation reads, "Amoebic dysentery while a prisoner of war. Treated upon liberation concomitant to above [noted] strain. No residual."[539]

Two days later, 7 November 1945, Don Dorfmeier signed his discharge separating him from the US Army Air Force after three and a half years of active duty service, collected $329.51 in pay for "mustering out and travel," and departed for California. His awards for this period of service were two campaign ribbons with two Bronze Star devices, identifying different phases of operations; a Good Conduct Medal, and an Air Medal. Surprisingly, there was no annotation or other reference

---

[537] Service medical records; Dorfmeier, Donald, 28 Sep 1945
[538] Ibid.,
[539] WD Form AGO 38; Physical Examination, 5 Nov 1945

on his discharge indicating that he had been a prisoner of war. It is also worth noting that Don signed his discharge and separation document in spite of multiple incorrect entries. Don's indifference to this and other administrative errors attests to the sense of urgency with which he, if not all servicemen, wanted to leave military service and return home after the war.

Home, and the desire to return home, held universal appeal for the "12,000,000 men and women serving in the US Armed Forces in May 1945."[540]* This was especially true for anyone who had served overseas. The all-consuming appeal of home with its familiarity and comforts, amid the chaos of war, became symbolic of safety, nurturance, and above all, predictability. Yet, few veterans understood how much they had changed as a result of their experiences in the service and that "home" would no longer provide the same sense of security. Their exposure to violent death and loss left many young men dazed and uncertain how to reorder their world. Sadly, it was this singular experience that caused many returning servicemen to feel isolated and disconnected from the very community they wanted to embrace.

Don returned home to California, without fanfare in early November 1945, one of 25,000 other men and women from Fresno County who served in the armed forces during the war.[541] He had hoped otherwise, having enlisted in the Air Force with aspirations of becoming a pilot and achieving personal recognition. Instead, he felt a sense of emptiness, later characterized by Dr. Robert Obourn, a psychiatrist and former POW, as "a sense of embarrassment," and inability to share the pride and success that was "the tradition of American Armed Forces."[542] Yet once settled, Don directed his attention toward school and registered the following week, in mid-semester, for six units of classes at Fresno State College. His admission ranked him as one of only 421 regular and part-time male students attending classes that fall at FSC. However, male enrollments more than doubled the following semester to 982 as some of the 2,700 FSC students who enlisted returned home and went

---

* In May 1945, US Armed Forces numbered 12,208,238 personnel assigned to the following services; US Army and Army Air Force, 8,267,958; US Navy & Marine Corps, 3,855,497; and US Coast Guard, 85,783.

[540] Cardozier, *The Mobilization of the United States in WWII*, 92
[541] Walker, *Fresno Community Book*, 210
[542] Williams, *Post Traumatic Stress Disorder*, 140

back to school to complete their education.[543]*

Don's decision to return to school was no surprise to his mother or his family. He indicated his intent to do so in several letters he wrote while interned as a POW. His decision was aided immensely by President Roosevelt's signing of the Serviceman's Readjustment Act in June 1944. The legislation, known as the GI Bill, contained various provisions for vocational and educational assistance to veterans enrolled in college, which offset "post-war demobilization problems. Students were authorized a stipend of $50.00 a month for single, and $75.00 a month for married veterans, in addition to maximum of $500.00 per year for tuition, fees, and books, an amount that greatly exceeded those costs in most colleges following the war."[544]

Other POWs interned with Don also went to school on the GI Bill. Former room and barrack's members Frank Dyer, Bob Cash, and Carl Moss all returned to college, as did John Anderson and George Guderley. Ultimately, 2,232,000 veterans attended college with support from this unique program, before its termination in 1956. A later report on the legislation's effectiveness noted most students "took their studies seriously and worked to get the most out of their experience."[545]

Initially readmitted to Fresno State as a returning sophomore, Don was eventually awarded an additional nine semester hours of academic credit for course work completed in summer 1943 when enrolled at Utah State Agricultural College. He also received another sixteen hours of credit for completing basic and preflight training while on active duty. Receipt of these additional credits allowed Don to carry a manageable course load the next three years in order to participate in the football and track programs while working part-time.

In 1946, the allowance for veteran students attending school on the GI Bill was increased by $15.00 dollars a month. Sometime later, the government notified all former POWs that they were going to receive

* One hundred and thirty-six graduates and former FSC students were killed while serving on active duty during WWII.[546]

[543] Walker, *Fresno Community Book,* 117
[544] Cardozier, *Colleges and Universities in WWII,* 223–224
[545] Cardozier, *Colleges and Universities in WWII,* 224
[546] Walker, *Fresno Community Book,* 117

a one-time compensation payment for having been interned during the war. Payment would be based on a rate of $1.50 a day for every day held by "an enemy government [that] continually failed to comply with one or more of the Articles of the Geneva Convention." However, the gesture and the criteria for assessing remuneration reflected little understanding of the hardships suffered by thousands of airmen who were shot down in hostile territory, and many of them were denied full compensation. George Guderley was denied $12.00 in payment once officials learned that he had successfully evaded capture for 8 days before being apprehended. Leonard Rose was also denied compensation for the 21 days he was held by the Russians prior to escaping from their detainment on 14 May 1945. Similarly, Don, Paul, and the three other men with whom they escaped were denied consideration for the seven days spent evading capture before being recovered by British forces on 21 April 1945.

Don registered at Fresno State College and joined the school's Alpha Fraternity, although he could have chosen from any number of organizations given his status as a returning servicemen and school athlete. He would have been comfortable with any brotherhood of veterans as he admired those who served in the military. He also enjoyed the active, if not excessive, social life of fraternity membership, which gave him an entrance into a world that had not been previously available. Physically attractive and animated, Don was engaging and immensely entertaining at any social gathering. Part of his charm was based on a self-deprecating humor and his ability to imitate the world leaders of his generation. Years later, Alton's wife June, recalled, "Don was hysterical with his mocking imitation of Mussolini" during a family party after he returned from the war.

Don was engaged with fraternity and other social activities, yet also renewed his participation in school sports. This primary focus became all the more pronounced several months later following Jean Lamoure's return from the Navy. The two men had known each other since high school and eagerly renewed their good-natured competition through sports. Don's scholastic interest was of secondary importance, although he clearly had the aptitude to have performed at a high academic level. It's worth noting, however, that individuals exposed to traumatic incidents frequently have difficulty with concentration and with persons in positions of authority. [547]

In contrast to the concerns expressed by Don's family, Jean liked the change in his high school friend, who he now perceived as "more assured and less anxious." Yet, Jean probably did not appreciate how much of Don's cavalier attitude, characterized as "more easy going and fun to be around," was a reflection of his increasing use of alcohol to cope with his post-service adjustment. One of the first individuals to recognize the returning veteran's adjustment difficulties, and conflict with authority at Fresno State College, was the football coach, Jimmy Bradshaw. Bradshaw, also known as "The Rabbit," was a former All-American at the University of Nevada and had coached at Fresno State for the past 10 years, accumulating an impressive 59–18–2 record in the California Coast Conference. Yet, the coach was frustrated by the attitude of his returning players. Although interested in playing football, these veterans had no intent in following rules that seemed trivial or irrelevant. Nor were they willing to comply with standards of behaviors restricting a player's use of alcohol. The problem eventually became so vexing for Bradshaw that he retired from coaching the following year. He had, according to his daughter, Beverly, become embittered by "today's youth who just weren't receptive to being coached." However, Bradshaw's replacement, Glen Gleason, fared no better. Most of his players, recalled Lamoure, "spent almost as much time in the clubs as on the practice field."

Jean also recalled, with much affection, some of the antics that characterized his relationship with Don as they traveled to Fresno State sporting events around California. On one such outing to San Jose, Don insisted a porter carry their bags upstairs to their room after they had checked into a local hotel. Once inside the room, Don looked expectantly at Jean to provide the tip. This good-natured tension between the two athletes lasted for a moment before Don thought to check the pockets of the coat he had borrowed from Jean, only to discover a bundle of bills in the front pocket. Then, grinning mischievously, Don retrieved the money from the coat and preceded to hand the expectant porter a "very generous tip," much to Jean's surprise.

However lighthearted or playful Don may have appeared to Jean following his return to Fresno, he was also, according to his future

[547] Williams, *Post Traumatic Stress Disorder,* 36

mother-in-law, "high-strung, quick-tempered, and nervous."* To help manage the intrusive thoughts that elicited these symptoms, Don and countless other veterans attempted to regulate their emotional well-being with alcohol. Little understanding or effective treatment models existed in 1945 for those traumatized by war, although the phenomena of soldiers distressed by conflict is a recurring theme throughout history. Former Civil War veteran and later Supreme Court Justice, Oliver Winslow Homes, characterized the experience of his generation as "having been touched by fire." Other metaphors from this and other earlier conflicts referred to war-related trauma as melancholia, soldier's heart, and shell shock

Following WWI, the medical and psychiatric community of the nation's military believed, incorrectly, that potential inductees into the US Armed Forces could be screened for susceptibility to trauma. Such thinking disqualified over one million individuals from military service during WWII. Still, one out of every four medical evacuations in the US Armed Forces during the war were psychiatric casualties, which were treated with mixed results.[548] Overseas, the Army Air Force managed these patients using a protocol developed during the previous war to establish "flak farms" in England in 1942–1943. With such facilities, service flight surgeons applied the principles of "proximity, immediacy, and expectancy," to treat individuals, and sometimes entire crews who were experiencing combat fatigue. However, long-term treatment for those evacuated from Theater consisted of little more than "[hiding them] in the back wards of [a] veteran's hospital."[549]

Stateside, the psychiatric community had little to offer returning veterans in need of psychological help for war-related trauma. The predominant treatment models at the time were based on variants of Freudian psychoanalytic theory of psycho-sexual development, asserting emotional problems were attributed to arrestment in the early stages of childhood development. These models were exceedingly deterministic and void of many of the constructs characteristic of later,

* Other symptoms experienced by returning POWs included over stimulation, difficulty with interpersonal relationships, and sleep disturbances.[550]

[548] Williams, *Post Traumatic Stress Disorder,* 2
[549] Tick, *War and the Soul,* 156
[550] Williams, *Post-Traumatic Stress Disorder,* 36

more humanistic models of psychology. Still, even the availability of a more compassionate treatment paradigm at the end of the war might have been too threatening for Don and his generation. Asking for psychological help was not a social norm for males in the post-war culture of 1945. However, Don did apply to the Veterans Administration for a rating disability and care related to his physical conditions in hope of receiving some type of treatment. His first application for assistance was filed on 19 February 1946, seeking compensation and treatment for "sacroiliac strain and amoebic dysentery." His claim was returned 11 months later on 21 January 1947 with a "zero percent rating" and denied recognition as a "combat related disability."[551] Later attempts to establish a disability rating for treatment of "nervousness" were also dismissed as not service-connected.

While Don struggled with his adjustment and other psychological problems he appeared to be doing well to others outside of his family. Many perceived him as an attractive, high-functioning individual with considerable interpersonal and athletic skills. Several favorable articles, published after his separation from active duty, buoyed this perception. A 1946 Fresno State College media guide noted, "Big and stalwartly built, Don Dorfmeier has been converted from fullback, where he played as a freshman in 1942, to end. He was a standout in the spring practice game this year and may break into the varsity ranks when he masters his new position. A veteran of three years in the AAF, during much of which he was a prisoner of war in Germany, Dorfmeier is also an able weight (shot put & discus) man on the track team."

Later that year, Don was again featured in another newspaper article titled, "Where Are They Now?" The article noted, "Donald D. Dorfmeier, manager of the Winther Brothers' Shell Service Station and Fresno State College student and football player was a former prisoner of war." Following this introduction, the columnist provided a more focused and comprehensive account of his service history and escape than the disjointed interview published the previous year. The article also mentioned that Don escaped with four other men, including Fresno resident, Paul McNally. The mention of McNally's name in the article might have given both men reason to reflect on the time they spent together as POWs. They had, after all, shared the same experiences throughout the nine long months of their captivity. Yet, for whatever

---

[551] VA Form 564; Adjudication of Claim, 21 Jan 1947

reason, the two former airmen did not maintain a relationship following the war. Perhaps this was inevitable, since they pursued different life goals that limited further contact. It's also possible the two men had a falling-out over some disagreement. However, the most reasonable explanation for their parting was that continued contact reactivated too many traumatic memories.

Early in 1947, Don met an attractive co-ed on campus at Fresno State College. Barbara Jean Harris was a 20-year-old local resident currently enrolled as a junior in the Fine Arts Department. Stunningly beautiful and vibrant, Barbara stood 5 feet, 7 inches and had a fair complexion with hazel eyes to complement her dark red hair. Born on 24 Jun 1926 in Sacramento, California, she was two years younger than Don. Her parents divorced when she was very young and, shortly thereafter, her father died in a diving accident at a local swimming pool. The family moved from Sacramento to Fresno, and Barbara was raised as an only child by her maternal grandmother, Mamie, while her mother, Helen, worked as the assistant manager of the Fresno Home Title Company. All three women lived together at 847 Yale Street in two of the four flats owned by Barbara's grandmother. The family matriarch lived upstairs in one unit, while Barbara lived with mother in the first-level apartment facing the intersection of Yale and Clinton.

Barbara attended St. Therese's Catholic elementary school where she excelled in all academic and secondary endeavors such as "drawing, neatness and deportment." She later attended Fresno High School, graduated, and enrolled at Fresno State as an art major. She joined the Omega Xi Omicron sorority in the spring semester of 1944. Barbara was also exposed to a wide variety of other experiences to round out her formal education. One of these activities included working as a volunteer with the local Red Cross, which gave her some understanding of the sacrifices required of a country at war and those who served in the nation's armed forces.

The "chance encounter" between the two students might have been contrived. Barbara only later admitted to "being struck," or more likely, swept off her feet, "one morning after catching her first glimpse of Don, striding across campus in a freshly ironed white shirt." Regardless of the circumstances around their first meeting, the couple fell in love quickly and soon became inseparable. Plans for a July wedding "came as a surprise to friends of the bride and bridegroom," according to an announcement in the local paper. However, both families supported the marriage–the couple appeared to be an ideal match.

A subsequent announcement in the Fresno paper reported, "The couple married and exchanged their wedding vows at the picturesque Carmel Mission on 27 Jul 1947 and honeymooned in the coastal community of Carmel, California." Three days later Barbara wrote to her mother a touching note that provided a glimpse of not only her relationship with Don but also of the very special bond that existed between the two women. Aside from Barbara's comments describing Don as "very considerate," this letter is most endearing for the seven accompanying sketches inserted in the margins and indentations of each paragraph, scenes of them having dinner, sunning themselves at the beach, and shopping.

Don & Barbara engagement photo   Author's collection

Don and Barbara returned from their honeymoon and found an apartment at 838 Clinton Street, where they lived while attending classes their senior year. In the spring, Don finished his last season of athletic competition by placing in the West Coast Relays. Several weeks later, 27 May 1948, their first son, David, was born at St. Agnes hospital. The following month, Don graduated in June with a degree in Social Science and, with focus toward the future, finished another 10 credits during the following summer session. The couple then moved from Fresno to the San Francisco Bay area, with all the attending excitement of a new adventure. Don had been accepted to graduate school at Stanford University in Palo Alto, and they had just enough time to find a house to rent before he stated classes in September.

EPILOGUE

Don started attending classes at Stanford University in the autumn quarter of 1948. He initially enrolled as a student in the school of Political Science, then changed his focus and graduated with a Master of Arts in Education on 6 January 1950. Three months later, a second

Don Dorfmeier, Stanford 1948
Author's collection

son, and brother, Darrell, was born in Palo Alto. Shortly thereafter, the young couple purchased a wooded lot in a desirable neighborhood of Menlo Park, California where they built a new, yet modest three bedroom home that reflected Barbara's developed sense of form and composition.

The town of Menlo Park was a small community with an avant-garde charm typical of municipalities located in close proximity to a major university. The Southern Pacific railroad had officially named the town in 1866, and soon after, residents of San Francisco purchased vast tracks of land for summer homes. A literary publication, later known as *Sunset* magazine was founded in 1898. Other institutions that enhanced the charm and attraction of the town were the Menlo Boys School, and later college, founded in 1915 and the Allied Arts Guild, a unique collection of shops and artists studios, established in 1929. Post-war expansion brought the formation of the Stanford Research Institute and the development of many older estates, which accommodated a rapid population growth following the war.

Don Dorfmeier 1950   Author's collection

Soon after moving into their new residence, Don was hired as a physical education instructor and coach for the recently constructed Menlo-Atherton high school, which opened in September 1951. Don's duties in the Boy's Athletic Department were to teach physical education, serve as head coach for the school's track team, and assistant coach for the varsity football program. These activities put him in daily contact with the department's athletic director, Bob Ayers, who characterized Don as, "an excellent teacher and coach who was well respected, outgoing, and very sociable." Ayers could have easily said the same of Howard Costello, whom he hired to be head coach of the varsity football team. The choice of both men was fortuitous for the school and fostered the development of a lifelong friendship.

Troy Ratliff and Dan Varty were two student-athletes who played on Menlo-Atherton's first varsity football teams. Both players recalled with fond recollection the excitement and challenges associated with participating in the development of a new program. Troy, who would eventually play four years as fullback and linebacker also remembered being "hammered in their first games, until they finally won the Peninsula Athletic League Championship in 1954." Such an accomplishment for a new school was an uncommon phenomenon and Troy attributed the team's success to effective coaching, citing both men as "strong leaders who elicited a willingness to perform."

Dan Varty also ran hurdles for the school's track team where he experienced similar problems with the start of another new program. In this instance, Don's biggest challenge as head coach was a shortage of equipment. "He had," according to a local newspaper article, "no track, no pits for the field men, and only a strip of weeds for the shot putters and discus heavers." Still, the school's B team went undefeated for the year and Don's efforts caught the attention of one sports writer who suggested he be recognized for his exceptional accomplishments. In a local Redwood City *Tribune* column titled, "Lookin' Em Over," sports editor Paul M. McCarthy asked the question, "How About Dorfmeier as Top Coach of the Year?"

In addition to teaching and coaching responsibilities at Menlo-Atherton, Don also served as a counselor for incoming freshman. His strongest asset in this role was his ability to speak clearly and directly, to provide guidance and direction. He also spoke at times to community organizations about character development. Years later, former school athletes Dan Varty and Earl Johnson clearly remember one such instance when Don spoke to their church youth group, drawing upon his experiences as a POW to illustrate effective leadership and teamwork. Don's willingness to acknowledge his former military status, much less talk about the experiences in any type of open forum, was unique and uncommon among ex-POWs, most of whom did neither. Bob Ayers, as well as others, also recalled that Don on some occasions would speak with them individually about his military service. Ayers noted such occasions were usually limited to their "lunch hour [where] he would tell me stories of his escape, but not often." However, other faculty members and colleagues who knew Don throughout his professional career were unaware of his wartime experiences.

Elizabeth Van Dalsem recalled meeting Don in 1953 when she started teaching at Menlo-Atherton as a field requirement for her doctoral program in psychology. At the time, Miss Van Dalsem taught English and history, in addition to serving as a freshman counselor where she "knew Don as a colleague and coach." Elizabeth's primary recollection of Don was that of his strong physical presence, always "well dressed and groomed . . . a handsome addition to the staff." She also recalled Don had "large, well-formed hands that were [always] manicured and used for gesturing or [touching someone] when he had something to say." Don also moved "easily and quickly, with long strides and purposeful movement without conveying the impression of hurrying." Lastly, Elizabeth recalled, "Don had a deep voice and he expressed his feelings clearly through his manner of speaking. His "laugh was [also] quick and fun," but he was "very serious and demanding [when arguing] his position." On another occasion she characterized Don as, "a good fellow well-hailed."

In 1955, my mother starting teaching Fine Arts at Menlo-Atherton, where she had previously substituted for classes taught by Van Dalsem. Elizabeth would later acknowledge the novel and efficient manner in which Barbara would manage a classroom and that "she was well liked by her students." Bob Ayers also remembered Barbara's presence on campus, noting "she was pretty, well dressed and polite, yet aloof and not engaging." However, this may have been just part of her public persona. She was very warm and gregarious with friends outside of work.

For the next three years, both of my parents taught at Menlo-Atherton as Don continued to enjoy notable success as coach of the school's track and field teams. Sportswriters would later recognize him as "one of Northern California's most successful track coaches" and characterized successive Sequoia District titles in 1956, 1957, and 1958 as a "Dynasty." As a result of this success, Don was selected for athletic director at one of two new district high schools scheduled to open in the fall 1958. Howard Costello was selected for the position at Ravenswood in Palo Alto, while Don was offered the assignment at

---

* The position of Athletic Director required administrative oversight of a progressive school physical education program and participation in a competitive inter-school athletic conference.

Woodside High School.*

Family home 1956   Author's collection

I have many fond memories of my father during these early years of my life, yet I also recall disturbing incidents where he drank to intoxication and was verbally abusive. Although these episodes were intermittent and usually restricted to weekends or holidays, they increased over time, caused much distress within the family, and created escalating tension between my parents. Still, their marriage seemed functional. My grandmother, Helen, even said as much years later, lamenting "I don't understand what happened? They had the world by the tail." And so it seemed. Both parents were successful in their professional endeavors, especially my father who had been promoted again to the position of assistant director of Attendance and Welfare for the Sequoia Union High School District. However, I had a limited understanding of my parent's marriage, and surprised when my mother filed for divorce several years later.

Prior to their separation, I started attending high school at Menlo-Atherton where I became fully aware of my father's iconic status within the community. I also discovered that my mother was perceived as an equally competent person. In addition to her teaching responsibilities, she was much respected for her creative design of stage sets used in the school's theatrical productions and her inspirational decorations of the administration building's front windows during the Christmas season.

The following summer, my mother filed for divorce, yet complicated her separation by dating another man, Joe Z, who, to my astonishment, was also a former POW. In later conversation with Joe, I learned that he had served in the Marine Corps and captured on Corregidor following the Japanese invasion of the Philippine Islands. I also deduced from our limited interactions that his experiences as a POW were as traumatic, if not more severe, than Don's ordeal in Germany. He had been held in captivity three times longer than my father, and, as events would later prove, considerably more emotionally disturbed.

Six months later, my father voluntarily admitted himself to a psychiatric facility in Belmont, California to seek treatment for "anxiety and depression together with acute alcohol intoxication."[552] However, the two-week hospitalization terrified him, reactivating all the anxiety and fears associated with his experience as a prisoner of war. The very institutional nature of the hospital, its staff hierarchy, schedules, and routines, in addition to protocols for using restraints and lockup, were too reminiscent of the internment camps in Germany.

Following his release, Don made another effort to petition the Veterans Administration and request recognition of a service-connected disability. As part of this effort, he sent several letters to his former mother-in-law, asking for a witness statement to support his claim. Helen responded to Don's request by sending him a two-page letter in early March 1964, stating she "would testify under oath . . . your troubles were caused by your war experiences," and that . . . "you came home high-strung, quick-tempered, and nervous." A lengthy postscript concluded, "Putting two and two together, it now seems obvious that you were headed for trouble."

Weeks later, my mother found the resolve to end her relationship with Joe, which was an endeavor fraught with risk. Still, when tragedy struck on 31 March 1964, it was more devastating than I could have imagined. The day started pleasantly enough with a cool spring morning, however, at noon, Joe met my mother at our home, where he

---

[552] VA Form Letter 21–121, Hospital summarization, 21 April 1964

shot and killed her, then killed himself.

The next day, the front page of the Redwood City Tribune announced the two deaths as a "murder and suicide." The paper further cited Police Captain William Kieler as stating "Joseph Z, 42, of San Jose shot Mrs. Barbara Dorfmeier, 35, then killed himself."[553] More precisely, Joe shot my mother, twice, in the back with a .25 caliber automatic pistol. He then shot himself in the chest, yet thought to have lived another minute before collapsing on the living room floor.

Sadly, my father was considered a suspect in the death of his estranged wife. Contrary to initial reports, "the possibility . . . of a double murder by a third party, [remained] under investigation" for several months. Don's supervisor, Mr. Sam Chaney, recalled that he and others in his office had been contacted by the police and questioned at length about my father's activities prior to and following the estimated time of the two deaths. My father also mentioned that he was not only a suspect, but had been repeatedly followed by the police until he was later cleared of suspicion. At the time I remember thinking this seemed all rather tragic and unwarranted. I had called my father shortly after discovering that my mother and Joe had been shot and I knew from his devastated reaction that he had not harmed either of them.

While under investigation, Don was seen by a VA psychiatrist for an evaluation to support his recent filing for a service-connected disability. The report, dated 9 June 1964, is complimentary, yet neither complete nor a valid assessment. Glaringly absent are any inquiries or reporting of Don's use of alcohol. Had this issue been raised, and assuming Don answered such questions truthfully, the psychiatrist would have undoubtedly had a much different impression of Don's level of functioning. In the absence of such questioning, I can only assume both men colluded in keeping the examination on a superficial level or at least deflected the conversation from focusing on what was most important. In the absence of any history of substance abuse, much less the relationship between his alcohol use and subsequent divorce, the psychiatrist could, in all good conscience, respond positively to Don who presented himself as an exceedingly fit and attractive forty-year-old man. Conversely, Don's focus on the tragedy of his wife's death kept the psychiatrist from discovering a critical link between his

[553] Redwood City *Tribune*, 1 April 1964

wartime service and twenty-year history of alcohol abuse.[554]

Regrettably, Don's claim for a service-connected disability, which would have allowed him to receive treatment at a VA hospital, was denied just weeks later.[555] The letter, stating "your nervous condition and essential hypertension were found to be non-service connected," would have been considered reprehensible by no less of an authority than Dr. Leslie Caplan, the acknowledged hero of the long Hunger March across northern Germany in 1945. Following the war, Caplan completed a rotation in psychiatry and spent the last part of his life as a clinical professor at the University of Minnesota and as a consultant to the VA. According to Caplan, "Every POW should automatically be service-connected for . . . malnutrition, gastritis, dysentery, respiratory and skin diseases, arthritis, frostbite, and nervous disorders."[556] He further noted that the long-term effects of acute malnutrition and captivity-related maladies contribute to such diseases as arteriosclerosis, hypertension . . . cirrhosis of the liver, peptic ulcers, and anemia. Caplan's assertions were validated in a later VA study that concluded WWII POWs were nine times more likely to suffer a stroke than other combat veterans, and had a considerably shorter life expectancy than the general population.[557] Shockingly, another twenty years would pass before the country would acknowledge the sacrifices of the WWII POWs, and provide the treatment advocated by Dr. Caplan.

The denial of Don's claim for a service-connected disability closed the therapeutic window through which he might have received treatment for his current diagnosis of "reactive depression." Arguably, he could have pursued treatment on his own, yet didn't. Instead, Don started dictating the first of twelve, fifteen-minute recordings of his military service and experiences as a POW. His intent was to publish a book on the 20th anniversary of his escape, and dedicate it to the memory of his wife, Barbara. I had been asked to design the jacket cover for the book, and although intrigued by the project, my primary focus at that time was spent in preparation for the forthcoming football season.

The start of the new school year at Menlo-Atherton was exciting

[554] VA Neuropsychiatric Examination, 6 Jun 1964
[555] VA Letter; Adjudication of Claim, 31 Jul 1964
[556] Carlson, *We Were Each Other's Prisoners*, 235–236
[557] Ibid., 236

and our football team won the 1964 South Peninsula Athletic League's championship in a classic night contest. Yet, in retrospect, our nine-game season served mostly as a personal distraction and once ended, my tentative connection to school became all too apparent. Shortly, military service emerged as an acceptable option for extricating myself from what seemed a hopeless situation. I even discussed the possibility with my father and Howard Costello one Sunday en route to a football game in San Francisco. Months later, at the end of my junior year of high school, I walked into a recruiter's office, declared my intent to enlist in the army and left home in early July, 1965.

I returned home, three years later, and started attending classes at a new Junior College in Redwood City, even as the doors in some of the new classrooms were being hung. However, my newfound serenity would be short-lived. In late October 1969, my brother, Darrell, was hit by a car while riding his motorcycle home from work. I received the notification from my father around 10:00 o'clock that evening. Thirty minutes later, arriving at the hospital, I learned that my brother had been pronounced dead on arrival, then revived and in a deep coma with a guarded prognosis.

For the next 72 hours, my father and I waited in the intensive care unit at Stanford Hospital in an on-going vigil as my brother hovered between life and death. The following six to eight weeks were equally difficult. Darrell's condition fluctuated through multiple crises resulting from continual internal bleeding, various infections and later, pneumonia. By mid-December, his situation seemed hopeless.

A week later, my uncle Alton drove up from Fresno, unannounced, to arrange a family intervention. Alton had become increasingly alarmed by my father's use of alcohol over the past several months and he hoped to elicit Don's willingness to seek treatment. Although touched by Alton's concern, my uncle really didn't understand that a successful intervention needed to be planned, if not rehearsed, and was almost certain to fail when initiated spontaneously. Moreover, Alton had no understanding that Don was terrified by his earlier hospitalization in 1964, and therefore was adamant in his refusal to admit himself again to a treatment facility.

In January 1970, Darrell began to slowly emerge from his coma, which allowed for a complete assessment of his injuries. Initial medical reports were not encouraging. Aside from significant weight loss and muscle atrophy, Darrell had damaged the left side of his brain, which controls motor functions of the right side of his body. Other injuries included a damaged larynx that affected his speech and broken femur in his left leg, which was later amputated.

The severity of Darrell's injuries required multiple operations over several months and a total of 140 units of blood, all of which were donated by his family, numerous friends, and others. The hospital was also contacted almost daily by countless persons in the community, expressing their concern. Many of these callers identified themselves as "former students or players who admired Don and wanted to help the man who had been so inspirational in their earlier life."

That summer, Darrell was moved from the Stanford ICU to another wing of the hospital and then later transferred to a rehabilitation center in San Jose, California. He would remain there, as an in-patient, for another year before being discharged to live on his own. Yet, while Darrell was starting to make a slow, limited recovery, our father slipped into the abyss of long-term addiction, unable to cope with any further loss or grief.

Sadly, I did not see my father again during the last eight months of his life. Still, I was thinking of him on the day he died. I had spent that morning and early afternoon, with twenty other students, excavating an archeology site in northern California. After returning to our camp, one of these students was caring for his infant son in a way that reminded me of an earlier photograph of my father attending to me in a similar manner. Moments later, after informed of a missed call, I learned that my 48-year-old father had died early that morning, 27 July 1972.

I arrived in Redwood City two days later, after my uncle Alton had initiated my father's funeral arrangements. A later autopsy report would cite the cause of his death as hypoglycemia, secondary to alcoholism. The finding was not surprising. Still, the reality of his death was shocking, and I was not able to absorb the emotional impact of his loss for some time. I had never seen him sick, miss a day of work, or otherwise physically incapacitated, except when intoxicated. These earlier, lifelong recollections of a seemingly indestructible man, who projected a larger-than-life persona, made his passing all the more difficult.

Sorting through my father's limited personal possessions following his death was equally sad and disturbing. Still, I was grateful to find his aircrew wings, German POW identification tag, and an engraved stopwatch given to him "In Appreciation" by the "1957 Menlo-Atherton Track Team." I also retrieved a letter of recommendation signed by Elizabeth Van Dalsem and his service tapes dictated years earlier.

Twenty-five years would pass before I was interested in listening to my father's tapes. In the interim, I completed undergraduate studies in anthropology, then years later, a master's degree in psychology and counseling. The latter effort was initiated to further a career in the army after returning to active duty in the late 1970s. Yet, upon finishing graduate school, I realized that my calling in life was to help others affected by trauma.

Over the next ten years, I served in various clinical positions with the Department of the Army, providing counseling services to active duty soldiers and their families. I also completed a two-year post graduate marriage and family training program that placed significant emphasis on therapists helping clients identify the various messages they received from their families of origin. It was the emphasis of this theme, and a renewed recognition of how my father had shaped my life, that prompted a latent interest in his service tapes.

A year later, I found an engineer who successfully recovered most of my father's original recordings, which allowed me to hear his service history for the first time, and to recognize the full extent of his wartime experiences. However, I was most captivated by the collective hardship of the long Hunger March across northern Germany, which served as the primary motivation to bring my father's story to publication. This incentive launched a fifteen-year effort to corroborate his recordings and provide an overarching context for his narrative, which was provided by many other veterans who served with my father or were interned with him in the same camps.

The intent of my endeavor is to provide further understanding of the plight of American POWs during the climatic months of the Second

World War in Europe, and how service members and their families are affected by the residual impact of war. On a more personal level, I have developed a greater appreciation of how my father and many other POWs returned home traumatized and highly anxious men, "deeply scarred by their experience." Some of these veterans would spend the rest of their lives with long-term psychological and substance abuse problems resulting in "impoverished interpersonal relationships, unemployment and [chronic] health problems."[558] Yet, in spite of such suffering, it is worth remembering that most of these men, including my father, "struggled to retain a sense of decency and self-worth in the face of truly horrifying and debilitating circumstances."[559]

---

[558] Williams, *Post-Traumatic Stress Disorder*, 104
[559] Carlson, *We Were Each Others Prisoners*, 226

POSTSCRIPT

Twenty years after the defeat of Nazi Germany, another generation of American youth was drawn to military service to honor their fathers, or other family members, who served in the US Armed Forces during WWII. I met the son of one of these veterans following my assignment to the 82nd Airborne Division, Fort Bragg, NC. Soon after meeting, I learned that my friend's father, Lieutenant Colonel Don Riggle, Sr., had also flown with the Eighth Air Force in Europe and had been similarly interned as a German POW during the war. The following spring, I had a chance to meet the former B-17 pilot while visiting the family home in Silver Springs, MD. Yet, I would only hear about the most dramatic aspect of his last mission years later.

In spring 1944, 24-year-old Lieutenant Don Riggle, Sr., of the 100th Bomb Group, was returning from his eighth mission after bombing Berlin. However, flak damage sustained during the bomb run forced him to leave the protective formation of his group. The lone Fortress was then attacked by six German ME-109 fighters. Within a few brief moments, his navigation and control systems were destroyed. A fire started in the right wing, and four crew members were wounded, two critically.

Determining his aircraft was inoperable and defenseless, Riggle ordered his surviving crew to abandon ship while he stabilized the damaged Fortress long enough for the others to escape. He then moved to the rear of the fuselage to ensure that everyone had gotten out safely. Yet, before making his own exit, he stopped long enough at the open window positions of the two dead waist gunners to attach static lines to their parachutes before he jettisoned their bodies from the burning aircraft.

Riggle's demonstrated concern for the members of his crew was emblematic of the compassion that existed among the airmen in POW camps in Germany and elsewhere during the Second World War. This theme was still present years later, in the many stories I heard from the men held at Stalag Luft IV and those on the long Hunger March out of Pomerania. It was this compassion, forever linked to the trauma of the war, which bind these men to the defining experiences of their lives.

In May 1945, Lieutenant Don Riggle, along with 116,128 other American prisoners of war, most of whom were repatriated to US Military Control in Europe, started to make their way home. The United States government would later acknowledged that 130,201 US service personnel, 32,730 of whom were combat crew members of the US Army Air Force,[560] had been captured during the war and held as enemy POWs. The majority of the 14,072 servicemen who died in captivity perished while interned as Japanese prisoners in Asia. However, these government figures are suspect and unreliable. As late as March 1945, the Supreme Headquarters Allied Expeditionary Forces in Europe had no idea of the correct numbers of airmen or soldiers who had been captured in their Theater of Operations. Moreover, a full accounting of those who died while in German captivity was compromised after the war for reasons of political expediency and further obscured by the fact that 78,773 service personnel from WWII were still listed as Missing in Action (MIA) as late as 1985.[561] Conceivably, many other airmen or soldiers who perished on the forced marches across Europe, or were detained by the Soviets during the closing months of the war, are included in the number of US personnel listed as MIA.

Once home, many repatriated prisoners of war, as well as other returning veterans, faced serious physical and emotional adjustment problems. Some, like Dr. Leslie Caplan, endured long periods of hospitalization for illnesses such as tuberculosis, which continued to cause high rates of morbidity for American POWs. Hundreds of other airmen required hospitalization for multiple surgeries related to wounds sustained in combat. Gilbert E. Stover, Sr. spent a year at the Newton D. Baker hospital at Martinsberg, West Virginia, where plastic surgery and reconstruction of his face hid the physical scars. Yet, years later, Stover readily admitted, "The emotional scars are still with me today."[562] Other problems, caused by "residuals of malnutrition, gastrointestinal disorders, and cardiovascular conditions,"[563] would continue to affect many former POWs for years. Walter D. Czawlytko, acknowledged his "war-related illnesses robbed me of my youth," and that his wife

[560] Carlson, *We Were Each Other's Prisoners*, xvii

[561] Williams, *Post Traumatic Stress Disorder*, 131

[562] Rutkowski, *"We Regret to Inform You . . . ,"* 223

[563] Cohen, *A Follow-Up Study of WWII Prisoners of War*, 65–67.

"suffered terribly because of "my recurring disabilities."[564]

Overwhelming numbers of other returning POWs suffered from psychoneurosis, and drank to quell the intrusive thoughts and nightmares associated with their wartime service. In time, this abusive behavior, in addition to numerous residual problems cited in a 1954 government survey of WWII POWs, dramatically affected the mortality rate of this group of veterans. Later protocol examinations, initiated by the Veterans Administration in the early 1980s, attempted to quantify the extent of these problems–and the results were shocking. Sixty percent of European Theater and 82 percent of Pacific Theater POWs manifested significant psychiatric symptoms of anxiety disorders, post-traumatic stress disorder, and depression.[565] However, public recognition of the plight of these veterans came too late for almost 40,000 former POWs, who by 1985 were "dying younger [and] suffering more severe psychiatric disability . . . than their comrades-in-arms."[566] These figures are particularly disturbing as those selected for military service, especially in the Air Corps, represented the healthiest and brightest segment of the US population in 1940–1944.

Sadly, some thirty-five years passed before the United States Congress recognized its moral responsibility to care for former POWs of the Second World War. In 1982, the first of several significant legislative measures were passed that established "life-long presumption of service-connected disabilities for ten specific diagnoses if they become manifest at any time after repatriation, even if there is no such record of disease documented during active duty service." Five of these diagnoses are related to malnutrition, while three of the other five conditions pertain to psychiatric disorders.[567] Formal recognition of these service-related disabilities allowed veterans access to financial compensation, in addition to medical services for treatment at no cost to the service member.

This belated recognition was driven, in part, by public support for returning Vietnam War POWs, as well as State Department personnel held hostage following the 1979 seizure of the US embassy in Iran. The

---

[564] Rutkowski, "We Regret to Inform You . . . ," 243
[565] Williams, *Post Traumatic Stress Disorder*, 138
[566] Ibid., 134
[567] Williams, *Post Traumatic Stress Disorder*, 134–135

mental health community, and in particular, the American Psychiatric Association (APA), had also come to understand the impact and lasting effects of exposure to life threatening events. Increasing numbers of neuropsychiatric disorders among returning Vietnam veterans, in addition to individuals exposed to natural disasters and acts of terrorism, were all exhibiting similar and identifiable reactions to severe and terrifying experiences.

A clinical reaction following exposure to traumatic experiences was first identified as Post-Traumatic Stress Disorder (PTSD) in 1978, and later introduced in the APA's 1980 publication of the Diagnostic and Statistical Manual of Disorders, Third Edition, (DSM III). The primary criterion for diagnosis was based on "exposure to a psychologically disturbing event outside the range of usual human experience" that elicited "intense fear, terror, and helplessness."[568] Recurring symptoms associated with exposure to trauma, which serve as supporting criteria for diagnosis, include persistent intrusive thoughts, painful memories, nightmares, emotional numbness, sleep disturbances, depression, anxiety, and irritability.

Although PTSD was (and remains) classified in later publications of the DSM as an anxiety disorder, the diagnosis is considerably more debilitating than implied by its classification.[569] Exposure to severe trauma will cause physiological changes in brain size, function, and chemistry. The most notable of these changes effect the regulation of the endocrine and autonomic nervous systems. However, psychiatrist Jonathan Shay argues that the two most debilitating manifestations of PTSD are the loss of "authority over memory," and the undoing of one's character.[570]

"Traumatic memory," Shay further notes, "is not narrative. Rather it is experience that reoccurs . . . as a relivable nightmare" that will cause many veterans to struggle with some residual symptoms of Post-Traumatic Stress Disorder for the rest of their lives. Equally destructive, exposure to severe combat trauma damages individual character by destroying the fabric of their belief system: eroding one's sense of correct behavior expressed through their "ideals, ambition,

---

[568] Ibid., 103

[569] Frances, *Diagnostic and Statistical Manual of Mental Disorders-IV*, 424–426

[570] Shay, *Achilles in Vietnam, Combat Trauma & . . .* , 169–172

and affiliation."[571] Individuals exposed to severe trauma are frequently left feeling chronically hostile, isolated, and threatened.[572]

The long-delayed recognition of a distinct trauma-related disorder helped improve the treatment for many WWII and later, Korean War veterans who were similarly ignored by an unresponsive VA.* Most of these men were previously misdiagnosed with inaccurate and more stigmatizing illnesses such as schizophrenia or bipolar affective disorder. Congressional legislation also funded the opening of numerous community counseling centers throughout the country that provided outpatient services for these veterans and increasing numbers of disenfranchised Vietnam-era service members, often contemptuous of the VA mental health system. Counseling in these centers was conducted in individual, group, and marital settings to help veterans and their families gain further insights related to their wartime service.

In 1988, a thoroughly discredited Veteran's Administration was reorganized into a cabinet-level Department of Veterans Affairs. Two generations later, community Vet centers continue to provide education, counseling services and other forms of assistance to help veterans develop more effective coping skills.** These centers remain an attractive alternative to the perceived indifference of VA hospitals. The later passage of the Caregivers and Veterans Omnibus Health Services Act of 2010 also allows veterans who served in previous conflicts, in addition to those service members returning from Iraq and Afghanistan, to access readjustment counseling in one of over 300 Vet Centers located throughout the United States. These and others services

---

* The Korean War, which lasted from 1950–53, has been long referred to as "America's Forgotten War." This is especially tragic as over 54,000 US service personnel were killed, and another 103,248 were wounded in action. Some 3,746 service members were captured during the three year conflict and held as enemy POWs, while 8,142 are still listed as missing in action.

** Cognitive Behavior Therapy (CBT) focuses on the relationship between thoughts, emotions and behaviors, and currently considered by the US Department of Defense as the standard of care for treatment of PTSD. A recent variant of CBT, Exposure Therapy, utilizes a more focused fear extinction paradigm.

[571] Ibid., 37
[572] Ibid., 169–172

are now available to all personnel, and their families, who have served in a designated combat theater, as a member of the armed forces of the United States.

SONG OF THE ARMY AIR CORPS

Off we go into the wild blue yonder,
Climbing high into the sun;
Here they come zooming to meet our thunder,
At 'em boys, Give 'er the gun! (Give 'er the gun!),
Down we dive, spouting our flame from under,
Off with one helluva of roar!
We live in fame or go down in flame. Hey!
Nothing'll stop the US Air Force!

Minds of men fashioned a crate of thunder,
Sent it high into the blue;
Hands of men blasted the world asunder;
How they lived God only knew! (God only knew then!)
Souls of men dreaming of skies to conquer
Gave us wings, ever to soar!
With scouts before and bombers galore. Hey!
Nothing'll stop the US Air Force!

Bridge: "A Toast to the Host"
Here's a toast to the host
Of those who love the vastness of the sky,
To a friend we send a message of his brother men who fly.
We drink to those who gave their all of old,
Then down we roar to score a rainbow's pot of gold
A toast to the host of men we boast, the US Air Force!

Off we go into the wild sky yonder,
Keep the wings level and true;
If you'd live to be a grey-haired wonder
Keep the noise out of the blue! (Out of the blue, boys!)
Flying men, guarding the nation's border,
We'll be there, followed by more!
In echelon we carry on. Hey!
Nothing can stop the US Air Force.

ORDER OF BATTLE:
US ARMY EIGHTH AIR FORCE 1944

The US Army Eighth Air Force conducted air operations over occupied Europe from 17 August 1942 through 25 April 1945. At peak strength, it numbered over 200,000 personnel assigned to 40 bomb groups, 15 fight groups, and two photo-reconnaissance groups operating out of 25 airfields located in south-eastern England. In September 1943, Eighth Air Force bomb groups were organized into three bombardment divisions, each consisting of four or more combat bomb wings (CBW) of three bomb groups (BG). The First and Third Bombardment Divisions (Heavy) were equipped with B-17s, while the Second Division flew B-24s.[573]

Bomb Group (BG) Assignment

First Bomb Division (H)	Second Bomb Division (H)	Third Bomb Division (H)
1st CBW	2nd CBW	4th CBW
91 BG	389 BG	94 BG
381 BG	445 BG	385 BG
398 BG	453 BG	447 BG
40th CBW	14th CBW	13th CBW
92 BG	44 BG	95 BG
305 BG	39 BG	100 BG
306 BG	492 BG	390 BG
41st CBW	20th CBW	45th CBW
303 BG	93 BG	96 BG
379 BG	46 BG	388 BG
384 BG	448 BG	452 BG
94th CBW	95th CBW	92nd CBW
51 BG	489 BG	486 BG
401 BG	491 BG	487 BG
457 BG	458 BG	34 BG
	96th CBW	93rd CBW
	466 BG	490 BG
	467 BG	493 BG

---

[573] Freeman, *The Mighty Eighth*, 110

ROOM ASSIGNMENT: STALAG LUFT IV

The following individuals were assigned to room 10, barracks 4, C-lager, Stalag Luft IV, September 1944.

Name	Rank	Service Number
Chavez, M.C.*	M/SGT	19028026
Dorfmeier, D.D.**	S/SGT	19111310
Dowell, A.E.	SGT	35707899
Doyle, I.F.	S/SGT	37342041
Doyle, L.E.	SGT	17042662
Dumphy, J.J.	SGT	12120001
Duran, P.W.	SGT	19105097
Dyer, F.E.	S/SGT	13077272
Elsrod, O.W.	T/SGT	15333617
Enghauser, E.J.	SGT	15118629
Eschbach, J.K.	S/SGT	20323591
Espinoza, F.L.	SGT	39243233
Feldkamp, H.G.	SGT	35799789
Ferris, E.L.	SGT	32845124
Fetteroff, J.R.	SGT	36741573
Fischer, J.D.	SGT	38430453
Flores, M.G.	SGT	39234900
Hartney, C.W.	SGT	36328510
Kauanaugh, J.L	SGT	12178260
Knothe, L.A.	T/SGT	15340533
Leone, C.F.	T/SGT	13137217

* Room Leader

** Barracks Leader

This roster was compiled by Norwood Browder in the fall of 1944. Browder retained possession of the lager's roster throughout the duration of the 86-day Hunger March of 6 February to 2 May 1945. Upon his death in 1986, the records were passed to his brother Jack, who, coincidentally, was already a POW at Stalag Luft IV when Norwood arrived at the camp in late July 1944.

Congressional Record 104th Congress
Vol. 141 8 May 1995 No. 75

Commemorating the 50th anniversary of the forced march of American POWs from Stalag Luft IV

Mr. Warner, Mr. President, today we commemorate the 50th anniversary of the end of World War II in Europe. Victory in Europe day is one of the milestone dates of this century. I rise today to honor a group of Americans who made a large contribution to the Allied victory in Europe while also enduring more than their fair share of personal suffering and sacrifice: the brave men who were prisoners of war.

I believe it is appropriate to commemorate our World War II POW's by describing one incident from the war that is emblematic of the unique service rendered by those special people. This is a story of a 86-day, 488-mile forced march that commenced at a POW camp known as Stalag Luft IV, near Gross Tychow, on February 6, 1945, and ended in [Borze] on [May 2, 1945]. The ordeal of 9,500 men, most of whom were US Army Air Force Bomber Command non-commissioned officers, who suffered through incredible hardships on the march, yet survived, stands as an everlasting testimonial to the triumph of the American spirit over immeasurable adversity and of the indomitable ability and spirit of camaraderie, teamwork, and fortitude to overcome brutality, horrible conditions, and human suffering.

Bomber crews shot down over Axis countries often went through terrifying experiences even before being confined in concentration camps. Flying through withering flak, while also having to fight off enemy fighters, the bomb crews routinely saw other aircraft in formations blown to bits or turned into fiery coffins. Those who were taken POW had to endure their own plane being shot down or otherwise damaged sufficiently to cause their crews to bail out. Often crew mates –close friends–did not make it out of the burning aircraft. Those lucky enough to see their parachutes open, had to then go through the perilous descent amid flak and gunfire from the ground. Many crews were then captured by incensed civilians who had seen their property destroyed or had loved ones killed or maimed by Allied bombs. Those civilians at times would beat, spit upon, or even try to lynch the captured crews.

[In the] case of Stalag Luft IV, once the POWs arrived at the railroad station near the camp, though exhausted, unfed, and often wounded, many were forced to run the [three and a half kilometers] to the camp at the point of bayonets. Those who dropped behind were either bayoneted or bitten on the legs by police dogs. And all that was just a prelude to their incarceration where they were underfed, overcrowded, and often maltreated.

In February 1945, the Soviet offensive was rapidly pushing toward Stalag Luft IV. The German high command determined that it was necessary for the POWs to be evacuated and moved into Germany. But by that stage of the war, German material was at a premium, and neither sufficient railways nor trucks were available to move prisoners. Therefore, the decision was made to move the Allied prisoners by foot in [a] forced march.

The 86-day march was, by all accounts, savage. Men who for months, and in some cases years, had been denied proper nutrition, personal hygiene, medical care, were forced to do something that would be difficult for well-nourished, healthy, and appropriately trained infantry soldiers to accomplish. The late doctor (Major) Leslie Caplan, an American flight surgeon who was the chief medical officer for the 2,500 man [C-lager] from Stalag Luft IV, summed up the [march;] it was a march of great hardship. We marched long distances in bitter weather and on starvation rations. We lived in filth and slept in open fields or barns. Clothing, medical facilities and sanitary facilities were utterly inadequate. Hundreds of men suffered from malnutrition, dysentery, tuberculosis, and other diseases.

A number of American POWs on the march did not survive. Others suffered amputations of limbs or appendages while many more endured maladies that remained . . . [with them for the rest] of their lives. For [86 days and nearly 500 miles], enduring unbelievably inhumane conditions, the men from Stalag Luft IV walked, limped, and in some cases crawled onward until they reached the end of their march, [and] . . . liberation . . . on [2 May 1945].

Unfortunately, the story of the men of Stalag Luft IV, [is not well known. It is a story], replete with tales of the selfless and often heroic deeds of prisoners looking after other prisoners, and helping each other survive under deplorable conditions. I therefore rise today to bring their saga of victory over incredible adversity to the attention of my colleagues. I trust that these words will serve as a springboard for wider awareness among the American people of what the prisoners from Stalag Luft IV–and all prisoners of war camps–endured in their pursuit of freedom.

I especially want to honor three Stalag Luft veterans who endured and survived the March–Corporal Bob McVicker, Staff Sergeant Ralph Pippens, and Sergeant Arthur Duchesneau–who brought this important piece of history to my attention and provided me with in-depth information. [All three NCO's], at different points along the march, were each too impaired to walk under their own power. Yet, they each survived, mostly because of the efforts of other . . . American crew mates, [who] compassionately and selflessly help[ed] buddies in need.

Mr. President, I am sure my colleagues join me in saluting . . . the survivors of the Stalag Luft IV march, and all brave Americans who were prisoners of war in World War II. Their service was twofold: First as fighting men putting their lives on the line, each day, in the cause of freedom; and then, as prisoners of war, stoically enduring incredible hardships and showing their captors that the American spirit cannot be broken, no matter how terrible the conditions. We owe them a great debt of gratitude and the memory of their service our undying respect.

Army psychiatrist, Dr. Robert Lambright, was the first person to suggest I write a book, yet offered no further opinion pertaining to scope or content. Years later, Dr. Leon Rappaport, professor of psychology at Kansas State University in Manhattan, Kansas agreed to supervise a yearlong independent study that guided my initial research for this project. It was during this period that I found Peter Meyer, an engineer with Dictaphone L & H, in Melbourne, Florida, who successfully recovered most of the information on the tapes my father recorded in 1964.

The staff of the McHale Library at Kansas State University also provided assistance with obtaining source material from other colleges and libraries. One such acquisition was a copy of the unpublished diary of former POW Gerald Ralston, who was interned in my father's lager at Stalag Luft IV. KSU climatologist, Mary Knapp, further assisted me in finding accurate weather data to document the severity of the European winter in 1944–1945.

The 398th Bomb Group Association's historian, Lee Bradley, and publication editor, Allen Ostrom, contributed immensely to furthering my understanding of the unit's formation, deployment, and participation in the air war over Europe. Through the association, I also made contact with Dr. Leonard Streitfeld, author of *Hell From Heaven*, and former crew members John Bell, Wallace Blackwell, Bob Carr, and Stanford Lewis. These men provided poignant and informative narratives to augment the wealth of information I received from John Anderson, who granted open and frequent access to his unpublished diary. Jack Browder, Leonard Deranleau, author of *Memories of an Aerial Gunner*, Joseph O'Donnell, author of *A History of Stalag Luft IV*, Don Riggle, Sr., Jim Skarles, Herman Steck, and Francis Troy, C-lager's Man of Confidence, all furnished rich details from their varied personal experiences.

US Special Operations Command librarian, Tom Tait, was most helpful in finding a copy of the War Department's 1944 *MIS-X Manual on Evasion, Escape, and Survival*. Other service members who supported my endeavor during my assignment to the J-7 Training Division include Sergeants Major Andrew Farkas, Joe Garrido, Bob Gron, and Kris O'Donnel. Retired Master Sergeant Jim Hetrick, a former advisor and longtime friend, maintained unwavering interest and steadfast focus on the applicability of the C-lager story to other generations of Americans serving in the nation's armed forces.

Archivist David Giodano of the National Archives in College Park, Maryland, assisted me in obtaining copies of the Eighth Air Force Tactical Operations Order for 4 August 1944 and the Missing Air Crew Report for my father's plane. Roland Gieger, author of "Das Stammlager de Luftwaffe VI in St. Wendel," graciously allowed me access to his research material documenting the establishment of a previously unacknowledged internment camp cited in his article. Captain Kim N. Thomsen, Chief, Nutrition Care Division, Fort Riley, Kansas, furthered my understanding of the adverse effects of malnutrition and directed my inquiry to Ancel Keys' definitive study of starvation.

Gilda Lintz and the staff of Kansas Senator Pat Roberts were instrumental in my obtaining hundreds of pages of my father's medical records from an unresponsive Veterans Administration. Paul McNally's son, Gary, Patrick Benker's daughter, Patricia, a National Service Officer with the American Ex-POW Association, and Dr. Caplan's daughter, Laura, provided invaluable information pertaining to their fathers' wartime service.

Stalag Luft IV Association chairman, Leonard Rose, sent me a copy of Norwood Browder's 1944 roster of men assigned to my father's room in C-lager, which enabled me to contact former room members Martin Chavez, Leone Clement, John Fetterolf, Jack Fischer, and Chuck Hartney, who offered informative annotates about my father, in addition to their own experiences as POWs. Barrack's members Bob Cash and Carl Moss contacted me on their own initiative.

Former POW Otha Huckaby and Thelma Dyer, the widow of roommate, Frank Dyer, provided copies of diaries written by Dallas Farris and an anonymous airman. March participants Stratton Beesley, Charles Brennan, and George Guderley, author of "The Thirteenth Mission," sent me copies of Al Zimmerman's documentary film, *Behind the Wire*, Dr. Caplan's medical journal, *Domain of Heroes* and an engineer's scaled drawing of the Stalag Luft IV compound. Other former prisoners of war Fred Campbell, a National Service Officer with the American Ex-POW Association, Tony Capon, Glen Jostad, Don Kirby, and Milton Price also expressed great interest in my writing and offered many personal accounts of their varied experiences.

Supervisors and colleagues Bob Ayers, Sam Chaney, and Dr. Elizabeth Van Dalsem, in addition to student-athletes Earl Johnson, Troy Ratliff, and Dan Varty shared their collective perceptions of Don's character and performance while coaching at Menlo-Atherton and functioning in other roles within the Sequoia Union High School District. Dr. Van Dalsem also provided unwavering support throughout the duration of my project, in addition to reading every draft and providing many unique insights.

Graphic designer, Dora Cora, and photographers, Jerry Wallace and Allison Neuru, contributed invaluable assistance with the design of my book jacket and numerous photo enhancements. Trine Marlen edited my first drafts and warrants special recognition for offering many helpful suggestions and encouragement. Later drafts were edited by Susan Nordlinger, Lynnea Hagen, and Susan Dill, who also formatted my final revisions for publication. All four women expressed great interest, much compassion, and an overall willingness to navigate the details of a complex and overarching narrative.

Barker, A. J., *Prisoners of War*, Universe Books, New York, NY, 1975

Beaumont, Roger, A., *Military Elites*, The Bobbs-Merrill Company, Inc, New York, NY, 1974

Beevor, Antony, *The Fall of Berlin 1945*, Viking, New York, NY, 2002

Bekker, Cajus, *The Luftwaffe War Diaries: The German Air Force in World War II*, Doubleday, Garden City, NY, 1968

Brendon, Piers, *The Dark Valley: A Panorama of the 1930s*, Alfred A. Knopf, New York, NY, 2000

Buss, Philip, H., & Mollor, Andrew, *Hitler's Germanic Legions*, Macdonald and Jane's, London, 1978

Caplan, Laura, *Domain of Heroes*, Jerry's Printing & Design, Edina, Minnesota, 2004

Cardozier, V. R., *Colleges and Universities in World War II*, Praeger, Westport, Connecticut, 1993

Cardozier, V. R., *The Mobilization of the United States in World War II*, McFarland & Company, Inc., Jefferson, NC, 1995

Carlson, Lewis H., *We were Each Other's Prisoners*, Basic Books, New York, NY, 1997

Churchill, Winston, S., *The War Speeches of Winston Churchill*, Houghton Mifflin Company, London, 1953

Carter, Kit C. & Mueller, Robert, *The Army Air Forces in World War II: Combat Chronology, 1941–1945*, The US Government Printing Office, Washington, D. C., 1973

Christiansen, Chris, *Seven Years Among Prisoners of War*, Ohio University Press, Athens, Ohio, 1994

Cohen, Bernard M., *A Follow-up Study of WWII Prisoners of War*, US Government Printing Office, Washington, D. C., 1954

Cooper, Mathew, *The German Air Force,1933–1945*, Jane's Publishing Inc., New York, NY, 1981

Cooper, Mathew, *The German Army, 1933–1945*, Stein & Day, Briarcliff Manor, New York, NY, 1978

Craven, Westley, F., *The Army Air Forces in WWII, (Volumes I–VI)*, University of Chicago Press, Chicago, IL, 1955

Dear, Ian, *Escape and Evasion*, The History Press, Stroud, Great Britain, 2010

Deighton, Lee, *Battle of Britain*, Jonathan Cape, Ltd., London, 1980

Doyle, Robert C., *A prisoners Duty*, Naval Institute Press, Annapolis, MY, 1997

BIBLIOGRAPHY

348

Duffy, Christopher, *Red Storm on the Reich: The Soviet March on Germany, 1945*, Macmillan Publishing Company, New York, NY, 1991

Durand, Arthur A., *Stalag Luft III*, Louisiana State University Press, Baton Rouge, 1988

Evans, Richard J., *The Third Reich at War*, The Penguin Press, New York, NY, 2009

Forman, Wallace R., *B-17 Nose Art Name Directory*, Phalanx Publishing, North Branch, MN, 1996

Forster, Arnold, *The World at War, Stein & Day*, NY, 1973

Foy, David A., For *You the War is Over*, Stein and Day, New York, NY, 1984

Frances, Allen, *Diagnostic and Statistical Manual of Mental Disorders, IV*, American Psychiatric Association, Washington, DC, 1994

Frankl, Viktor, *Man's Search for Meaning*, Beacon Press, Boston, 1962

Freeman, Roger, A., *The Mighty Eighth: A History of the Units, Men and Machines of the US 8th Air Force*, Crown Publishers, Inc., New York, NY, 1970

Gabbard, Glen O., *Treatments of Psychiatric Disorders, Second Addition*, American Psychiatric Press, Inc., Washington, DC, 2005

Gander, Terry & Chamberlain, Peter, *Weapons of the Third Reich*, Doubleday & Company, Garden City, NY, 1979

Garraty, John A., *The Great Depression*, Harcourt Brace Jovanovich Publishers, San Diego, CA, 1986

Gilbert, Martin, *The Day the War Ended*, Henry Holt and Company, New York, NY, 1995

Ginzberg, Eli, *The Lost Divisions*, Columbia University Press, New York, NY, 1959

Gray, J. Glenn, *The Warriors: Reflections on Men in Battle*, Harcourt, Brace & Company, New York, NY 1959

Hallion, Richard P., *D-Day 1944; Air Power Over the Normandy Beaches and Beyond*, Air Force History and Museums Program, 1994

Hastings, Max, *Armageddon, Battle for Germany, 1944–45*, Alfred A. Knopf, New York, NY, 2004

Hoyt, Edwin, P., *Angles of Death: Goering Luftwaffe*, Tom Dohery Associates, New York, NY, 1994

Jablonski, Edward, *Flying Fortress: The Illustrated Biography of the B-17s and the Men Who Flew Them*, Doubleday, New York, NY, 1965

Jennings, Peter & Brewster, Todd, *The Century*, Doubleday, New York, NY, 1998

Kaplan, Philip & Smith, Rex A. *One Last Look*, Abbeville Press, Inc. New York, NY, 1983

Keegan, John, *The Second World War*, Viking Penguin, New York, NY, 1990

Keys, Ancel, *The Biology of Human Starvation*, The University of Minnesota Press, The North Central Publishing Company, St. Paul, MN, 1950

Korda, Michael, *Ike: An American Hero*, Harper Collins, New York, NY, 2007

Laffin, John, *Americans in Battle*, J. M. Dent & Sons Ltd, London, 1973

Levine, Alan J., *The Strategic Bombing of Germany, 1940–1945*, Praeger Publishing, Westport, CT, 1992

Lucas, James, *The Last Days of the Third Reich*, William Marrow & Company, Inc., New York, NY, 1986

Lucas, James, *The Third Reich: Experiences of War*, The Sterling Publishing Co. Inc., New York, NY, 1990

Lucas, James, *War on the Eastern Front 1941–1945*, Bonanza Books, New York, NY, 1982

Mark, Joanna & Humphries, Steve, *London at War*, Sedgwick & Jackson, London, 1985

Marwick, Arthur, *Britain in Our Century*. Thames & Hudson, Inc., New York, NY, 1984

McKee, Alexander, *Dresden 1945: The Devils Tinderbox*, E.P. Dutton, New York, NY, 1982

Middlebrook, Martin, *The Peenemünde Raid: The Night of 17–18 August, 1943*, Bobs-Merrill, New York, NY, 1982

Moorehead, Roger, *Berlin at War*, Basic Books, New York, NY, 2010

Muller, Richard, *The German Air War in Russia*, The Nautical & Avn Publishing Company of America, Baltimore, MD, 1992

O'Donnell, Joseph P., *The Shoe Leather Express; The Evacuation of Kriegsgefangenen Lager, Luftgangsters Marching Across Germany, The Pangs of the Thorn, & A History of Stalag Luft IV* Triangle Reprocenter, Trenton, NJ, 1982

Overy, Richard J., *The Air War*, Europe Publications Limited, London, 1980

Overy, Richard, J., *Why the Allies Won*, W.W. Norton & Company, Inc., New York, NY, 1995

Price, Alfred, *The Battle over the Reich*, Charles Scribner's Sons, New York, NY, 1973

Price, Alfred, *The Bomber in World War II*, Charles Scribner's Sons, New York, NY, 1976

Poynter, Dan, *The Parachute Manual (Volume I & II), Third Edition*, Para Publishing, Santa Barbara, CA, 1984

Rehart, Catherine Morison. *The Heartland's Heritage: An Illustrated History of Fresno County*. Heritage Media Corp., Carlsbad, CA, 2000

Ross, Gregory, *America 1941, A Nation at the Crossroads*, The Free Press, New York, NY, 1989

Russell, Edward T., *Leaping the Atlantic Wall*, Air Force History and Museum Program, 1999

Rutkowski, Bill, *"We Regret to Inform You . . . ,"* Aardvark Global Publishing Company, LLC, Largo, MD, 2006

Ryan, Cornelious, *The Last Battle*, Simon & Schuster, 1966

Seaton, Albert, *The Russo-German War 1941–45*, Arthur Barker Limited, London, 1971

Shay, Jonathan, MD, *Achilles In Vietnam; Combat Trauma and the Undoing of Character*, Touchstone, New York, NY 1994

Skinner, Richard, M., & Loosbrock, John, F., *The Wild Blue, The Story of American Airpower*, G.P. Putnams Sons, NY, New York, 1961

Shirer, William L., *The Rise and Fall of the Third Reich*, Simon and Schuster, NY, 1960

Streitfeld, Leonard, *Hell from Heaven*, The Laureate Press, Egg Harbor City, NJ, 1994

Sweeting, C, G., *US Combat Flying Clothing: Army Air Forces Clothing During World War II*, Smithsonian Institute Press, Washington, DC, 1984

Tick, Edward, *War and the Soul*, Quest Books, Wheaton, IL, 2005

Toliver, Raymond, F., *The Interrogator: The Story of Hanns Scharff, Luftwaffe's Master Interrogator*, Aero Publishers, 1978

Waiczis, Michael R., and William B. Secrest, Jr. *A Portrait of Fresno, 1885–1985: A Publication of the Centennial History Committee*. Centennial History Committee, Fresno, 1985

Walker, Ben Randal. *The Fresno County Blue Book,* A.H. Cawston, Fresno, 1941.

Wells, Mark, K. *Courage and Air Warfare*, Frank Cass & Co, Ltd., London, 1995

Westermann, Edward, B., *Flak*, University Press of Kansas, Lawrence, KS, 2001

Williams, Tom, *Post-Traumatic Stress Disorder, A Handbook for Clinicians*, Disabled American Veterans, Cincinnati, Ohio, 1987

Ziemke, Earl, F., *Stalingrad to Berlin*, Barnes & Noble, New York, NY, 1996

Government Publications

War Department, MIS-X Manual on Escape, Evasion, and Survival, Washington, DC, Feb 1944

HQ Eighth Air Force, Tactical Mission Report-514, 4 Aug 1944

War Department, HQ AAF, Missing Air Crew Report-7707, 8 Aug 1944

War Department, HQ AAF, Missing Air Crew Report-7907, 17 Aug 1944

Articles, Periodicals & Special Collections

Guderley, George W., "The Thirteenth Mission." *Friends Journal* 27. 2 (Summer 2004) : 9–44

Phillips, John, "The Long March: The Forgotten Journey of a POW." *Destination Discovery* 9.11(Feb 1994) : 32–39

Editor, "Waist Gunners." *Flak News* 22.1 (Jan 2007) : 10

Frazier, Willis, "Operations Officer." *Flak News* 21.3 (Jul 2006): 4–8

Kraft, Bob, "The Art of Bunching Up." *Flak News* 20.3 (Jul 2005): 5–9

Henningsson, Par, "American Internees in Sweden." *Flak News* 14.3 (Jul 1999) : 5–9

Mikulus, John, "Stalag Luft Became A Happy Place." *Flak News* 17.1 (Jan 2002) : 9

Zdiarsky, Jan, "Bloody Encounter." *Flak News* 22.4 (Oct 2007) : 6–10

CSU-Fresno, Special Collections Library

Electronic Media:

Documentary:

Behind the Wire, Al Zimmerman, video Eighth AF Historic Site, 1994

Interviews:

Dyer, Francis E., video Andersonville National Historic Site, 1992
Fischer, Jack, video Andersonville National Historic Site, 1994

Internet:

Blackwell, Wallace. "Timeless Voices." www.398th.org
Core, Ben. "Combat Diaries." www.398th.org
Lyman, Derald R. "Combat Diaries." www.398th.org
Mellis, Charles J. "Combat Diaries." www.398th.org

Unpublished accounts & diaries:

Deranleau, Leonard, *Memories of an Aerial Gunner*
Suchsland, Otto, "Course Twelve"
Anderson, John,
Anonymous
Farris, Dallas
Ralston, Gerald
Steck, Herman, H.

Author's Interviews & Correspondence:

Anderson, John, H.
Anderson, Hazal
Ayers, Bob
Beesley, Stratton, W
Bell, John, E.
Benker, Patrica
Blackwell, Wallace
Bradley, Lee
Browder, Jack, L.
Campbell, Fred
Caplan, Laura
Capone, Tony
Carr, William, R.
Cash, Robert, L.
Chaney, Sam
Chavez, Martin, C.
Costello. Bill
Deranleau, Leonard, J.
Dorfmeier, June
Dyer, Thelma
Fetterolf, John, R.
Fischer, Jack, D.
Hilliard, George
Huckaby, Otha
Huckaby, Mildred
Gieger, Roland

Giodano, David
Guderley, George, W.
Hartney, Charles, W.
Johnson, Earl
Jostad, Glen
Kirby, Don
Lamoure, Jean
Lamoure, Beverly
Leone, Clement, F.
Lewis, Sanford, A.
Lintz, Gilda
McNally, Gary
Moss, Carl
O'Donnell, Joseph
Ostrom, Allen
Price, Milton, O., Sr.
Ratliff, Troy
Riggle, Don, E., Sr.
Rose, Leonard
Skarles, Jim, A.
Steck, Herman
Streitfeld, Leonard
Thomsen, Kim
Troy, Francis
Van Dalsem, Elizabeth
Varty, Dan

354

ABOUT THE AUTHOR

Mr. David Dorfmeier is a Vietnam veteran, retired Army Sergeant Major, and clinical therapist who has a personal and professional interest in working with service members suffering from Post Traumatic Stress Disorder. He has a master's degree in Psychology & Counseling from the University of Northern Colorado and has completed a two-year post graduate Marriage & Family Training Program at the Menninger Clinic in Topeka, Kansas. In addition to a long career in the Army Reserve, the author was employed for 20 years with the Department of the Army providing clinical counseling services to active duty soldiers and their family members. Following retirement, he served another four years as a clinical consultant working with the Department of Defense providing adjustment counseling to service members returning from Iraq and Afghanistan.

For more information, visit
www.C-LAGER.com

Made in the USA
San Bernardino, CA
26 December 2016